PROFESSIONAL ORCHESTRATION.
VOLUME 1

The First Key: Solo Instruments & Instrumentation Notes

BY PETER LAWRENCE ALEXANDER

Professional Mentor workbook for Volume 1 and downloadable audio package from eClassical.com containing a majority of the book's examples are available from www.alexanderpublishing.com/musictraining.

Professional Orchestration. Volume 1, 3rd Edition
The First Key: Solo Instruments & Instrumentation Notes
Copyright ©2008 by Peter Lawrence Alexander

Alexander Publishing
P.O. Box 1720
Petersburg, VA 23805
www.alexanderpublishing.com

Alexander Publishing is the
Publishing division of Alexander University, Inc.

Professional Orchestration is a service mark of Alexander University, Inc.

Paperback edition published 2008
ISBN-13: 978-0-939067-70-1

Printed in the United States of America

Cover design and layout by Caroline J. Alexander

Alexander, Peter Lawrence, 1950-

*For Henry Mancini who helped start the process,
& Jerry Goldsmith who helped polish it.*

Thanks

This book was written with a lot of help from some really great people.

Johnny Mandel graciously loaned me his copy of Widor's *Technique of the Modern Orchestra* which was the basis for the instrumentation notes of this volume.

Concertmaster Paul Shure laboriously and cheerfully checked and revised Mr. Widor's observations about violin performance. This master violinist, who also performed under Toscanini and is currently the Concertmaster for the Pasadena Symphony Orchestra, checked all the string stops, updated bowing definitions, provided insights not found in any orchestration book, and never failed to demonstrate how to be a gracious gentleman in the Entertainment Capitol of the World.

Pamela Goldsmith provided extra insights on the viola. Armand Kaproff checked the Cello chapter. Composer and bassist Arni Egilsson pointed out all kinds of things the bass could do that weren't in any book.

Dominc Fera provided insights on the clarinet and symphonic seating of the woodwind section as a whole. Jim Kantor gave me three hours of solid clarinet instruction and never failed to be able to do on the clarinet what someone said couldn't be done.

Ross DeRoche provided excellent insights for the Tuba chapter. Composer Mike McQuistion clued me into his use of the Contrabass Trombone in the Batman cartoon series. Thanks, Buddy!

Bill Motzing provided the fundamentals on the harp while Ann Remson demonstrated many of them to me.

Larry Bunker and Emil Richards provided pertinent insights for being a studio percussionist.

Mike Lang: just thanks for being the special friend you are.

Any mistakes in these chapters should be laid at my feet and not those of the musicians who counselled me.

Special thanks to Sandy DeCrescent, who looked the other way during breaks while I nabbed musicians at three Jerry Goldsmith film scoring sessions and for her assistant Denise who provided quick phone answers to unique questions from an orchestration book writer.

Jo Anne Kane and her staff at 20th Century Fox provided score examples to demonstrate how it should be set up professionally.

Bob Bornstein at Paramount clarified how to notate string harmonics on the bass.

Arthur Morton, one of the world's great orchestrators, said more in a more paragraph of conversation to me then I ever learned in an orchestration class.

Judy Green of Judy Green Music graciously sent score page samples so you'd know how it's done in the Entertainment Capitol of the World.

Ken Hall taught me about musically setting up click tracks.

Bruce Botnick never failed to demonstrate the partnership required between the composer and his recording engineer.

Lois Carruth made all the arrangements for me being at Jerry's sessions.

And finally, many thanks to Mrs. Kathryn Hunley who ran the shop while I spent time in the studios, and with great professional care and dedication designed and produced this book, doing her best to make this a readable, usable work for you.

Table of Contents

Foreword

Rimsky-Korsakov's *Principles of Orchestration* has long been a familiar and much-used handbook of mine. More than just a compendium of orchestral devices, I have found the book valuable for its sound aesthetic advice. One of the most important sections of the book is actually the author's preface in which he counsels the aspiring orchestrator/composer to write for the group which is to perform the music rather than for an ideal group, and to understand that music which is easy to perform generally sounds best. Though since Rimsky's day the art of orchestration has advanced into sonic areas which he could never have imagined, what he had to say regarding the students "phases" is still worth considering.

When I was studying orchestration in school, I was told that Rimsky's book was too old-fashioned to be of much use today. After many years of orchestral experience, however, I have found that the *opposite* is true. The book, after all, was written to demonstrate the *principles* of orchestration, and it does that effectively. As the author points out, the art of poetic orchestration, i.e., creativity, is something which cannot be taught.

At the risk of being presumptuous, however, I would quibble with Rimsky on one point. There is much to be learned in the works of earlier composers, such as Mozart, Haydn, and Bach, if one wants to be considered a true master of this very special art. Even though the manner in which the baroque and classical composers voiced instrumental combinations was often specific, working as composers-for-hire they frequently heard their works performed when the ink was barely dry. Their musical emphasis was *not* primarily one of sonority and color as it increasingly is today, but we can see in these earlier scores experimentation and orchestral craft. This is true particularly with regard to their string writing.

With the aid of the optional MP3 audio package, this new marvelously expanded edition of *Principles of Orchestration* (retitled as *Professional Orchestration.*) offers more opportunities to see and hear the combinations which formerly could only be imagined. One has to keep in mind, however, that the examples quoted were solutions for specific compositional problems. Instrumental choice, tessitura, and balance are in most respects the result of a musical idea. The decision as to which combination is best based upon what needs to be expressed. It is interesting to compare the different works of a master orchestrator such as Ravel to see how he orchestrated each piece differently in order to accommodate the preciseness of his imagination. Orchestration truly is an art, not a science.

As a final note to the student, be assured that even if you absorb all the ideas in this book and all of those in every other orchestration text, you will still find yourself stumped, frustrated and perplexed when actually orchestrating. If you are working in a commercial medium, Such as film or television, the emotional and dramatic responses which will be derived from the orchestral sound add yet another burden to the choices being made. It is surely a subject about which, as my grandfather used to say, "the more you know, the less you know." Fortunately, this revised and augmented edition by Peter Alexander, along with consistent, relentlessly critical listening of your own work, should do a great deal in making the mysteries of musical expression somewhat less formidable.

Bruce Broughton

Emmy winner

Supervising Composer for *Tiny Toons*®

Composer:

Silverado, Young Sherlock Homes,

Harry and the Hendersons,

The Old Man and the Sea,

George Washington: The Forging of A Nation

The Call

It was the summer of 1981 when I arrived in Southern California to begin my career as a film composer. It was also the summer that *Raiders of The Lost Ark* was released. I remember sitting in the theatre hearing John Williams' score. I was mesmerized by it. As the end credits rolled everyone in my group wanted to leave, but I wanted to stay long enough to see who had orchestrated this score. Finally the name came up! It was Herb Spenser.

Fresh from Boston, I didn't know anyone in town, much less out of town! But I was determined that I was going to meet Herb Spenser. I wanted to orchestrate just like that. Notice I said orchestrate. I was always pretty confident in my ability to compose, but coming out of college, I'd only had the obligatory one semester of orchestration that colleges offer in the senior year. It's not enough. Then or now.

Consequently, I found myself way behind the power curve in my ability to get out there and compete with other composers. I needed to learn more than I knew. I wanted to know what the top Hollywood guys knew. I could hear these combinations in my head when I went to write, but I lacked the experience to know exactly what it was I was hearing. So I would spend hours going through score after score trying to identify what my inner ear was hearing.

Talk about time consuming!

So, I concluded the best way to start was at the top. I had no illusions about getting an interview with John Williams, but I did think I had a decent chance of getting one with Herb Spenser.

Not knowing him, or where he even lived, I was somewhat stumped on how to proceed. Fortunately, after a little prayer, it occurred to me that Herb Spenser would be a member of the Musicians Union. Since I was living in Ventura, California at the time, I placed a call to the local union. I left a message on their machine.

To my delight, a few days later, the local Ventura office called me back with Herb Spenser's phone number. They had checked and gotten permission for me to call and speak with him.

Being a busy professional, Herb Spenser gave me five minutes. Let me tell you something about five minutes. With a dodo, five minutes can be the biggest waste of time in your whole life. But with a professional who knows how to advise and teach, it can change the course of your entire life.

And it did.

In five minutes, Herb Spenser told me exactly what I needed to know. "If you're going to be successful," he explained, "you have to know about a thousand devices because that's the language of orchestration."

And so began the journey to organize and compile this device list on my own and to learn the craft that would empower my music to sing and soar.

Here's the thing about working with any top professional. They'll put you in the right direction, but don't expect to be spoon fed. It's up to you to do the digging.

And dig I did.

Ultimately, I came up with the device list. To explain, "device" was Herb's way of saying combinations and doublings. As a jazz arranger, I knew plenty of those. There was no mystery there.

The beginnings of this list is right here. It's the "secret sauce" list. I know that to be true, because after I finished volume 1, I was over at Warner Brothers with Jerry Goldsmith (*Planet of The Apes, Star Trek, Outland, The Blue Max*, and about 297 other film scores) sitting in the back of the control room with his orchestrator, who blurted out so loudly that everyone turned and looked at me, "Holy Sh*t! You've got everything in here we steal from!"

Indeed I did.

And now, so do you.

What you're holding is multi-volume. Now, to explain what you've got, I have to explain it from an academic viewpoint so it will make sense.

Whenever you see a book labeled *Orchestration*, generally, it's not about orchestration. It's about instrumentation. All of the college texts are designed to be covered in a single semester with a workbook. In that one semester you learn about the individual instruments and how to write for them. That's instrumentation.

When you look at the music examples in all the books, you mostly see single lines of musical examples, not the entire score. So if you're studying say the flute, you'll be given a technique and a single line example to illustrate the technique. Typically, because of copyright issues, that's all you get.

That's where *Professional Orchestration* is different. A huge majority of the musical examples in this book are full page/full score examples. So now you can see, and with the optional audio package, can *hear* the examples in context of the score.

That's a huge help! But with this present volume, there's one other huge benefit you get from my approach (which follows what both Berlioz and Rimsky-Korsakov did in their books).

When you're looking at these examples, organized by the low, medium, high and very high registers for most of the instruments, you're learning the first set of orchestral devices and combinations that covers how to write an orchestral accompaniment to a solo instrument. You'll also discover that there are certain ranges (called "sweet spots" by orchestrators) that composers consistently write for in dramatic writing, regardless of whether it's for film/TV or the concert hall.

Just in Volume 1, *Solo Instruments and Instrumentation Notes*, you have nearly 200 devices mapped out for you, provided you do the score analysis.

The next learning advantage you have comes with the computer and programs that come with orchestral sample libraries. As part of your analysis, you can key the examples into your notation or sequencing program to compare to recordings and live performances when these pieces are performed locally.

If you're working with orchestral sample libraries beyond what comes with the various notation programs, you're also:

- testing your samples to see which ones work and which don't
- building your sequencing skills
- building your recording and mixing skills

All from one full page/full score example.

And because you have "playback" with the orchestral sample libraries, you can also re-orchestrate the example to see why the composer made the choice he did.

Now, a warning.

With all this electronic power, don't think for a second that you don't need to go hear live concerts and talk with musicians, because you do. If you do everything electronically, including restricting your listening to CDs and MP3s, you can make tragic mistakes in your scores that if performed live, will set you back.

Sample libraries are great tools, but they are only musical snapshots of a technique performed in a moment of time.

Having said that, I now want to explain about The 8 Keys to Learning Professional Orchestration since each volume is dedicated to one of the eight keys. This means that each volume is problem/solution driven. Here they are:

Volume 1: The First Key - *Solo Instruments and Instrumentation Notes*

Volume 2A: The Second Key - *Orchestrating the Melody Within the Strings*

Volume 2B: The Second Key - *Orchestrating the Melody Within the Woodwinds and Brass*

Volume 3: The Third Key - *Orchestrating the Melody by Combining Orchestral Sections*

Volume 4: The Fourth Key - *Orchestrating Harmony Within Each Orchestral Section*

Volume 5 : The Fifth Key - *Orchestrating Harmony by Combining Orchestral Sections*

Volume 6: The Sixth Key - *Solving Practical Scoring Issues*

Volume 7: The Seventh Key - *Scoring For Voice and Orchestra*

Volume 8: The Eighth Key - *Scoring For Voices*

One thing else to point out. The Eight Keys are how you approach score study for the examples in this book, and any other study score you might have.

With a highlighter, you mark the score:

1. where the solo instrument is performing (usually the melody or counter-theme)
2. where the melody is being performed in the strings and with what technique(s)
3. where the melody is being performed in the woodwinds and with what technique(s)
4. where the melody is being performed in the brass and with what technique(s)
5. where the melody is being performed with combined sections and with what technique(s)
6. where the melody is being harmonized in three or more parts per section (ensemble writing)
7. where the melody is being harmonized in three or more parts when sections are combined
8. how the tutti's, *ppp, fff*, etc., are written
9. how the orchestra is written behind the solo voice and whether or not the composer doubled the voice with an instrument to help the singer.

These are very simple observations. By applying them to any score, you'll quickly begin to discover how it was written.

I've included examples that have been recorded. I've worked to keep the examples within a restricted group of works so that you would learn a few, well, thus giving you a library of resources that fit into a couple of bookshelves.

As you can see, a lot came from that phone call with Herb Spenser in the Summer of 1981. So please, use this knowledge, and be blessed.

Peter Lawrence Alexander
Petersburg, Virginia
October, 2008

String Section Overview

The purpose of this chapter is to give you basic information about the string section for seating location for live and recording work, and writing insights for various sized ensembles. This information is important because for all recording work, the composer's responsibility is to tell the studio how he wants the ensemble seated. In some cases, composers go so far as to specify which mikes to use, which for work outside of major recording centers is a solid idea to insure quality of sound.

Seating Plan

This is the most common string seating plan for the orchestra.

EXAMPLE 1-1

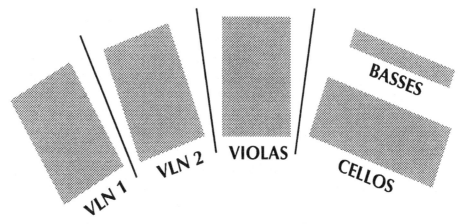

Here, Violin 1 and Violin 2 occupy the far left quadrant. The Violas are mostly in the middle. The Cellos and the Basses are off to the right. The advantage of this seating arrangement is that the tone colors represented by each string section are grouped from left to right as high (violins), medium (violas) and low (cellos/basses). So, each is given its own *space* in which to sound.

The other advantage of this setup is for the violas. The brilliant sounding instruments are placed to the left (violins) and to the right (cellos). The violas, being a middle register instrument, and also being an instrument that doesn't project the same way the violins do, are placed in the middle so that they can be heard. The virtue of this setup can be immediately appreciated by the end of one symphony concert.

The studio setup for a large string section is very similar. The only difference is that each section is given more space in which to work. This is a recording concession. Mikes are placed throughout each section. In the control room, the recording engineer has his faders marked Violin 1, Violin 2, Violas, Cellos, and Basses. In the hands of a competent composer, this seating arrangement enables the beautiful, rich texture of the violas to shine through, rather than be covered.

Outside of major recording centers like Los Angeles and New York, it may not be possible to set up the strings in this exact way since recording studios vary in size. To handle a full session, smaller studios may have to group instrument sections in either booths or rooms. Here are two setups for one such date:

EXAMPLE 1-2

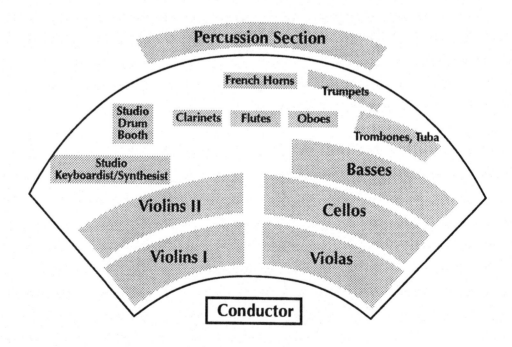

EXAMPLE 1-2A

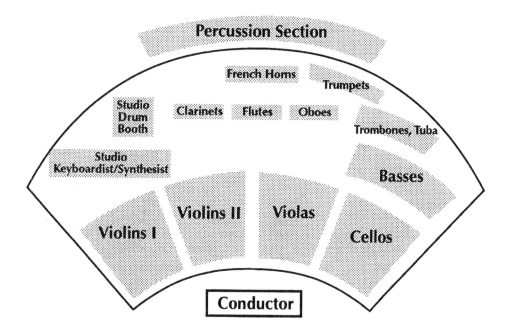

Here, the strings are grouped quite close together. Example 1-2 represents a smaller string section where the violins are grouped to the left. Violas, Cellos, and Basses are grouped to the right. Example 1-2A represents the symphonic string setup of Example 1-2.

To insure the quality of the final mix (for which the composer is generally held responsible in a recording session), it's the composer's responsibility to come down from the podium, go into the control room and hear the *take*. This is an incredibly important task for the composer since even in major recording centers, there are always only a handful of recording engineers who are so immersed in the symphonic sound that you can trust their judgment. Even then, because the final product is the responsibility of the composer, it's necessary that the composer go in and listen to the *take* while the ensemble is seated rather than when everyone has gone home. That way if there's a problem, it can be fixed right then.

Problems in maintaining an effective balance in the mix will generally come from one of three sources: a poorly written score, a poor engineer, or a poorly written score *and* a poor engineer.

String Ensemble Sizes

The composer/orchestrator must know the size and quality of the string ensemble being written for in order to know which orchestral string devices[1] and combinations he can

---

[1] The word *device* is a term some orchestrators use in place of the word *effect*. String *devices* include divisi, fingered tremolo, tremolo, pizzicato, snap pizzicato, col legno, sul tasto, sul ponticello, natural and artificial harmonics, glissandi/portamento, etc. The word *technique* is not appropo because that refers back to the skill of the performer.

successfully use in that project. The chart below shows typical sized string ensembles for both orchestral and studio scoring.

	Full Orchestra	Medium Orchestra	Small Orchestra	One Hour TV Show	Cartoon Show String Section
Violins 1	16	12	8	5	3
Violins 2	14	10	6	5	3
Violas	12	8	4	4	2
Cellos	10	6	3	4	2
Basses	8-10	4-6	2-3	1-2	1-2

To be a constant reminder as to which string devices can be used, Hollywood composers and orchestrators write to the left of the instrument name on *each* score page the number of stringed instruments available per section. You can do almost anything with a large ensemble and it will come off. But with a smaller ensemble, greater care must be taken because some devices just may not work the way expected. (See example below.)

EXAMPLE 1-3

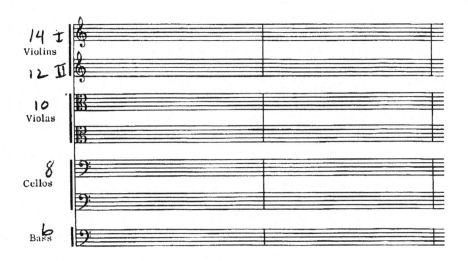

This numbering of available players also helps focus thinking as to which smaller string ensembles within the larger string ensemble can be successfully used. For example, in *Don Juan*, Strauss divides the basses into four parts. Numerically, that device can only be used with two of the listed ensembles in the chart above: the large and medium orchestra. For Debussy's *La Mer*, where the cellos are divided into four parts, it's expected that 16 cellos be used. This means that even for the large orchestra listed above, additional players have to be booked to perform the parts. Four cellos could play each individual part, but the result would be a very chamber-like ensemble sound rather than the big full lush sound expected.

Writing Insights

This section gives you some basic insights to keep in mind when writing for strings based on the size ensemble available for which to write.

Divisi

Divisi is where the individual section is divided into 2, 3 or 4 parts. It's used so that an entire string department (like all the violins) can usually perform a complete 3 - 4 part chord.

Most often the section is divided in half. As a general rule of thumb, unless a chamber sound is specifically desired, it's unwise to divide when there are less than 6-8 instruments per section. This allows for a minimum of three to four players per harmony part. A minimum of four players per harmony part is much more the ideal.

When the section is divided in half, half the players perform the top note, the second half perform the bottom note. When the section is divided into threes, a third play the top note, a third the second note of the chord, and a third the third chord tone. When the section is divided by four (rare), 25% of the section play the top note, and so on. Examine the chart below. Underlining indicates the most successful sounding *divisi* depending on the section size.

VIOLIN 1

Players per Part	4-6 Violinists	8-10 Violinists	12 Violinists	16 Violinists
Div a 2	2-<u>3</u>	<u>4-5</u>	<u>6</u>	<u>8</u>
Div a 3	1.4-2	2.6-<u>3.3</u>	<u>4</u>	<u>5</u>
Div a 4	1-1.5	2-2.5	<u>3</u>	<u>4</u>

With six violinists and up in a section, you can comfortably divide the section in half. But again, six is the minimum. To divide the section by 3, you can get away with 10 violinists, but 12 is preferred. To divide the section by 4, at least 12 violins should be available.

Violas

It's best not to divide the violas when fewer than 8 are available. However, 6 available would be the minimum. Violas are usually divided to serve three purposes.

The first, as used frequently by Ravel, is to fill in triadic chordtones with the divided violins so that the harmonized melody is sounding in octaves:

Violin 1	*Melody*
Violin 2	*Harmony*
Violin 2	*Harmony*
Violin 1	*Melody 8vb*
Violas	*Harmony 8vb*
Violas	*Harmony 8vb*

Notice that the divided Violin 1 plays the melody in octaves. Divided Violin 2 plays the harmony immediately below the melody. The divided violas play the harmony an octave lower under the melody which also is an octave lower.

A second voicing that produces the same sonic result is this one:

Violin 1	*Melody*
Violin 1	*Harmony*
Violin 2	*Harmony*
Violin 2	*Melody 8vb*
Violas	*Harmony 8vb*
Violas	*Harmony 8vb*

The first method is the one more frequently used because on the score, the composer's intent is quickly understood.

The second use is when the violas are divided with divided cellos, and optional added basses, to create a rich, warm ensemble by either performing the melody or a pad with viola lead. When any of these techniques are used, the violins are most often either in octaves performing the melody or a counterline, or they're in unison playing the melody or a counterline. The most common combinations are:

Four Part Harmony	Five Part Harmony	Six Part Harmony
Violas *Div a 2*	Violas *Div a 2*	Violas *Div a 2*
Cellos *Div a 2*	Cellos *Div a 2*	Cellos *Div a 2*
	Basses	Basses *Div a 2* (rare with less than 4 basses)

In each of the above devices, the violas carry the melody. With four-part ensemble writing, another effective ensemble (used by Ravel in *Rapsodie Espagnole*) is viola (melody), cello (harmony), viola (harmony), cello (harmony or melody 8vb.)

The third use is when the violas are divided to perform the melody as a soli in two part writing. This does not happen as often as it should. But to work, 6-8 violas are the minimum.

Cellos: The Exception

An exception to this for smaller ensembles is with the cellos. If there are 4 violas, 4 cellos and 2 basses for example, you can divide the cellos in half for a fourth harmony part. Some film composers feel that since cellos have such a dominant brilliant sound over the violas, the violas are best n*ot* divided in smaller ensembles, but rather kept all on *one* harmony part. So the tendency of some film composers is to divide the cellos instead. Other composers, like Henry Mancini, don't feel that way, and prefer to divide the violas 2 & 2 and the cellos 2 & 2. *(For reference, please see Mr. Mancini's book & CD,* Sounds and Scores, *available from music stores.)*

Using Three Part Harmony

For smaller ensembles where sustained harmony is desired in the score, a strong writing technique is three part harmony with the violas, cellos and basses and *all* the violins playing the melody in unison or octaves.

A second option is to divide the cellos in half, and create an ensemble for sustained harmony of basses, cellos, cellos. This allows the violas to be either doubled with the violins in unison, or for the violas and violins to be added together as a "high" ensemble and then divide the writing into no more than two parts: octaves, sixths, thirds, etc.

For example with 10 violins (5 and 5) plus 4 violas, for a total of 14 players, you could write Violin 1 on the melody (5), divide Violin 2 on the melody and harmony (2 and 3 players respectively per harmony part) and then write the violas unison with the lower Violin 2 part. This now gives you seven players on the melody and seven on either the melody an octave below, or the harmony part. Observe:

Melody   Violin 1 (5) + Violin 2 (2)

Melody 8vb   Violin 2 (3) + Violas (4)

Pad [2]   Cellos, Cellos, Basses

This should point out the *danger* of writing for a mythical ensemble vs. the actual group most likely to perform the score.[3]

Doubling Woodwinds With Divided Strings

Care should be taken as to the number of woodwinds doubled with divided strings. The French school of orchestration suggests 1 woodwind for every four violins at *p*. At this dynamic level, and depending on the range, the violins are colored by the woodwind, but the violin sound remains the dominant color. When two woodwinds are added in unison to four violins at *p*, the woodwind color begins to predominate. When three woodwinds are added in unison to four violins at *p*, the woodwinds now dominate. Excellent examples of this concept can be found in Ravel's orchestration of *Pictures At An Exhibition* and Debussy's *Iberia* [4].

Double Stops

Double stops occur when two notes on adjacent strings are sounded at once. Double stops are either indicated in brackets or with the score expression *non-div*. The notes in a double stop can be sustained, articulated in rhythm with the bow, or plucked for pizzicato. The most common use for double stops is to add a harmony part. This is best done on a sustaining part

---

[2] The word *pad* is a term that means sustained chordal harmony.

[3] Many of the score examples demonstrate devices in late 19th and early 20th century works that required either the large orchestra, or in many cases, an *expanded* large orchestra. The composer must train his mind to scope the sound of these devices, which sound so brilliant in the large orchestra, *down* to the ensemble actually being written for. In general for live performance, it usually takes a *minimum* of three string players on a part, or device, to create a *sectional* feel.

[4] This concept of orchestration is covered in detail in volumes 2-5: *Orchestrating the Melody Within Each Section*, *Orchestrating the Melody By Combining Orchestral Sections*, *Orchestrating Harmony Within Each Section*, and *Orchestrating Harmony by Combining Orchestral Sections*.

and not a rapidly moving rhythmic line. When done on a rapidly moving rhythmic line, the Concertmaster of the string section may, if there are sufficient strings, order the passage to be performed *divisi* instead. For adding harmony, scoring stage experience has found that double stops are best employed in the cellos, especially on sustaining chords where there is little rhythmic movement. When deploying the double stop in the cellos, it's common to double the root of the chord in octaves with the basses while most often sustaining in the double stop the fifth of the chord.

Pizzicato

Because there are four different stringed instruments, there are four different pizzicato sounds, except for special effect and harsher percussive results. In general, pizzicato writing is best kept to the lower three strings on each instrument. The exception is the cello, where all 4 strings are good.

There are nine basic uses for pizzicato, each of which is fully illustrated in this present volume. These nine uses are:

1. *One string section accompanying a solo instrument*

2. *The complete string section accompanying a solo instrument*

3. *Accenting key rhythmic points in the melody*

4. *A walking or a marching effect*

5. *Mixed with sustained harmony*

6. *Within double, triple, or quadruple stops*

7. *To simulate a guitar or other plectrum instrument*

8. *To carry the melody*

9. *For dance and other driving rhythms optionally doubled by low brass*

Basic String Ensembles

The string section can be broken down into six smaller, highly coloristic ensembles with vertical harmony that do not require *divisi* at all. These are:

Violin 1	Violin 1	Violin 1	Violin 2	Violas	Violin 1 + Violin 2
Violin 2	Violin 2	Violin 2	Violas	Cellos	Violas + Cellos
Violas	Violas	Violas	Cellos	Basses	Basses
	Cellos	Cellos*	Basses		
		Basses			

For an added sixth harmony part, a double stop can be used in the cellos as described above.

The first ensemble is most often used for close triadic writing. It produces a rich, lush, warm sound, especially when the violins are in the medium and low registers.

The second and fourth ensembles are used for four-part writing. The second ensemble, lacking the bass, has a rich, warm intimate sound, especially when the violins are kept in the medium register. The fourth ensemble has great depth with the addition of the bass. Used as a pad, Violin 1 is free to carry the melody.

The third ensemble is the full string section written with five-part harmony and the option of the sixth-part with a double stop used on a sustaining chord tone in the cellos as described earlier.

The fifth ensemble is mostly used for rhythm and pads in three-part harmony. All the violins are free to be either used on the melody in unison, or octave, or in two-part open harmony.

The sixth ensemble is for three-part writing and creates a very large sound. Beethoven frequently used it.

Unison and Octave Combinations

These devices are fully illustrated in Volumes 2A and 2B, *Orchestrating the Melody Within Each Section*. However, for the moment, a complete list can be found in the *Professional Mentor* for Volume 1. Go through a number of scores to look specifically for how, when, and in what context composers used these devices. This exercise will do much to eliminate the early nausea experienced when such fearful question arise like, "What's this going to sound like?!" or "Oh, my gosh, what am I *doing*?!"

This way, you know what the device sounds like *before* scoring begins, thus eliminating much of the angst, anxiety, and *Maalox* consumed during the first efforts.

Chapter 2

The Violin:
Basic Information

This chapter covers the basics about the violin. We'll start by looking at the instrument itself. Please study the examples on the following pages.

Parts Of The Violin

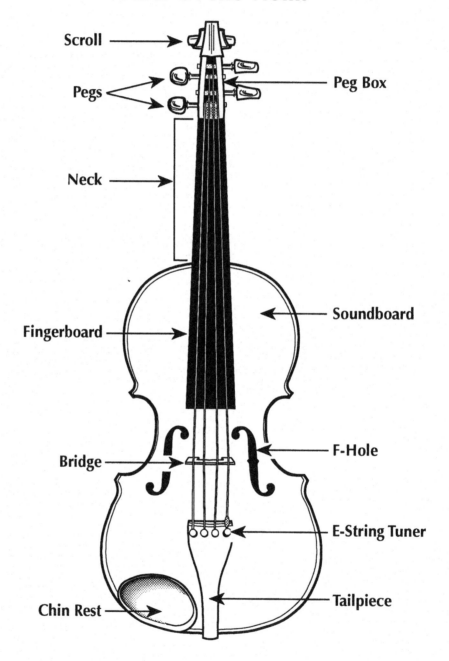

Scroll

Pegs

Peg Box

Neck

Soundboard

Fingerboard

Bridge

F-Hole

E-String Tuner

Chin Rest

Tailpiece

EXAMPLE 2-1A

Side View Of The Violin

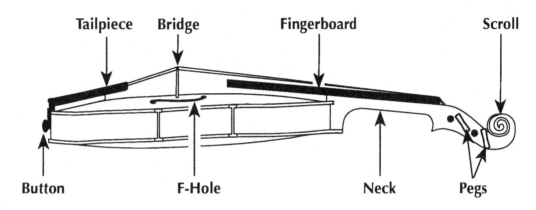

Tailpiece Bridge Fingerboard Scroll

Button F-Hole Neck Pegs

EXAMPLE 2-2

Parts Of The Bow

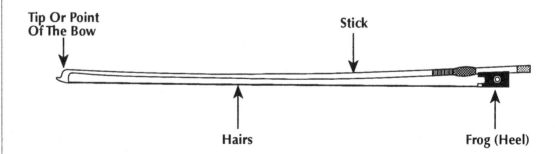

Tip Or Point
Of The Bow Stick

Hairs Frog (Heel)

Range Definitions

The maximum range of the violin can be set at 3 octaves and a fifth:

EXAMPLE 2-3

The comprehensive chart below shows the names of the strings for each instrument, the clefs used, the practical professional range, practical school and community orchestra ranges.

EXAMPLE 2-4

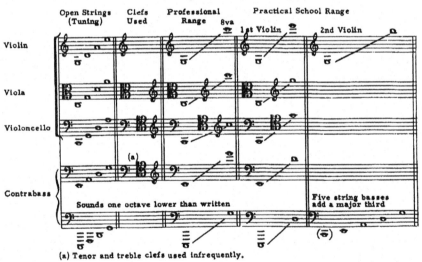

Rimsky-Korsakov has divided this range for the violins into low, medium, high, and very high. The chart below shows the range breaks and on which string the violinist is most likely to perform the passage.

EXAMPLE 2-5

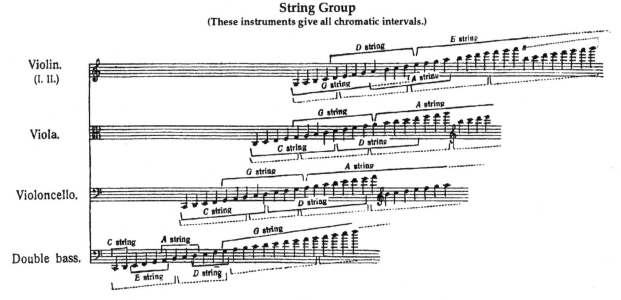

String Group
(These instruments give all chromatic intervals.)

Black lines on each string denote the general range in orchestral writing.
The dotted lines give the registers, low, medium, high, very high.

The examples on the following pages demonstrate how the violins sound in each register.

Score Reference 2-6 Low Violins   **Mozart** *Symphony #36, 4th Movement*

Score Reference 2-6 Low Violins   Mozart *Symphony #36, 4th Movement*

Score Reference 2-6 Low Violins Mozart *Symphony #36, 4th Movement*

Score Reference 2-6 Low Violins   Mozart *Symphony #36, 4th Movement*

Score Reference 2-7 Medium Violins   Beethoven *Symphony #6 1st Movement*

Score Reference 2-7 Medium Violins   Beethoven *Symphony #6 1st Movement*

Score Reference 2-8 High Violins   Prokofiev *Peter and the Wolf*

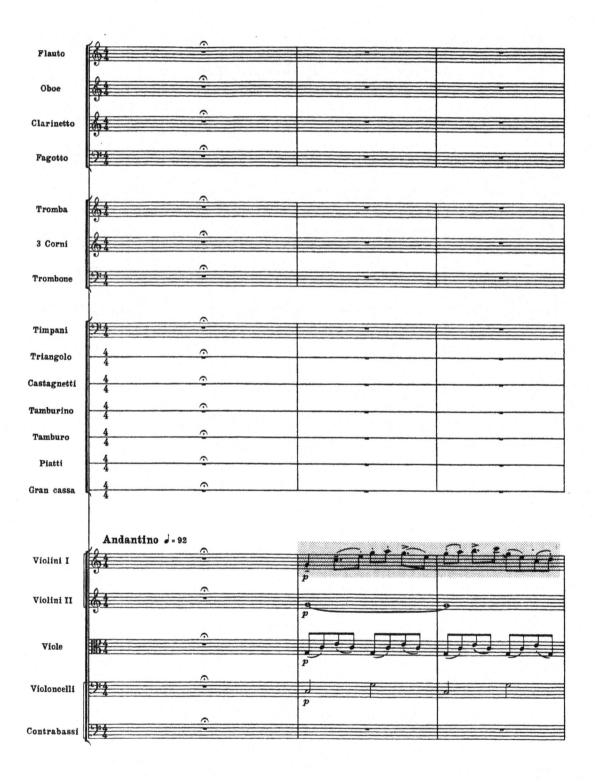

Score Reference 2-8 High Violins   Prokofiev *Peter and the Wolf*

Score Reference 2-8 High Violins   Prokofiev *Peter and the Wolf*

Score Reference 2-9 Very High Violins   Dvorak *New World Symphony, 4th Movement*

Score Reference 2-9 Very High Violins   Dvorak *New World Symphony, 4th Movement*

The Four Strings

There are four strings on the violin: G, D, A, and E. Each of these strings is numbered with the highest being the first string and the lowest being the fourth string. Thus, the highest string, E, is the first string. The lowest string, G is the fourth string. The E string is also called the *chanterelle*. In conversation with violinists, or any string player, always talk about the specific string rather than the actual string number.

Positions and Fingerings

All string playing is a technique of position. By position, it's meant the position of the left hand and the notes across all fours strings, both diatonic and chromatic, that are performable under each of the four fingers as the left hand moves up and down the fingerboard. There are seven basic positions with the highest note on the seventh position being Bb above high C. For notes higher than this, additional positions are used. But most practical writing is contained within the seven positions. The example below shows all the diatonic notes available in each position. The numbers above the notes refer to which finger executes that pitch.

EXAMPLE 2-10

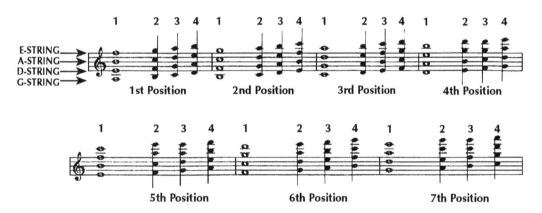

This chart shows that leaps that are impossible to perform on the piano, or other instruments, are *easily* do-able on the violin. Here's a practical example from Bach's *Concerto for Two Violins*:

EXAMPLE 2-11

For the writer with contrapuntal skill, this means that violin parts can be written in two registers at the same time (but mostly for soloists, not practical day-to-day orchestral scoring). Here's an example from Bach's *3rd Violin Concerto*:

EXAMPLE 2-12

Let's look at each of the positions laid out as a scale:

EXAMPLE 2-13

Below is a chart of the first position showing all the available diatonic and chromatic notes.

EXAMPLE 2-14

IV	III	II	I
G	D	A	E
A♭	E♭	B♭	F
A	E	B	F#
B♭	F	C	G
B	F#	C#	G#
C	G	D	A
D♭	A♭	E♭	B♭
D	A	E	B

ETC.

Now, here's the grid with the first position fingering marked as illustrated in Example 2-13.

EXAMPLE 2-15

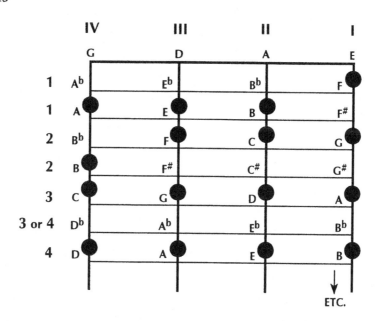

	IV	III	II	I
	G	D	A	E
1	A♭	E♭	B♭	F
1	A	E	B	F#
2	B♭	F	C	G
2	B	F#	C#	G#
3	C	G	D	A
3 or 4	D♭	A♭	E♭	B♭
4	D	A	E	B

ETC.

Note that in first position, except for the open G on the G string, open notes aren't used on the melody, but are in rapid passages.

29

Chromatic Notes

There are two techniques for performing chromatic notes. The older method is to slide the finger to the chromatic note desired. The modern method taught today is for the violinist to treat the chromatic note as an exact fingering position rather than as a note to be slid to. At one time, it was taught that chromatic scales weren't as performable because the chromatic note could only be obtained by sliding the finger from the true note to the altered note, particularly in a rapid tempo. Again, because of newer methods taught, this is not the case, especially with modern 20th century writing.

The ascending chromatic scale is quite practicable. Depending on the caliber of the players, a descending chromatic scale might cause some difficulties in execution especially if the line is very high since when coming down, the fingers are very close to each other.

At one time, it was believed dangerous to perform without preparation the notes contained in the highest third:

EXAMPLE 2-16

but because of improved training, this is no longer true for a professional orchestra, but could be true for an amateur or student group.

Maximum Stretch on One and Two Adjacent Strings

The maximum stretch on one string cannot exceed a perfect fifth. Beyond the fifth, it's not practical unless a soloist has a large hand.

EXAMPLE 2-17

In any *tempo.*

———— Excellent tremolos. ————

From the perfect fifth upwards, inclusively, two adjacent strings have to be used, and then the execution becomes heavy, the bow having to move back and forth from one string to the other. The result is a softer, less delineated sound.

EXAMPLE 2-18

Impossible in
quick *tempo.*

The most practical stretch possible for the hand on two strings (in orchestral playing) is the minor ninth, which should be used carefully. However, a stretch of a tenth across two adjacent strings is quite possible, but it's not practical to assume that all players can reach it.

Tone Quality

Each string has a different tone quality. The outer strings, G and E, are the most brilliant. The second and third strings have a subdued timbre. You can have the violin section play on a specific string by writing the word *sul* followed by the string name. On any of the four strings, you can write up to an octave and a fourth. This is true of all the strings. The lower octave will be the loudest with the power in tone being in proportion to the length of the string. Above an octave and a fourth, you get a cloudy, airy quality that's valid as an effect. It's valid, but not easy.

The Viola:
Basic Information

This chapter covers basics about the viola which is tuned a perfect fifth below the violin. All the information about positions and fingering for the violin applies equally to the violas. The strings of the viola are C (C below middle C), G (above middle C), D, and A. The violas are mostly written in the alto clef, but for very high parts can be written in the treble clef.

The comprehensive chart on the next page shows the strings for the viola, the clefs used, the practical professional range, practical school and community orchestra ranges.

EXAMPLE 3-1

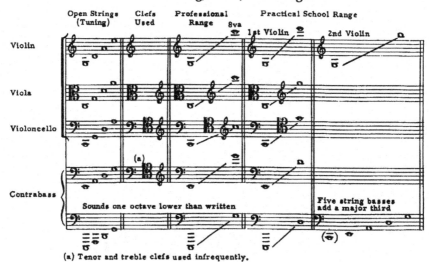

Comprehensive Chart for Strings
Tuning, Clefs, and Ranges

(a) Tenor and treble clefs used infrequently.

Rimsky-Korsakov has divided the range of the violas into low, medium, high, and very high. The chart below shows the range breaks and on which string the violist is most likely to perform the passage.

EXAMPLE 3-2

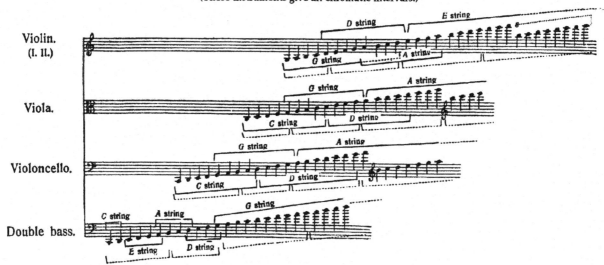

String Group
(These instruments give all chromatic intervals.)

Black lines on each string denote the general range in orchestral writing.
The dotted lines give the registers, low, medium, high, very high.

The examples on the following pages demonstrate how violas sound in each register. In general, the lower and middle registers tend to have a rich, mellow, distinctive, and unusual quality, while the upper registers have a much more creamy texture to them. Violas are often found written an octave below violins that are in the high and very high registers. They're also written in unison with the cellos, and in octaves with the cellos where the viola has the lead. When cellos have the lead, and a light bass is required, violas can be used to fill that function, mindful that the lowest note is C below middle C.

Score Reference 3-3 Low Violas *Schumann* Symphony #1, 1st Movement

Score Reference 3-3 Low Violas *Schumann* Symphony #1, *1st Movement*

Score Reference 3-3 Low Violas *Schumann* Symphony #1, 1st Movement

Score Reference 3-4 Medium Violas   Mahler *Symphony #1, 1st Movement*

Score Reference 3-4 Medium Violas Mahler *Symphony #1, 1st Movement*

Score Reference 3-5 High Violas   Wagner *Parsifal Overture*

Score Reference 3-6 Very High Violas   Wagner *Tristan and Isolde*

Score Reference 3-6 Very High Violas   Wagner *Tristan and Isolde*

The Four Strings

As stated earlier, there are four strings on the viola, C, G, D, and A. Each is numbered with the highest (A) being the first string and the lowest (C) being the fourth string.

Positions and Fingerings

Like the violin, there are seven different positions for the viola. The example below shows all the diatonic notes available in each position. The numbers above the notes refer to which finger executes that pitch.

EXAMPLE 3-7

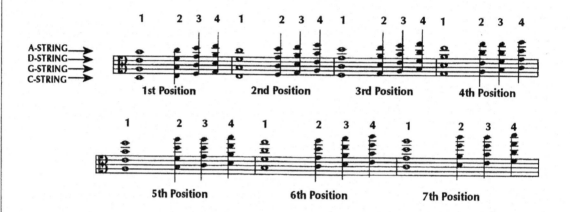

Here are each of the positions laid out as a diatonic scale:

EXAMPLE 3-8

Below is a viola grid of the first position showing all the available diatonic and chromatic notes.

EXAMPLE 3-9

IV	III	II	I
C	G	D	A
D^b	A^b	E^b	B^b
D	A	E	B
E^b	B^b	F	C
E	B	F$^#$	C$^#$
F	C	G	D
G^b	D^b	A^b	E^b
G	D	A	E

ETC.

Now here's the viola grid with the first position fingering marked as illustrated in Example 3-8.

EXAMPLE 3-10

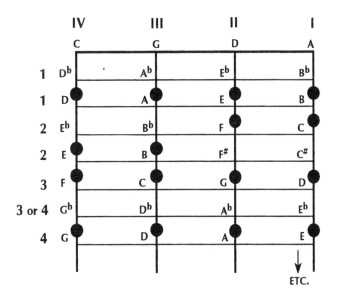

Note that in the first position, except for the open note C on the C string, no other open strings are used. Fast passage work takes advantage of the open strings for tonal clarity. But on the melody, violists are more likely to use covered strings for tone color consistency.

All the information about performing chromatic notes on the violin applies equally to the viola.

Maximum Stretch on One and Two Adjacent Strings

For the violins, it was said that the maximum safe stretch on a single string was a perfect fifth and a tenth on the second string. On the violas, because it's a larger instrument, the perfect fourth on one string and the octave on two strings is the limit.

EXAMPLE 3-11

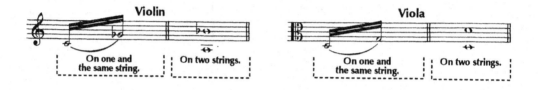

Tone Quality

On the viola, violists consider C and G as the most sonorous. The D string is considered foggy. The A string above 3rd position G becomes more strident.

The Cello: Basic Information

Like the viola, the cello is also tuned C, G, D and A, but sounding an octave below the violas. Thus, since the lowest note on the cello is C two octaves below middle C, the cello can function as either a tenor or a bass.

Range Definitions

The professional range is C two octaves below middle C to E, two octaves above middle C. Soloists can play an octave, sometimes a tenth above that.

EXAMPLE 4-1

The comprehensive chart below shows the names of the strings for the cello, the clefs used, the practical professional range, and the practical school and community orchestra range.

EXAMPLE **4-2**

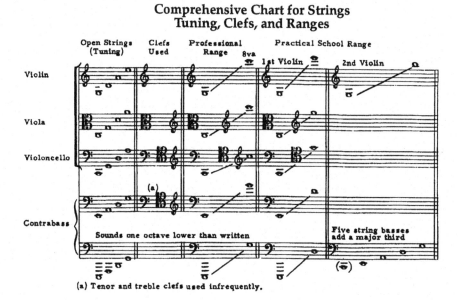

Rimsky-Korsakov has divided this range for the cellos into low, medium, high, and very high. The chart on the following page shows the range breaks and on which string the cellist is most like to perform the passage.

EXAMPLE 4-3

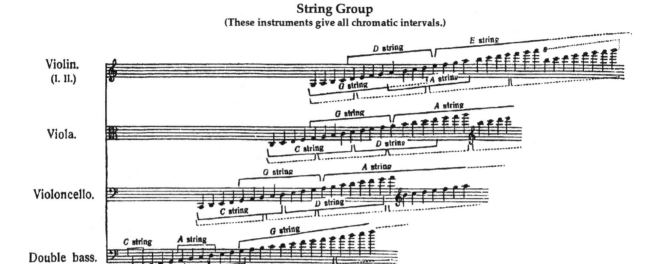

String Group
(These instruments give all chromatic intervals.)

Black lines on each string denote the general range in orchestral writing.
The dotted lines give the registers, low, medium, high, very high.

The examples on the following pages demonstrate how the cellos sound in each register.

Score Reference 4-4 Low Cellos   Sibelius *Swan of Tuonela*

Score Reference 4-4 Low Cellos   Sibelius *Swan of Tuonela*

Score Reference 4-5 Low and Medium Cellos   Mahler *Symphony #1, 4th Movement*

Score Reference 4-5 Low and Medium Cellos   Mahler *Symphony #1, 4th Movement*

Score Reference 4-6 Medium Cellos   **Beethoven** *Symphony #9, 4th Movement*

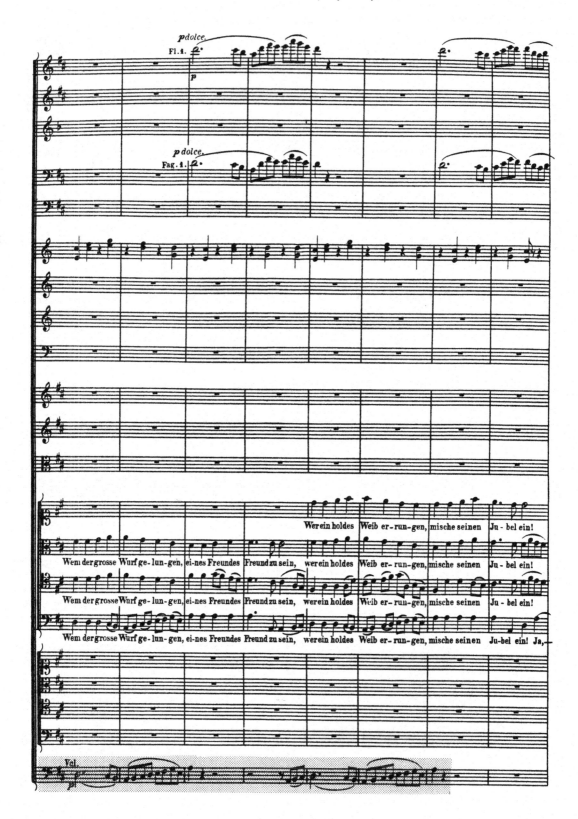

Score Reference 4-6 Medium Cellos   Beethoven *Symphony #9, 4th Movement*

Score Reference 4-7 High and Very High Cellos   Strauss *Don Juan*

Score Reference 4-7 High and Very High Cellos   Strauss *Don Juan*

Score Reference 4-8 Very High Cellos   **Wagner** *Tristan and Isolde Overture*

Score Reference 4-8 Very High Cellos   Wagner *Tristan and Isolde Overture*

Score Reference 4-8 Very High Cellos   Wagner *Tristan and Isolde Overture*

The Four Strings

There are four strings on the Cello: C, G, D, and A. Each string is numbered with the highest string being I and the lowest being IV. The cello range is an octave below the violas.

Positions and Fingerings

Like the violins and violas, there are seven basic positions on the cello. But, because the instrument is larger, the distance that the fingers can comfortably reach is limited to a third, with a maximum stretch of a fourth being possible. However, all fingerings are based around combinations of chromatic notes within the interval of a third. As a result, the cellist might be said to have smaller positions to accommodate chromatics.

Seven Positions Applied on the C-String

Below are the seven basic positions as applied to the C-String only. As with the violin and viola, the cellist has a broad range within each position when all the positions are presented for the G, D, and A strings.

EXAMPLE 4-9

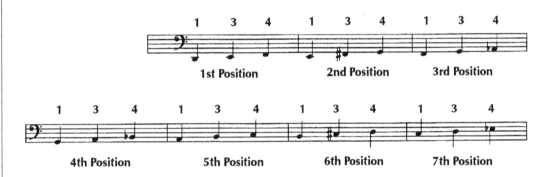

Observe first that only three notes are presented within the positions using a fingering labeled 1, 3, 4 (first, third and fourth fingers). The largest interval the cellist can stretch for in the regular positions is a fourth. Compare to the violin and viola where the maximum stretch on a single string is a perfect fifth.

Fingerings Within Each Position

Within each position are a series of fingerings to account for chromatic notes. The chart below shows the fingerings.

The first bar is the open or natural position.

EXAMPLE 4-10

The second bar with D, Eb, F, has the second finger catching the chromatic note.

The first bar, with D, D#, E, F also has the second finger catching the chromatic note.

EXAMPLE 4-11

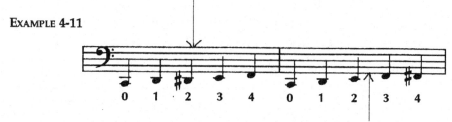

The second bar with D, E, F, and F# has the fourth finger catching the chromatic note.

All these fingering variations are found in just the first position on the C string. This is repeated across all four strings in each of the seven positions.

There are additional "sub-positions" below each of these listed that enable the cellist to account for all chromatic opportunities. Each of these subpositions work within the 3rd interval.

This means that the cellist, unlike the violinist or violist, must change positions more frequently. Also, these shifting positions create mini-portamentos that aren't heavily noticeable, but that are nonetheless present. A large move can produce an exaggerated portamento which can be definitely noticed in a large cello section.

Chromatic Scales
Chromatic scales are fingered with a repetition of the 1,2,3 pattern.

EXAMPLE 4-12

Tone Quality

Like the Violin and Viola, the first string of the Cello is the most brilliant, the one to which the melody is usually given, and which creates the most intense impression. Also like the Violin and Viola, the two outer strings, the 1st and 4th, are the most sonorous. The attack can be more vigorous, because the bow is not hampered as it is when playing on the middle strings, where it constantly runs the risk of grazing the neighboring strings.

The veiled quality of the second string is also very useful. The third string even, may be used in a solo with very good effect, but it more frequently has the bass of the harmony to play, like the fourth, whose full quiet tone is able to sustain the weight of a considerable orchestral mass.

Cellos On the Bass Line Without the Basses

It frequently happens that a composer chooses to put the cellos on the bass line and omit the basses. This creates a warm intimate ensemble sound. When the basses are added, a noticeable change in orchestration occurs whereby intimacy is expanded to depth. Here then, on the following pages are seven specific techniques showing how this is done.

1. Cellos on the bass line doubled by bassoon 2.
2. Cellos on the bass line reinforced by the harp.
3. Cellos pizzicato on the bass line.
4. Divisi cellos on the bass line.
5. Cellos and violas in octaves on the bass line.
6. Cellos on the bass line in an intimate passage.
7. Cellos on a sustaining bass line without the basses.

Score Example 4-13 Cellos On the Bass Line Doubled by Bassoon 2
Beethoven *Symphony #5, Andante*

Score Example 4-14 Cellos on the Bass Line Reinforced by the Harp   Bizet *Carmen, Seguidilla*

Score Example 4-14 Cellos on the Bass Line Reinforced by the Harp   Bizet *Carmen, Seguidilla*

Score Example 4-15 Cellos Pizzicato on the Bass Line at *pp*
Ravel *Mother Goose Suite, Laideronnette*

Score Example 4-16 Divisi Cellos at *pp* Performing the Bass Line
Debussy *Pelleas et Melisande Act 2, Scene 2*

Score Example 4-17 Cellos and Violas in Octaves on the Bass Line
Bizet *Carmen Street Boys Chorus Act 1*

Score Example 4-18 Cellos On the Bass Line in an Intimate Passage
Ravel *Mother Goose Suite, The Fairy Garden*

Score Example 4-18 Cellos On the Bass Line in an Intimate Passage
Ravel *Mother Goose Suite, The Fairy Garden*

Score Example 4-19 Cellos on the Bass Line in an Intimate Passage
Wagner *Overture to Parsifal*

Score Example 4-20 Cellos on a Sustaining Bass Line Without the Basses
Ravel *Mother Goose Suite, Laideronnette*

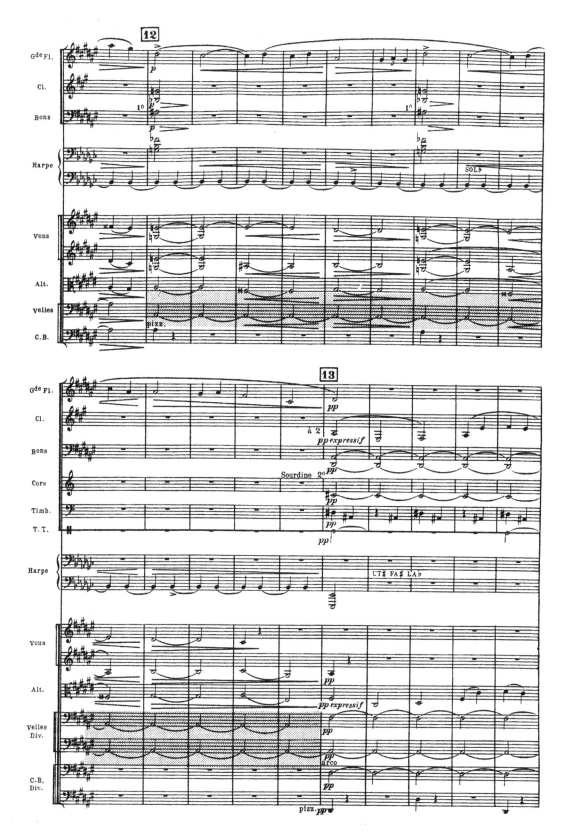

The String Bass: Basic Information

The bass is tuned E,A,D, and G, but sounding an octave *below* where written. This makes the bass the only transposing string instrument. Modern bass parts are now written down to the low C. To do this, bass players either have a device called an *extender* which lowers the E string down to C, or a five string bass where the lowest note is a C. This then gives the bassist C, E, A, D, and G strings.

In major recording centers, writing the basses down to low C is reasonable to do. Outside of those centers with schools and community orchestras, you can't assume that the players will have basses equipped to reach the lower notes. In that case you're safer not writing below the open E. When contracting bass players for a recording session, be sure to specify (especially outside of Los Angeles and New York) that the basses need to reach low C.

Range Definitions

With either the extender or the fifth C-string, plus the use of steel strings, the professional range (sounding) is C three octaves below middle C to D above middle C. Virtuosi can play a perfect fourth above this. It's even possible on some basses to reach the low Bb. The written part will be one octave higher. Example 5-1 on the following page reflects the "safe" range.

Note, however, that it's advisable not to write the basses above E above middle C, or G above middle C for practical daily writing.

EXAMPLE 5-1

The comprehensive chart below shows the names of the strings for the basses, the clefs used, the practical professional range, and the practical school and community orchestra range.

EXAMPLE 5-2

**Comprehensive Chart for Strings
Tuning, Clefs, and Ranges**

(a) Tenor and treble clefs used infrequently.

Rimsky-Korsakov has divided this range for the basses into low, medium, high, and very high. The chart on the following page shows the range breaks and on which string the bassist is most likely to perform the passage.

EXAMPLE 5-3

String Group
(These instruments give all chromatic intervals.)

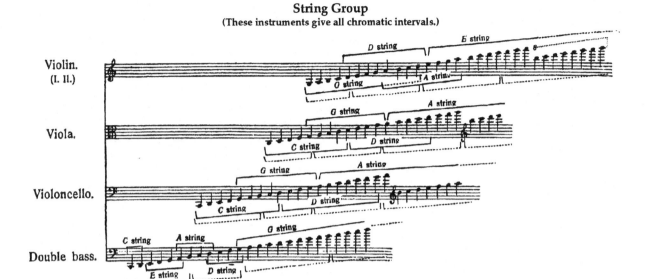

Black lines on each string denote the general range in orchestral writing.
The dotted lines give the registers, low, medium, high, very high.

The examples on the following pages demonstrate how the basses sound in each register.

Score Reference 5-4 Low Basses   Strauss *Salome's Dance*

Score Reference 5-4 Low Basses **Strauss** *Salome's Dance*

Score Reference 5-5 Medium Basses with Cellos   Beethoven *Symphony #9 4th Movement*

Score Reference 5-5 Medium Basses with Cellos **Beethoven** *Symphony #9 4th Movement*

Score Reference 5-6 High Basses   Beethoven *Symphony #9 4th Movement*

Score Reference 5-6 High Basses   Beethoven *Symphony #9 4th Movement*

Score Reference 5-7 Very High Basses   Mahler *Symphony #1 3rd Movement*

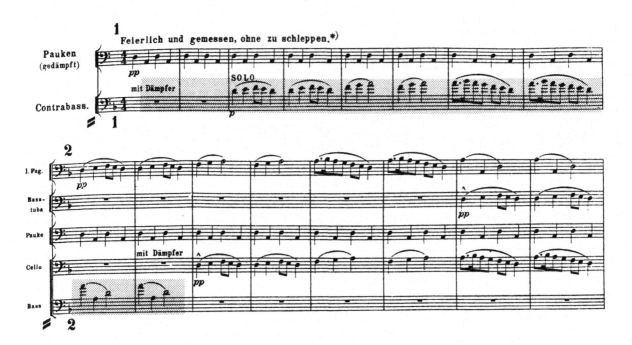

Fingering

Like the other stringed instruments, the bass also has seven positions. The positions are broken down into half positions. See below with the example on the G-string. Notice that through position 5, the fingering is 1,2,4. From position 6 up, the fingering is 1, 2, 3.

EXAMPLE 5-8

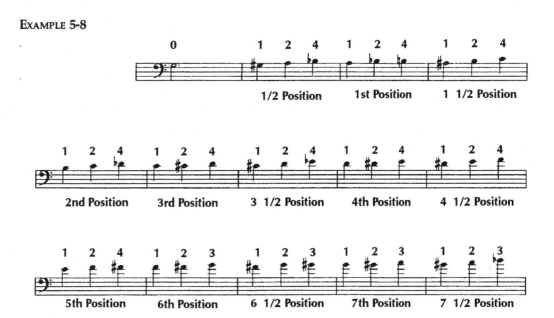

Runs

Rapid runs are often written for the Basses. They are effective and powerful. With runs, cellos usually double the basses. See the example below.

EXAMPLE 5-9

21 Bass Writing Techniques

There are many subtle ways of creating interesting and effective bass parts. The score examples in the following section gives you 21 common techniques. Please note that many of the techniques are from selected works by Bizet (*Carmen*), Debussy (*Pelleas et Melisande*), and Wagner which are not recorded on the accompanying tapes. Both full scores and recordings are available of these works which should be in every composer's library. If you lack the recordings, but have access to synthesizers and samplers, then sequence the examples to give yourself the flavor of techniques most young students aren't aware of.

1. Cellos and basses in octaves, cellos doubled by timpani.

2. Cellos and basses in octaves and tremolo.

3. Basses doubling a motive in the cellos part.

4. Cellos and basses in octaves and pizzicato.

5. Two part section: cellos and basses in octaves on 1 line, remaining strings in octaves on another line.

6. Cellos and basses in unison.

7. Cellos arco, basses pizzicato, and both unison.

8. Cellos/basses unison on bass line with arco cellos.

9. Basses reinforcing a rhythmic cello line.

10. Arco basses, pizzicato cellos.

11. Different rhythm with basses and cellos.

12. Unison accent note with bass reinforcing cello arpeggio.

13. Basses performing a 5th independent line.

14. Basses as part of a sectional pizzicato chord.

15. Basses and cellos in interlocking 4-part harmony.

16. Basses divided and tremolo.

17. Basses divided playing fifths.

18. Basses divided in octaves.

19. Basses and cellos doubled by bassoon.

20. Divided basses reinforced by bassoons.

21. Basses with melodic theme.

Score Reference 5-11 Cellos and Basses in Octaves, Cellos Doubled by Timpani
Bizet *Carmen, Act 1, Scene 2*

Score Reference 5-12 Cellos and Basses in Octaves in Tremolo
Bizet *Carmen Act 1, Cigarette Girl Chorus*

Score Reference 5-13 Basses Doubling a Motive in the Cello Part
Beethoven *Symphony #7, 2nd Movement*

Score Reference 5-14 Cellos and Basses in Octaves and Pizzicato
Beethoven *Symphony #6, Andante*

Score Reference 5-15 Violas, Cellos & Basses in Octaves to All Strings in Octaves
Bizet *Carmen, Street Boy Chorus*

Score Reference 5-16 Cellos and Basses in Unison Beethoven *Symphony #6, 1st Movement*

Score Reference 5-17 Cellos Arco, Basses Pizzicato in Unison
Bizet *Carmen, Cigarette Girl Chorus*

Score Reference 5-18 Cellos/Basses Unison on Bass Line with Arco Cellos, Pizz Bass and the Cello Note Value Extended **Bizet** *Carmen, Duet of Don Jose and Micaela*

Score Reference 5-18 Cellos/Basses Unison on Bass Line with Arco Cellos, Pizz Bass and the Cello Note Value Extended   **Bizet** *Carmen, Duet of Don Jose and Micaela*

Score Reference 5-19 Basses Reinforcing a Rhythmic Cello Line   Bizet *Carmen, Habanera*

Score Reference 5-19 Basses Reinforcing a Rhythmic Cellos Line   Bizet *Carmen, Habanera*

Score Reference 5-20 Basses Arco with Cellos Pizzicato
Debussy *Pelleas et Melisande, Act 3, Scene 4*

Score Reference 5-21 Different Rhythm With the Bass and Cello and Rest of the Strings
Bizet *Carmen, Gypsy Song*

Score Reference 5-21 Different Rhythm With the Bass and Cello and Rest of the Strings
Bizet *Carmen, Gypsy Song*

Score Reference 5-22 Unison Accent Note with Bass Reinforcing Cello Arpeggio
Bizet *Carmen Act 4*

Score Reference 5-23 Basses Performing a Fifth Independent Line
Mozart *Symphony #41, The Jupiter, Finale 6*

Score Reference 5-24 Basses As Part of a Sectional Pizzicato Chord   Bizet *Carmen, Entr'acte 1*

Score Reference 5-25 Basses and Cellos in Interlocking 4-part Writing
Debussy *Pelleas et Melisande Act 3, Scene 2*

Score Reference 5-25 Basses and Cellos in Interlocking 4-part Writing
Debussy *Pelleas et Melisande Act 3, Scene 2*

Score Reference 5-26 Basses Divided, Tremolo, Sul Tasto with Bassoon Harmony
Debussy *Pelleas et Melisande Act 2, Scene 2*

Score Reference 5-27 Basses Divided Playing Perfect Fifths
Ravel *Mother Goose Suite, The Fairy Garden*

Score Reference 5-27 Basses Divided Playing Perfect Fifths
Ravel *Mother Goose Suite, The Fairy Garden*

Score Reference 5-28 Basses Divided Playing Octaves with Viola, Cello, Bass Ensemble
Debussy *Pelleas et Melisande, Act 4, Scene 2*

Score Reference 5-29 Basses and Cellos Doubled by Bassoon
Mendelssohn *Midsummer Night's Dream, No. 5*

Score Reference 5-29 Basses and Cellos Doubled by Bassoon
Mendelssohn *Midsummer Night's Dream, No. 5*

Score Reference 5-30 Divided Basses Reinforced by Bassoons playing at *f*
Debussy *Pelleas et Melisande, Act 2*

Score Reference 5-31 Divided Basses Doubled in Octaves by Bassoons
Wagner *Overture to Tristan and Isolde*

Score Reference 5-32 Basses With Melodic Theme   Beethoven *Symphony #5, Scherzo*

Bowings, Effects, & Bowing Effects

Bowing uses a back and forth, or push/pull motion. A **downbow** is when the bow moves towards the point of the bow. An **upbow** is when the bow moves towards the frog (or heel) of the bow.

EXAMPLE 6-1

Down-bow ⊓

Up-bow V

String coloristic techniques, excluding vibrato, pizzicato and harmonics, are created by fingering; by specific types of bowing that are used for effect or for specific types of musical/rhythmic figures; by bowing at specific points on the instrument (regular, at the bridge, or at the fingerboard), or a combination of types of bowing combined with location (at the bridge or at the fingerboard). The bowing indication continues in force until the score is marked *position naturale* or *ordinario*.

Basic Bowings

Basic bowings that take place between the fingerboard and the bridge are detached, *legato*, *spiccato/staccato*, *martellato*, *saltando*, *louré*, *punta d'arco*, and *au tallone*.

Detached

English	French	German
Detached	Detaché	Gestrichen

Unless otherwise called for (see specific examples in this chapter), detached (or *detaché* in French) is the basic back and forth bow stroke used on all stringed instruments.

Grand Detaché - means the full stroke of the bow is being used in the passage from the heel of the bow to the point and vice versa. Fastest recommended tempo is quarter = 132-144.

EXAMPLE 6-2

Detaché Moyen - means about a third of the bow is being used. Fastest recommended tempo is MM120 when 16th notes are being written.

Petit Detaché - means that the point of the bow is being used. Fastest recommended tempo is MM144 where 16th notes are being written.

Legato

English	Italian	French	German
Legato	Legato	Legato	Legato

If detached means one note per bow stroke, then legato means two or more notes under the bow stroke. For a louder sound, put fewer notes under a single bow. For faster playing, put more notes under a single bow. As the most general guideline, in moderate tempo with sustaining notes (pads) in the strings, the legato should not exceed four bars in length. A figure like the one below should not go for longer than two bars under the same bow:

EXAMPLE 6-3

Note:

In studio work, the composer can merely mark the lyrical phrasing he wants, and then prior to recording (or even during the session), meet with the concertmaster to explain what he's looking for. As the piece progresses during rehearsal, the concertmaster, with a watchful eye on the composer/conductor to see if he's being pleased, will call out instructions and alternate bowings. Although it's faster for the composer to work out his bowings ahead of time, it should be remembered that for a film score, it's not unusual to have to write, orchestrate, and copy parts for 45 minutes of music in under six weeks. By comparison, Stravinsky took close to a year to write the *Rite of Spring* which is also about 45 minutes long. For concert work, the opposite is true. Bowings must be worked out before rehearsal, but can be and are often corrected in rehearsal with new pieces. How do you gain this knowledge? There are really only three ways. The first is going to concerts where you have the scores and where you both watch and hear the bowings (not to mention asking questions after the concert). The second method is to write short passages that you can have a string player perform for you. The third way is after the piece is written, bring in a top flight violinist to go over the piece and help you work out the bowings.

Spiccato

English	Italian	French	German
Spiccato	Spiccato	Staccato	Abgestossen

Used in slow or moderato tempos. Here the bow is bouncing off the string. This bowing is created by making the middle of the bow rebound after each note. It's best suited to passages requiring great lightness of execution. The quicker the rate of movement, the better the effect. Fastest recommended tempo is MM 80 - 144 when 16th notes are being written in the passage. The loudest dynamic possible is *mf - f*.

EXAMPLE 6-4

Martelé

English	Italian	French	German
Martelé	Marcato	Martelé	Markiert
	Martellato		
	Martello		

This bowing is played at the upper part of the bow each note being attacked abruptly, as if with a hammer. It can be used *p* as well as *f*. Fastest recommended tempo is MM120 where eighth notes are the basis of the passage. Note the little inverted triangle marking used over each note. For triplet passages, as shown below, bring the tempo down to MM100.

EXAMPLE 6-5

Saltato, Saltando (Sautillé, Jeté)

English	Italian	French	German
Saltando	Saltando	Sautillé	Springbogen
		Jeté	

Here the bow is "thrown" on the string so that the bow bounces much like a drum stick. The maximum notes under one bow is 2-6.

Louré

Notes are said to be played louré when each one is articulated, although a number are played with the same bow. This is indicated by little dashes over each note under the slur. This is best used in cantabile passages.

Example 6-6

Punta d'Arco

English	Italian	French	German
Tip of bow	Punta d'arco	Avec la pointe	An der spitze des bogens

Used in fast staccato passages. The music is played at the point of the bow. This is not a technique, only an indication of where the passage is played.

At The Frog

English	Italian	French	German
At the frog	Au tallone	Au talon	Am frosch

This is the opposite of *punta d' arco*. Here the music is played at the heel of the bow. This effect is used for short, forceful playing.

Effects

Glissé/Portato

This is a sliding of the finger, most often on the same string, from one note to another producing a chromatic slide. Can be done across two adjacent strings. Also frequently used with harmonics. A gliss between two notes is indicated with a straight line.

Effect Bowings

Effect bowings include *sul ponticello, sul tasto, col legno, tremolo, fingered tremolo*.

EXAMPLE 6-7

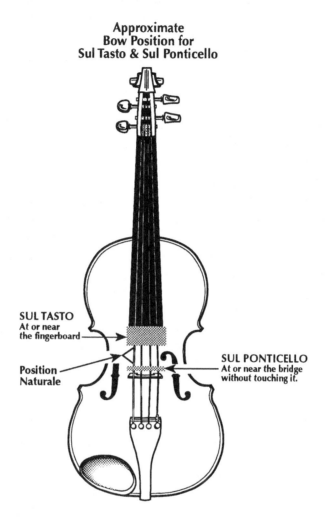

**Approximate
Bow Position for
Sul Tasto & Sul Ponticello**

SUL TASTO
At or near
the fingerboard

**Position
Naturale**

SUL PONTICELLO
At or near the bridge
without touching it.

Sul Ponticello

English	Italian	French	German
Near the Bridge	Sul Ponticello	Sur le chevalet	Am Steg

This means that the string player bows the passage close to the bridge. Frequently done with mutes. Twentieth Century music also has glissandi within *sul ponticello* bowing, along with pizzicato, tremolo and fingered tremolo.

Sul Tasto

English	Italian	French	German
Sul tasto	Sul tasto	Sur le touce	Am griffbrett

This means that the string player bows the passage close to the fingerboard and creates a soft, floating sound. Frequently done with mutes for quiet delicate passages. Maximum dynamic possible is *mf*. Twentieth Century music also has glissandi within *sul tasto* bowing along with *pizzicato, tremolo* and *fingered tremolo*.

Col Legno

English	Italian	French	German
Col legno	col legno	Avec le bois	Col legno gestrichen

Means that the strings are struck with the back of the bow. The sound produced is like a dry "cleek." Col legno can be written with or without specific pitches. Long rhythmic values indicate multiple bounces creating a type of *cleeky* bubbling effect as heard in the film *Close Encounters of the Third Kind* when the aliens leave the ship. Also used for rhythmic accents.

Tremolando

English	Italian	French	German
Tremolo	Tremolo	Tremolo	Tremolo

This is a rapid back and forth movement of the bow on a single string playing a specific note. Occasionally, but not often, double stops are also tremoloed. Used for dramatic moments usually indicating mystery, warning, danger, or high anticipation.

Fingered Tremolo

The difference between a fingered tremolo and a trill is that a trill is restricted to either a step or half step. A fingered tremolo is a minor third or larger up to a perfect 5th. Both are performed on the same string. For consistency of tone quality, fingered tremolos are best when *not* written for open strings. There are two types: non-measured, as illustrated below creates a floating effect:

EXAMPLE 6-8

type 2 is a measured fingered tremolo used when rhythmic precision is wanted.

> ### *Note:*
> To enhance readability, bowings have not been highlighted on the following score references since they are clearly marked on the score.

Score Reference 6-9 Detached   Stravinsky *Petrushka*

Score Reference 6-9 Detached Stravinsky *Petrushka*

Score Reference 6-10 Detached   Tchaikovsky *Symphony #6, 1st Movement*

Score Reference 6-10 Detached   Tchaikovsky *Symphony #6, 1st Movement*

Score Reference 6-11 Successive Downbows   Rimsky-Korsakov *Capriccio Espagnole*

Score Reference 6-12 Successive Downbows   Stravinsky *Petruchka*

Score Reference 6-12 Successive Downbows Stravinsky *Petruchka*

Score Reference 6-13 Successive Upbows **Prokofiev** *Peter and the Wolf* at 1

Score Reference 6-14 Legato & Spiccato   Mendelssohn *Symphony #4, The Italian*

Score Reference 6-15 Spiccato & Jeté   Rimsky-Korsakov *Capriccio Espagnole,* Solo Violin

Score Reference 6-15 Spiccato & Jeté   Rimsky-Korsakov *Capriccio Espagnole,* Solo Violin

Score Reference 6-15 Spiccato & Jeté Rimsky-Korsakov *Capriccio Espagnole,* Solo Violin

Score Reference 6-16 Spiccato Rimsky-Korsakov *Capriccio Espagnole,* Solo Violin

Score Reference 6-17 Spiccato   Mendelssohn *Midsummer Night's Dream, Scherzo*

Score Reference 6-17 Spiccato **Mendelssohn** *Midsummer Night's Dream, Scherzo*

Score Reference 6-17 Spiccato Mendelssohn *Midsummer Night's Dream, Scherzo*

Score Reference 6-17 Spiccato   Mendelssohn *Midsummer Night's Dream, Scherzo*

Score Reference 6-17 Spiccato **Mendelssohn** *Midsummer Night's Dream, Scherzo*

Score Reference 6-18 Saltando (Sautille, Jete)   Rimsky-Korsakov *Capriccio Espagnole* Vln 1- Vln 2

Score Reference 6-19 Saltando (Sautille, Jeté)
Rimsky-Korsakov *Capriccio Espagnole,* Vln1, Vln2, Violas, Cellos

Score Reference 6-19 Saltando (Sautille, Jeté)
Rimsky-Korsakov *Capriccio Espagnole,* Vln1, Vln2, Violas, Cellos

Score Reference 6-20 Saltando (Sautille, Jeté)
Ravel *Rapsodie, Espagnole Malaguena,* Vln 1, Vln2, Violas

Score Reference 6-21 Glissando/Portamento
Ravel *Rapsodie Espagnole, Malaguena,* First Violins

Score Reference 6-21 Glissando/Portamento
Ravel *Rapsodie Espagnole, Malaguena,* First Violins

Score Reference 6-22 Glissando/Portamento   Ravel *Rapsodie Espagnole, Feria* Vln 1 to Vln2

Score Reference 6-22 Glissando/Portamento   Ravel *Rapsodie Espagnole, Feria* Vln 1 to Vln2

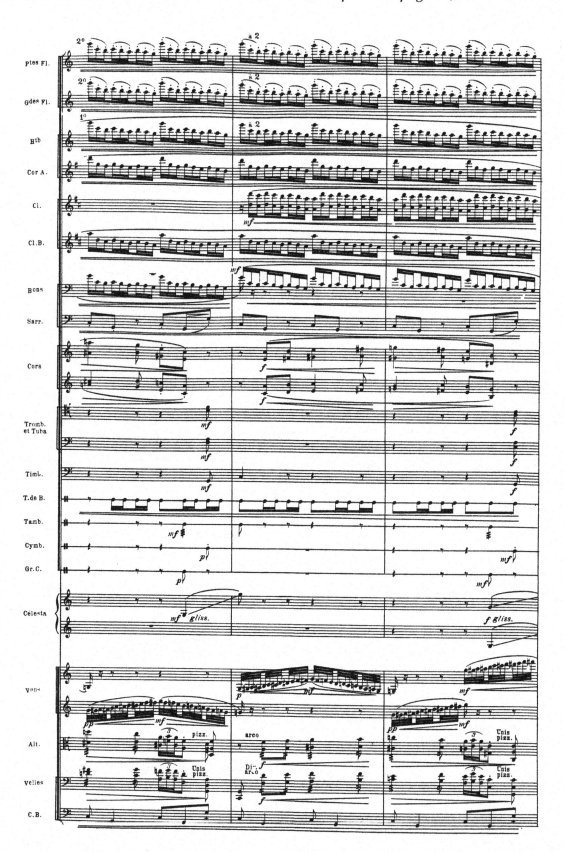

Score Reference 6-23 Glissando/Portamento Mahler *Symphony #1 2nd Movement* Vln1 -Vln2

Score Reference 6-24 Glissando/Portamento
Ravel *Rapsodie Espagnole, Malaguena,* Violas, Cellos & Basses

Score Reference 6-25 Glissando/Portamento Ravel *Daphnis and Chloe* [92]

Score Reference 6-26 Glissando/Portamento in Harmonics
Ravel *Rapsodie Espagnole, Feria* Cellos & Basses

Score Reference 6-27 Glissando/Portamento in Harmonics
Ravel *Mother Goose Suite, Beauty and the Beast* Vln 1 solo

Score Reference 6-28 Punta d'Arco   Berlioz *Symphony Fantastique*

Score Reference 6-29 Sul Ponticello with Au Tallone   Debussy *La Mer* at [62] Vln2 - Violas

Score Reference 6-30 Sul Ponticello   *Prokofiev* Peter and the Wolf

Score Reference 6-30 Sul Ponticello *Prokofiev Peter and the Wolf*

Score Reference 6-30 Sul Ponticello *Prokofiev* Peter and the Wolf

Score Reference 6-31 Sul Ponticello with Glissando
Ravel *Rapsodie Espagnole, Feria,* Viola and Cello

Score Reference 6-32 Sul Tasto **Ravel** *Rapsodie Espagnole, Habanera* Vln 1

Score Reference 6-32 Sul Tasto Ravel *Rapsodie Espagnole, Habanera* Vln 1

Score Reference 6-33 Sul Tasto
Ravel *Rapsodie Espagnole, Malaguena* Vln1, Vln2, Violas, Cellos

Score Reference 6-33 Sul Tasto
Ravel *Rapsodie Espagnole, Malaguena* Vln1, Vln2, Violas, Cellos

Score Reference 6-34 Sul Tasto with Glissando
Ravel *Rapsodie Espagnole, Feria* Vln1, Violas, Cellos

Score Reference 6-35 Sul Tasto with Glissando
Ravel *Daphnis & Chloe*, Violas, Cellos, Basses at 73

Score Reference 6-36 Col Legno   Prokofiev *Peter and the Wolf* [48] 5 following

Score Reference 6-36 Col Legno   Prokofiev *Peter and the Wolf* [48] 5 following

Score Reference 6-37 Tremolo **Bizet** *Prelude to Carmen,* Vln 1, Vln2, Violas

Score Reference 6-37 Tremolo **Bizet** *Prelude to Carmen,* Vln 1, Vln2, Violas

Score Reference 6-37 Tremolo   Bizet *Prelude to Carmen,* Vln 1, Vln2, Violas

Score Reference 6-38 Tremolo
Ravel *Rapsodie Espagnole, Malaguena,* Vln1, Vln2, Violas, Cellos

Score Reference 6-38 Tremolo
Ravel *Rapsodie Espagnole, Malaguena,* Vln1, Vln2, Violas, Cellos

Score Reference 6-39 Tremolo   Debussy *La Mer,* Across the Whole Section

Score Reference 6-39 Tremolo   Debussy *La Mer,* Across the Whole Section

Score Reference 6-40 Tremolo with Col Legno   Sibelius *Swan of Tuonela*

Score Reference 6-40 Tremolo with Col Legno   Sibelius *Swan of Tuonela*

Score Reference 6-40 Tremolo with Col Legno   Sibelius *Swan of Tuonela*

Score Reference 6-41 Tremolo with Sul Ponticello
Prokofiev *Peter and the Wolf* [23]2 following

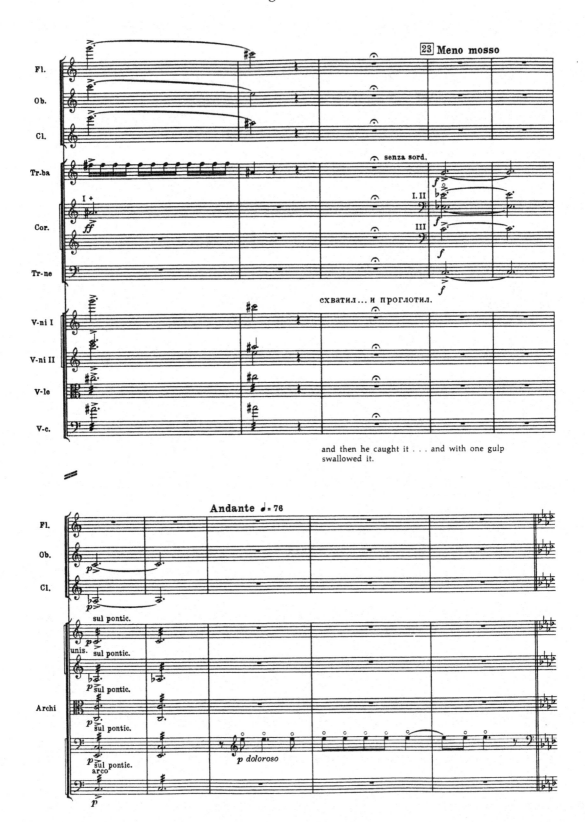

and then he caught it . . . and with one gulp
swallowed it.

Score Reference 6-42 Tremolo with Sul Tasto
Ravel *Rapsodie Espagnole, Prelude a la Nuit,* Vln1, Vln2, Violas

Score Reference 6-43 Tremolo with Sul Tasto
Ravel *Rapsodie Espagnole Prelude a la Nuit,* Across the Section

Score Reference 6-43 Tremolo with Sul Tasto
Ravel *Rapsodie Espagnole Prelude a la Nuit,* Across the Section

Score Reference 6-44 Fingered Tremolo
Ravel *Mother Goose Suite, The Fairy Garden* Vln1, Vln2, Violas

Score Reference 6-44 Fingered Tremolo
Ravel *Mother Goose Suite, The Fairy Garden* Vln1, Vln2, Violas

Score Reference 6-45 Fingered Tremolo with Sul Tasto
Ravel *Mother Goose Suite, Laideronnette*

Score Reference 6-45 Fingered Tremolo with Sul Tasto
Ravel *Mother Goose Suite, Laideronnette*

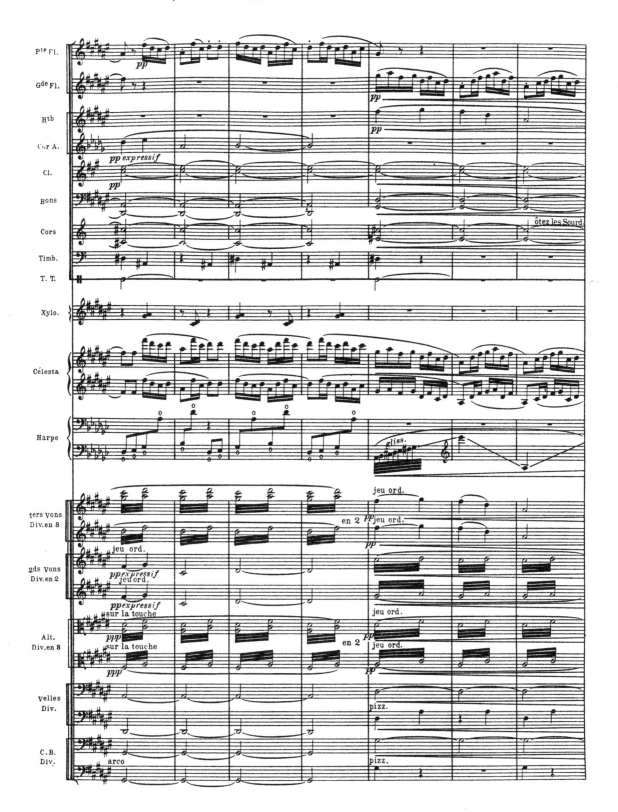

Score Reference 6-45 Fingered Tremolo with Sul Tasto
Ravel *Mother Goose Suite, Laideronnette*

Score Reference 6-46 Fingered Tremolo with Sul Tasto
Debussy *Prelude to the Afternoon of a Faun*

Score Reference 6-46 Fingered Tremolo with Sul Tasto
Debussy *Prelude to the Afternoon of a Faun*

Score Reference 6-46 Fingered Tremolo with Sul Tasto
Debussy *Prelude to the Afternoon of a Faun*

Score Reference 6-47 Fingered Tremolo with Sul Ponticello   Debussy *La Mer*

String Stops

In this chapter, we cover the issue of string stops for the quartet. This includes a complete listing per instrument chromatically of many of the available triple and quadruple stops.

General Comments

There are three kinds of string stops: double, triple and quadruple. Stops can be bowed, played pizzicato, or strummed for guitar-like effects. Stops are sounded across two or more adjacent strings. Depending on the sound desired by the composer or the use of the lowest string played open, string players generally work out the fingerings so that no open strings sound, thus creating an evenness of tone. Traditional part writing is not really possible with stops. Instead, the arranger/orchestrator should concentrate on creating parts with clean smooth harmony. Ease of fingering is the objective. Also, the composer should make no effort to try creating complete harmonic chords per instrument, but rather across the section as a whole. Voicings for triple and quadruple stops can be used to setup effective bowed arpeggio figures.

About the Triple & Quadruple Stop Listings

This chapter contains a thorough listing of triple and quadruple stops for the violin, viola, and cello. This is by no means an exhaustive list, but rather a solid beginning to show the student how to construct stops on almost any chord.

Double Stops

Example 7-1

How Double Stops Work

There are 3 possible pairs of strings for double stops for all string instruments.

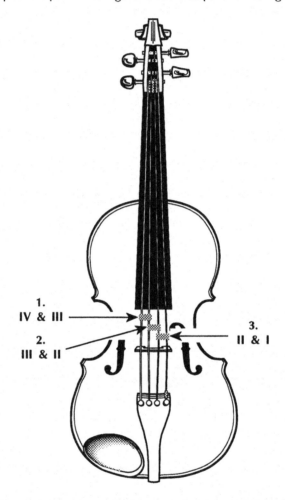

A *double stop* happens when two notes on adjacent strings are plucked, bowed or sustained. Both notes can be sustained. Double stops are most often used to add a harmony part. Bowed double stops are best used within the section on sustaining chord tones vs. even lightly rhythmical passages. If successive double stops are written in a rhythmical passage, the Concertmaster may elect to divide the section. (Sustained double stops can be very effective in the cellos especially when only a smaller section is available.) For the player to perform the double stops, the hand must stretch over two strings to do the fingering. (Thus, the largest practical stretch on the violin is a minor 9th across two strings.) Unless the player has large hands, it's generally not possible to reach the major ninth.

List Of Double Stops In The Order Of Increasing Difficulty
The following list applies almost evenly to all the stringed instruments.

EASY: all major and minor sixths:

EASY: all major, minor, and diminished sevenths:

EASY: major and minor thirds:

POSSIBLE: all perfect and augmented fourths:

POSSIBLE: all diminished and augmented fifths:

POSSIBLE: octaves:

POSSIBLE: major seconds.

RISKY: minor seconds, which should only be used with great care.

Professional studio players report that fourths are particularly difficult because care must be taken to assure proper tuning. So, some additional setup time should be allotted.

Triple Stops

EXAMPLE 7-2

How Triple Stops Work

There are 2 possible sets of strings for triple stops for all string instruments.

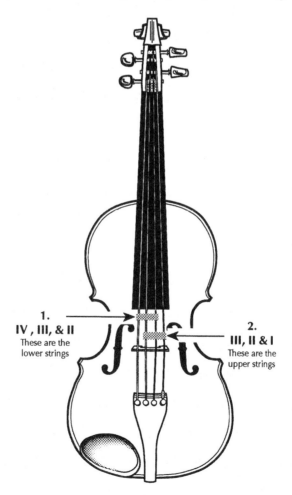

1.
IV , III, & II
These are the
lower strings

2.
III, II & I
These are the
upper strings

Triple stops happen when three adjacent strings are used. They can be plucked or bowed. (On the piano, this is the equivalent of a snap roll technique.) Since two notes can be sustained, only the top two notes of the triple stop are sustainable.

Quadruple Stops

Example 7-3

How Quadruple Stops Work

All four strings are plucked or bowed from low (IV) to high (I).

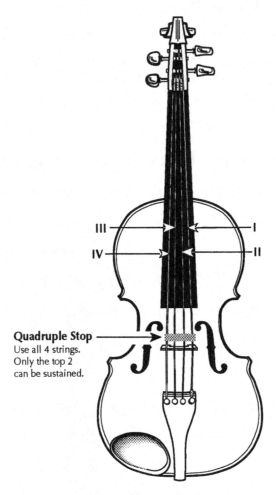

III ─ IV
I ─ II

Quadruple Stop
Use all 4 strings.
Only the top 2
can be sustained.

All four strings are used in a quadruple stop. They can be plucked or bowed. Since two notes can be sustained, only the top two notes of the quadruple stop are sustainable.

The Violin

As follows is a review of double, triple and quadruple stops for the violins.

Double Stops

It's easy to play all double stops that include an open string. For professional studio and orchestra players, the upper limits can be extended by three half-steps.

List of double stops in the order of increasing difficulty:
EASY: all major and minor sixths:

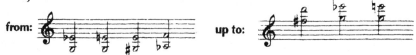

EASY: all major, minor, and diminished sevenths:

EASY: major and minor thirds:

POSSIBLE: all perfect and augmented fourths:

POSSIBLE: all diminished and augmented fifths:

POSSIBLE: octaves:

From this D upwards they become more and more difficult.

POSSIBLE: major seconds.

RISKY: minor seconds. Only use them with great care.

Triple Stops

As follows is a review of triple stops for the violins presented chromatically by the dominant seventh chord and with resolutions.

Key of C: 3-part Dominant Seventh Chords and Resolutions

In 3 parts

Resolutions

Key of Db: 3-part Dominant Seventh Chords and Resolutions

In 3 parts

Resolutions

possible in the minor mode only.

Key of C#: 3-part Dominant Seventh Chords and Resolutions

In 3 parts

Resolutions

possible in the minor mode only.

Key of D: 3-part Dominant Seventh Chords and Resolutions

In 3 parts

Resolutions

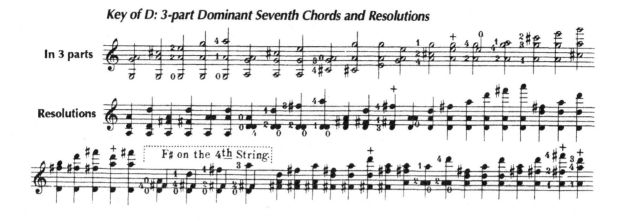

F♯ on the 4th String.

Key of Eb: 3-part Dominant Seventh Chords and Resolutions

In 3 parts

Resolutions

Key of E: 3-part Dominant Seventh Chords and Resolutions

In 3 parts

Resolutions

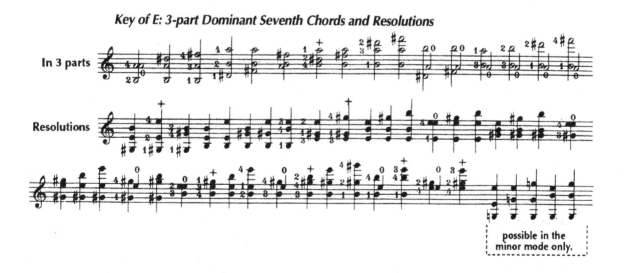

possible in the
minor mode only.

Key of F: 3-part Dominant Seventh Chords and Resolutions

In 3 parts

Resolutions

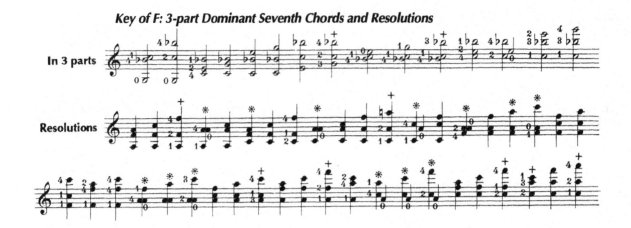

Key of F#: 3-part Dominant Seventh Chords and Resolutions

In 3 parts

Resolutions

possible in the
minor mode only.

Key of G: 3-part Dominant Seventh Chords and Resolutions

In 3 parts

Resolutions

Key of Ab: 3-part Dominant Seventh Chords and Resolutions

In 3 parts

Resolutions

Key of A: 3-part Dominant Seventh Chords and Resolutions

In 3 parts

Resolutions

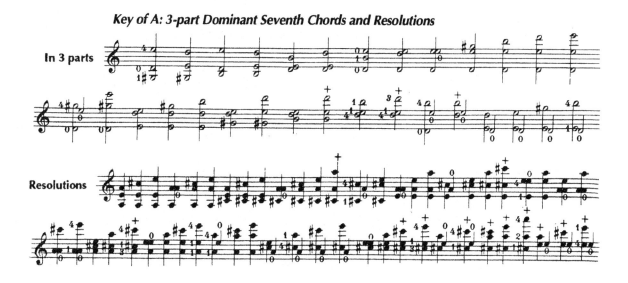

Key of Bb: 3-part Dominant Seventh Chords and Resolutions

In 3 parts

Resolutions

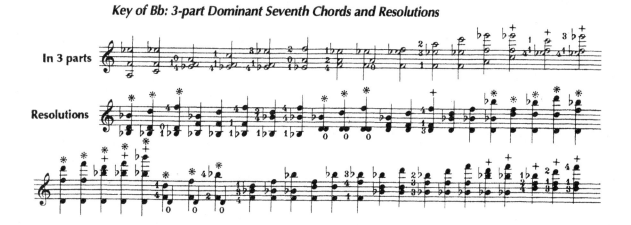

Key of B: 3-part Dominant Seventh Chords and Resolutions

In 3 parts

Resolutions

possible in the minor mode only.

Quadruple Stops

As follows is a review of quadruple stops for the violins presented chromatically by the dominant seventh chord and with resolutions.

Key of C: 4-part Dominant Seventh Chords and Resolutions

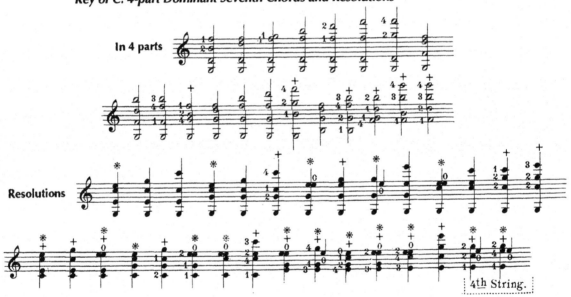

In 4 parts

Resolutions

4th String.

Key of Db: 4-part Dominant Seventh Chords and Resolutions

In 4 parts

Resolutions

possible in the minor mode only.

Key of C#: 4-part Dominant Seventh Chords and Resolutions

In 4 parts

Resolutions

possible in the
minor mode only.

Key of D: 4-part Dominant Seventh Chords and Resolutions

In 4 parts

Resolutions

Key of Eb: 4-part Dominant Seventh Chords and Resolutions

In 4 parts

Resolutions

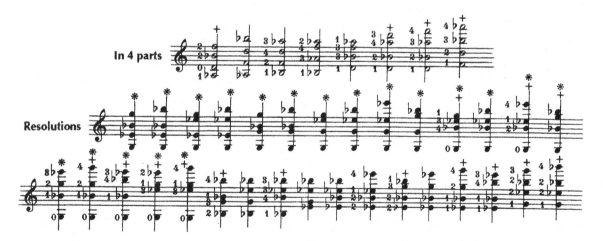

Key of E: 4-part Dominant Seventh Chords and Resolutions

In 4 parts

Resolutions

possible in the minor mode only.

Key of F: 4-part Dominant Seventh Chords and Resolutions

In 4 parts

Resolutions

Key of F#: 4-part Dominant Seventh Chords and Resolutions

In 4 parts

Resolutions

possible in the
minor mode only.

Key of G: 4-part Dominant Seventh Chords and Resolutions

In 4 parts

Resolutions

Key of Ab: 4-part Dominant Seventh Chords and Resolutions

In 4 parts

Resolutions

Key of A: 4-part Dominant Seventh Chords and Resolutions

In 4 parts

Resolutions

Key of Bb: 4-part Dominant Seventh Chords and Resolutions

In 4 parts

Resolutions

Key of B: 4-part Dominant Seventh Chords and Resolutions

In 4 parts

Resolutions

possible in the
minor mode only.

Diminished Seventh Chords

On the 3 Lower Strings

**In 3 parts.
On the three
lower strings.**

On the 3 Higher Strings

**On the three
higher strings.**

In 4-Parts

In 4 parts

Major and Minor Ninth Chords
On the 3 Lower Strings

**In 3 parts.
On the three
lower strings.**

On the 3 Higher Strings

**On the three
higher strings.**

In 4-Parts

In 4 parts

Augmented Fifth Chords

These are easy in four parts within these limits:

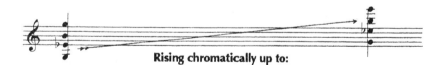

Rising chromatically up to:

The Viola

As follows is a review of double, triple and quadruple stops for the violas.

Double Stops

It's easy to play all double stops that include an open string. For professional studio and orchestra players, the upper limits can be extended by three half-steps.

List of double stops in order of increasing difficulty:

EASY: all major and minor sixths:

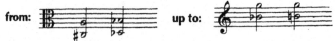

EASY: all major, minor, and diminished sevenths:

EASY: major and minor thirds:

POSSIBLE: all perfect and augmented fourths:

POSSIBLE: all diminished and augmented fifths:

POSSIBLE: octaves:

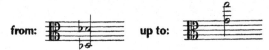

From this D upwards they become more and more difficult.

POSSIBLE: major seconds.

RISKY: minor seconds. Only use them with great care.

Triple Stops

As follows is a review of triple stops for the violas presented chromatically by the dominant seventh chord and with resolutions.

Key of C: 3-part Dominant Seventh Chords and Resolutions

In 3 parts

Resolutions

Key of Db(C#): 3-part Dominant Seventh Chords and Resolutions

In 3 parts

Resolutions

Key of D: 3-part Dominant Seventh Chords and Resolutions

In 3 parts

Resolutions

Key of Eb: 3-part Dominant Seventh Chords and Resolutions

In 3 parts

Resolutions

Key of E: 3-part Dominant Seventh Chords and Resolutions

In 3 parts

Resolutions

possible in the
minor mode only.

Key of F: 3-part Dominant Seventh Chords and Resolutions

In 3 parts

Resolutions

Key of F#: 3-part Dominant Seventh Chords and Resolutions

In 3 parts

Resolutions

possible in the
minor mode only.

Key of Gb: 3-part Dominant Seventh Chords and Resolutions

In 3 parts

Resolutions

possible in the
minor mode only.

Key of G: 3-part Dominant Seventh Chords and Resolutions

In 3 parts

Resolutions

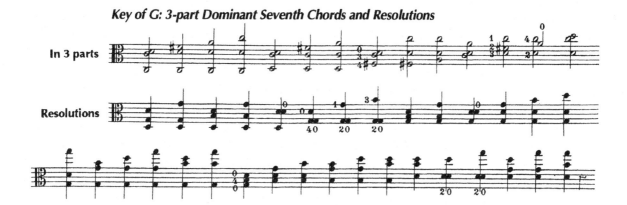

Key of Ab: 3-part Dominant Seventh Chords and Resolutions

In 3 parts

Resolutions

Key of A: 3-part Dominant Seventh Chords and Resolutions

In 3 parts

Resolutions

Key of Bb: 3-part Dominant Seventh Chords and Resolutions

Key of B: 3-part Dominant Seventh Chords and Resolutions

possible in the minor mode only.

Quadruple Stops

As follows is a review of quadruple stops for the violas presented chromatically by the dominant seventh chord and with resolutions.

Key of C: 4-part Dominant Seventh Chords and Resolutions

Key of Db(C#): 4-part Dominant Seventh Chords and Resolutions

Key of D: 4-part Dominant Seventh Chords and Resolutions

Key of Eb: 4-part Dominant Seventh Chords and Resolutions

Key of E: 4-part Dominant Seventh Chords and Resolutions

possible in the minor mode only.

Key of F: 4-part Dominant Seventh Chords and Resolutions

In 4 parts

Resolutions

Key of Gb: 4-part Dominant Seventh Chords and Resolutions

In 4 parts

Resolutions

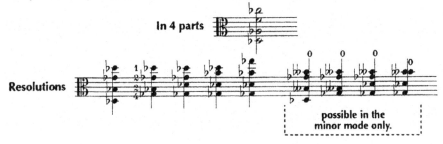

possible in the
minor mode only.

Key of F#: 4-part Dominant Seventh Chords and Resolutions

In 4 parts

Resolutions

possible in the minor mode only.

Key of G: 4-part Dominant Seventh Chords and Resolutions

In 4 parts

Resolutions

Key of Ab: 4-part Dominant Seventh Chords and Resolutions

Key of A: 4-part Dominant Seventh Chords and Resolutions

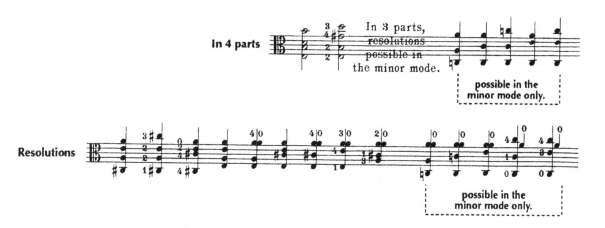

Key of Bb: 4-part Dominant Seventh Chords and Resolutions

Key of B: 4-part Dominant Seventh Chords and Resolutions

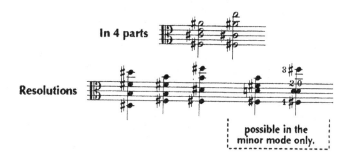

Diminished Seventh Chords

On the 3 Lower Strings

In 3 parts.
On the three
lower strings.

On the 3 Higher Strings

On the three
higher strings.

In 4-Parts

In 4 parts

Major and Minor Ninth Chords

On the 3 Lower Strings

In 3 parts.
On the three
lower strings.

On the 3 Higher Strings

On the three
higher strings.

In 4-Parts

In 4 parts

Augmented Fifth Chords

These are easy in four parts within these limits:

On the 3 Lower Strings

In 3 parts.
On the three
lower strings.

Easy up to:

On the 3 Higher Strings

In 3 parts.
On the three
higher strings.

Easy up to:

In 4-Parts

In 4 parts

Easy up to:

The Cello

As follows is a review of double, triple and quadruple stops for the cellos.

Thumb Positions

The highest note obtainable with the ordinary method of fingering is this B natural:

Above this note, the thumb is taken from its position on the backside of the cello and is placed firmly across and at right angles to the string, thus acting as a kind of artificial "nut." Their use is indicated by the sign which is placed above the note on which the thumb is to rest:

Ọ

Thumb-positions should not be leaped into and out of. Once set, however, other thumb positions can be made easily. Thumb-positions are sometimes used in the medium, or even in the low register. Thumb-positions should, in general, only be employed with considerable care. Skipping suddenly from a note produced by the usual fingering to a note that involves the use of the thumb is very risky, unless, this note happens to be the first harmonic of an open string, in which case the danger is minimized, because this first harmonic will come out, even if the position of the finger is not mathematically accurate.

Thumb Position and Double Stops

The thumb position is also used to stop the lower note of an octave double stop when the lower note is *not* an open string.

Double Stops

Seconds and Octaves

Seconds and octaves, which involve the use of the thumb, are to be avoided in orchestral writing, unless one or other of the notes is an open string:

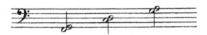

Thirds

Thirds can be classified as follows:

The following thirds can be awkward for orchestral players, and might best be used in a fortissimo:

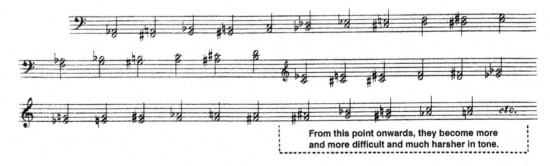

From this point onwards, they become more and more difficult and much harsher in tone.

Perfect and Augmented Fourths:

(Avoid writing higher than this for the orchestra)

Perfect Fifths
Perfect fifths are more satisfactory than on the Violin. They may be considered practicable:

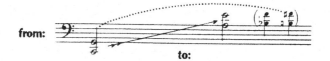

Major and Minor Sixths
All major and minor sixths are excellent:

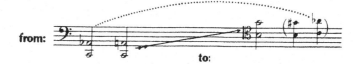

Minor Sevenths
Minor sevenths are more difficult, and their intonation more doubtful.

Triple Stops
The following is a listing of cello triple stops.

Major and Minor Chords
Up to Eb are the best.

First Inversions
First Inversions also pose no problem.

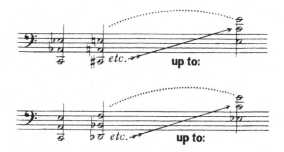

Second Inversions
Second Inversions are also possible.

Augmented Fifth Chords

Diminished Fifth Chords

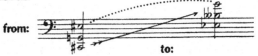

First Inversion of Augmented Fifth Chords

Diminished Fifth Chords

Diminished Fifth Chords, First Inversion

Dominant Seventh Chords

Chords of the Leading Seventh

Chords of the Leading Seventh Second Inversion

Diminished Seventh Chords

Quadruple Stops

The following are practicable:

Common Chords

Their First Inversions

Their Second Inversions

Augmented Fifth Chords

Augmented Fifth Chords First Inversions

Dominant Seventh Chords

Minor Seventh Chords

Ninth Chords

The Double-Bass

Double stops

The following double stops are practicable:

All minor and major thirds:

All perfect fourths:

This is extremely easy for the bassist since the instrument is tuned in fourths (E-A-D-G) while the other string instruments are tuned in fifths.

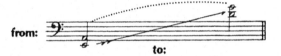

All perfect fifths:

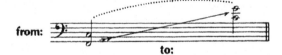

Sixths, Sevenths and Octaves

Sixths are ill advised except in the high register, where they can be played by *virtuosi*, but are *impractical* in the orchestra. The same remark applies to sevenths and octaves (unless the lower note happens to be an open string):

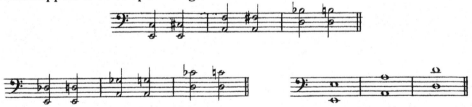

Score Examples With Stops

The following pages contain score examples with stops.

Score Reference 7-110 Double Stops   Prokofiev *Peter and the Wolf*

Score Reference 7-110 Double Stops   Prokofiev *Peter and the Wolf*

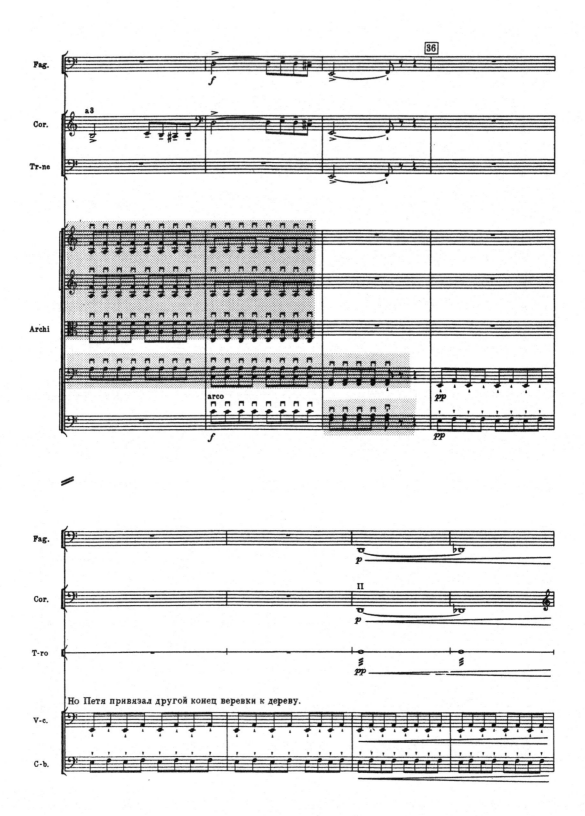

Score Reference 7-111 Double and Triple Stops Mixed   Prokofiev *Peter and The Wolf* [11]

Кошка подумала: „Птичка занята спором? Сейчас я ее сцапаю." И неслышно, на бархатных лапках подбиралась к ней.

Score Reference 7-111 Double and Triple Stops Mixed   Prokofiev *Peter and The Wolf* [11]

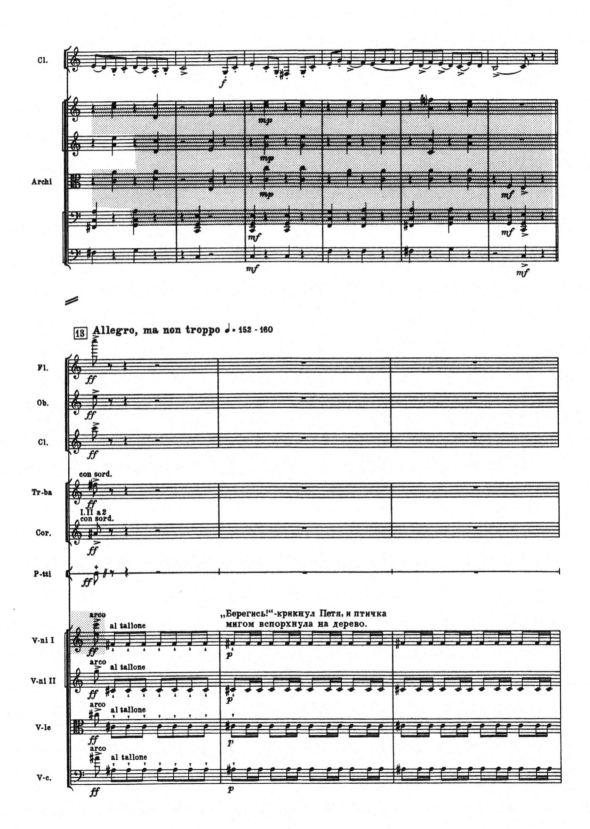

Score Reference 7-112 Triple and Quadruple Stops Mixed Against Woodwind Unison
Prokofiev *Peter and the Wolf* [39]

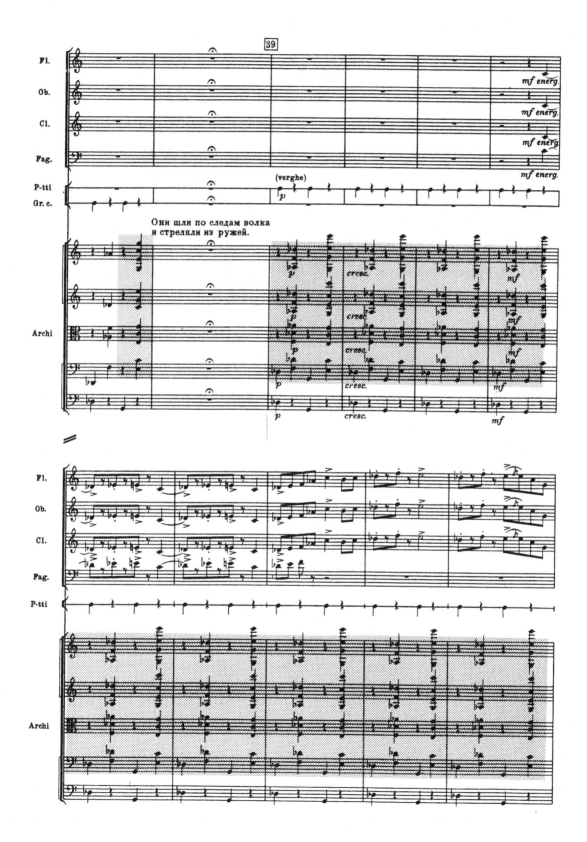

Score Reference 7-112 Triple and Quadruple Stops Mixed Against Woodwind Unison
Prokofiev *Peter and the Wolf* [39]

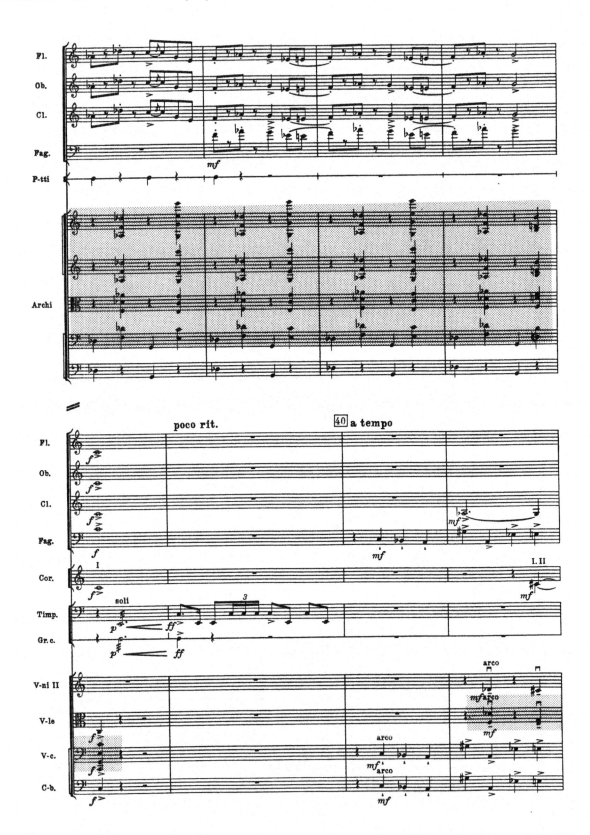

Score Reference 7-113 Triple and Quadruple Stops Reinforcing Brass Punches
Prokofiev *Peter and the Wolf* [31]

Птичка почти задевала крыльями морду волка, и волк сердито прыгал за ней во все стороны.

Score Reference 7-113 Triple and Quadruple Stops Reinforcing Brass Punches
Prokofiev *Peter and the Wolf*

Score Reference 7-113 Triple and Quadruple Stops Reinforcing Brass Punches
Prokofiev *Peter and the Wolf*

Ах, как птичка раздражала волка! Как он хотел схватить ее!
Но птичка была ловкая, и волк ничего не мог с ней поделать.

Score Reference 7-113 Triple and Quadruple Stops Reinforcing Brass Punches
Prokofiev *Peter and the Wolf*

Score Reference 7-113 Triple and Quadruple Stops Reinforcing Brass Punches
Prokofiev *Peter and the Wolf*

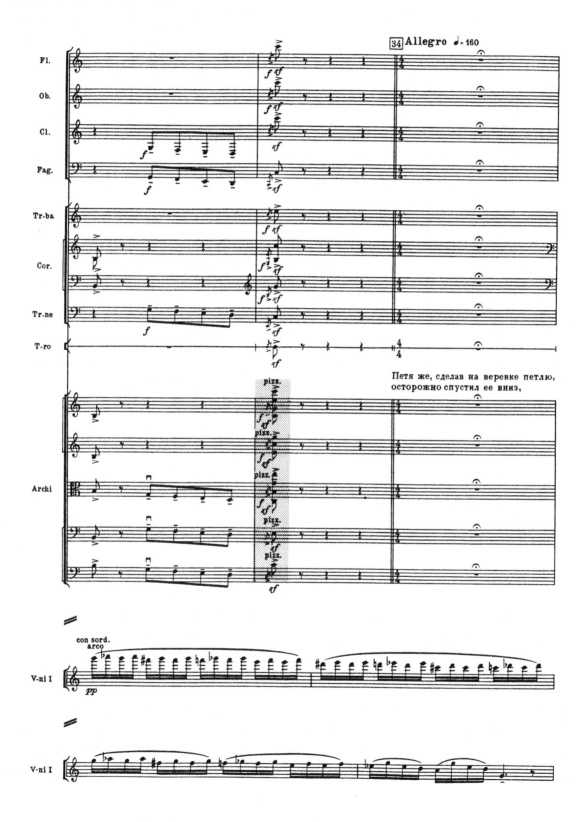

Score Reference 7-114 Stops Used as Basis For Arpeggios   Wagner *Overture to Parsifal*

Score Reference 7-114 Stops Used as Basis For Arpeggios   **Wagner** *Overture to Parsifal*

Score Reference 7-114 Stops Used as Basis For Arpeggios **Wagner** *Overture to Parsifal*

Score Reference 7-114 Stops Used as Basis For Arpeggios **Wagner** *Overture to Parsifal*

Score Reference 7-114 Stops Used as Basis For Arpeggios   Wagner *Overture to Parsifal*

Score Reference 7-114 Stops Used as Basis For Arpeggios   Wagner *Overture to Parsifal*

Imitating the Guitar or Balalika

A mixture of stops played pizzicato can be used to make the strings "sound like" either a guitar or balalika. The two most famous examples of this are Ravel's *Bolero* and Prokofiev's *Troika Song* from *Lt. Kije*. Frequently, the harp and piano are used to double the strings with this technique. The diagram below shows how the violins and violas are played with this technique.

EXAMPLE 7-115

For Guitar & Balalika Effects in Pizzicato

The violin and violas are turned to the side and strummed like a guitar,
(up and down motion) but with a single finger.
Two notable examples are Ravel's *Bolero* and Prokofiev's *Lt. Kije*.

Score Reference 7-116 Stops Used to Imitate a Balalika Doubled By Harp
Prokofiev *Lt. Kije, Troika Song*

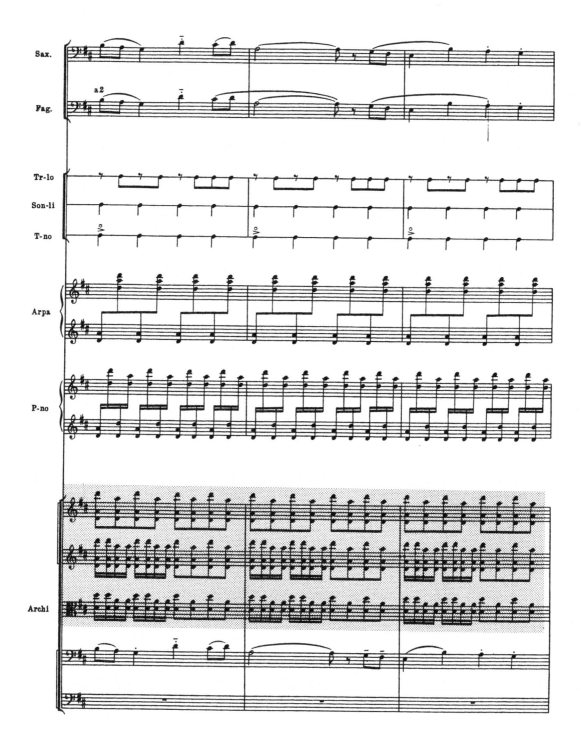

Score Reference 7-116 Stops Used to Imitate a Balalika Doubled By Harp
Prokofiev *Lt. Kije, Troika Song*

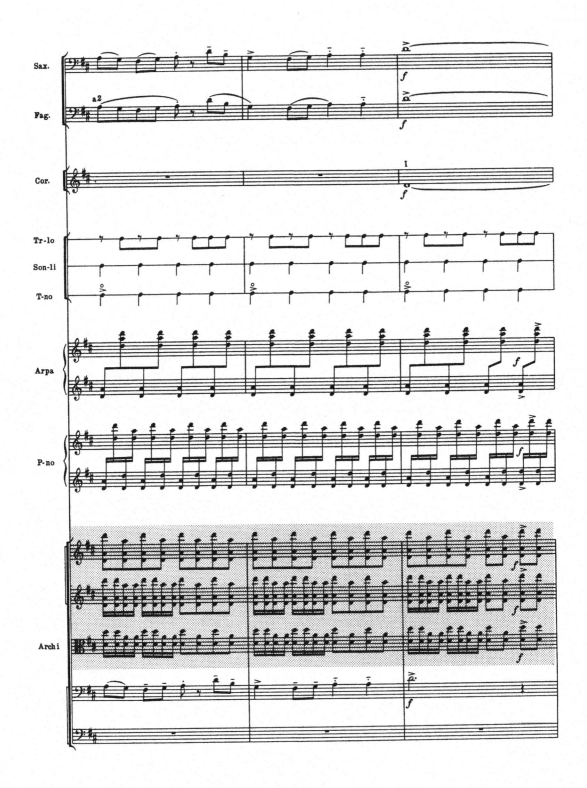

Score Reference 7-116 Stops Used to Imitate a Balalika Doubled By Harp
Prokofiev *Lt. Kije, Troika Song*

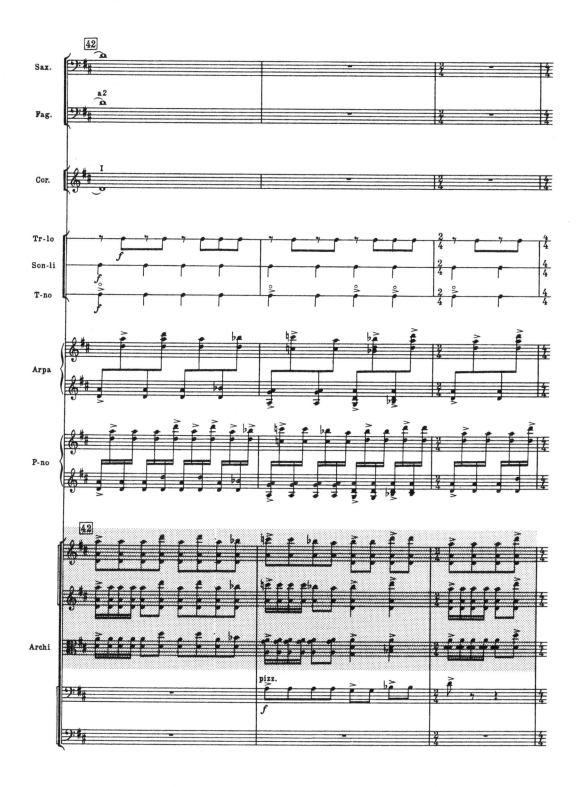

Chapter 8

Divisi

Divisi means that an individual string section is cut into typically two, three, or four smaller divisions to accommodate either an expanded vertical harmony stack, to write two or more independent parts (as is so prevalent in late 19th and early 20th century music as represented by Richard Strauss, Wagner, Debussy, Ravel, Stravinsky, etc.), or to create smaller coloristic ensembles within the larger string section. Divisi writing is also done to build to a full harmonic climax at the end of the phrase where the strings are often doubled by the woodwinds. In film scoring, divisi is almost always used to create lush harmonic textures with expanded vertical stacks of chords, to create smaller coloristic ensembles within the larger string ensemble, and to build to a full climax.

Standard Divisions and Score Markings

Practically, an individual section is not divided into more than 4 parts. Typically, a section is divided into two parts (marked *Div a 2*), sometimes three parts (marked *Div a 3*), and less frequently into four parts (marked *Div a 4*). When you want the section to go back to non-div, the score is marked *Unis* (for unison) at the point where the unison is to begin. The score can also be marked *non-div*, *all*, or *together*.

Number of Players Needed for Successful Divisi Writing

While not a hard and fast rule, it's generally recognized in studio writing that no less than three players from Violins through Violas should be available *per* part if a full, lush sound is wanted. When there are only 2 on a part, matching the pitch is harder than with 3 people since notes can phase in and out.

This concept of the number of players per part is very important because the writer frequently does not get to work with a standard sized symphonic string section. For example, below is a breakdown of the strings used by composer Jerry Goldsmith in the movie *Forever Young* vs. the string ensemble used in the *Batman* cartoon series and a standard one-hour TV show string section.

	Forever Young	*Batman*	*One Hour Show*
Violin 1	14	3	5
Violin 2	12	3	5
Violas	12	2	4
Cellos	10	2	4
Basses	6	1	2

Looking at the chart, all the strings can easily be divided *Div a 2* and even *Div a 3* with the *Forever Young* orchestra. But with the other sized strings, *no* divisi is possible for the *Batman* cartoon section, and only *some* divisi is possible with the *One Hour* show section. This brings up the golden rule of writing: *Know who and how many you're writing for!* If you don't, disaster *can* be yours. To keep in mind how many strings are being written for, many composers and orchestrators on both the left side of the sketch score and the left side of the full score mark on every page how many strings for each section. This is an important mental tool since the number of players per scoring session can vary greatly. See the example on the following page.

Example 8-1

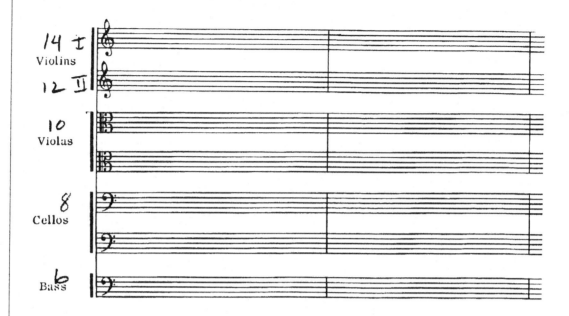

Score Paper Selection

For daily writing, professional composers and orchestrators use standard score pads that are pre-ruled 4 bars to the page with the clefs already in place. The score pages on the following pages are from from the Judy Green catalog, courtesy Judy Green Music Papers, Reseda, CA, 818-654-0033/877-685-6397. Example 8-1 shows staves in place for the Violin 1 and 2, but divided already for the violas and cellos. The next papers have three lines for the violins. Example 8-3 can be used for an expanded pop session. Violins are marked A, B, C allowing for a smaller section to complete basic triadic writing with violas, cellos and basses as a separate ensemble. Another option is to write 4-part modern harmony with the first three parts in the violins (A, B, C) and the fourth part in the violas. It's not uncommon on a scoring session to only have violins and a few violas. A similar accommodation is found with examples 8-4 and 8-5.

E<small>XAMPLE</small> **8-2**

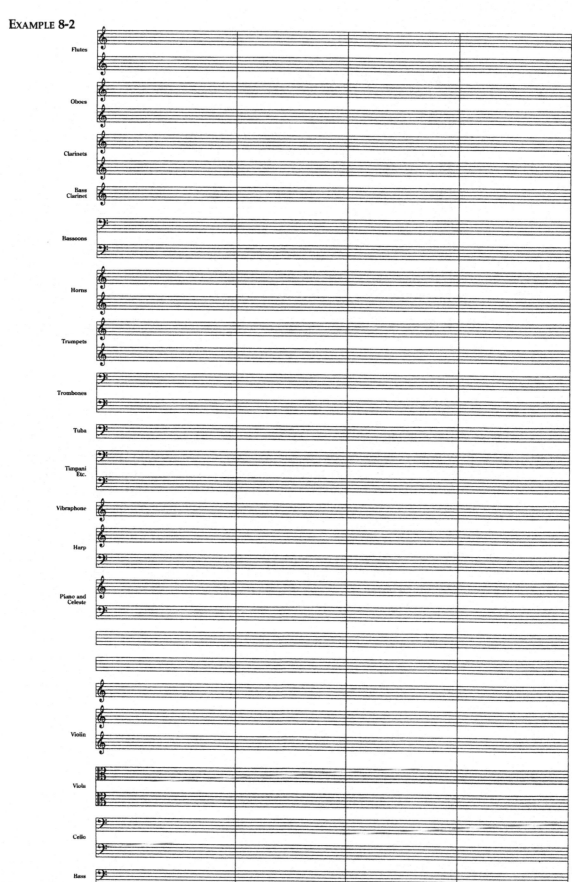

JUDY GREEN MUSIC Hollywood, CA 90028 (213) 466-2491

EXAMPLE 8-3

Example 8-4

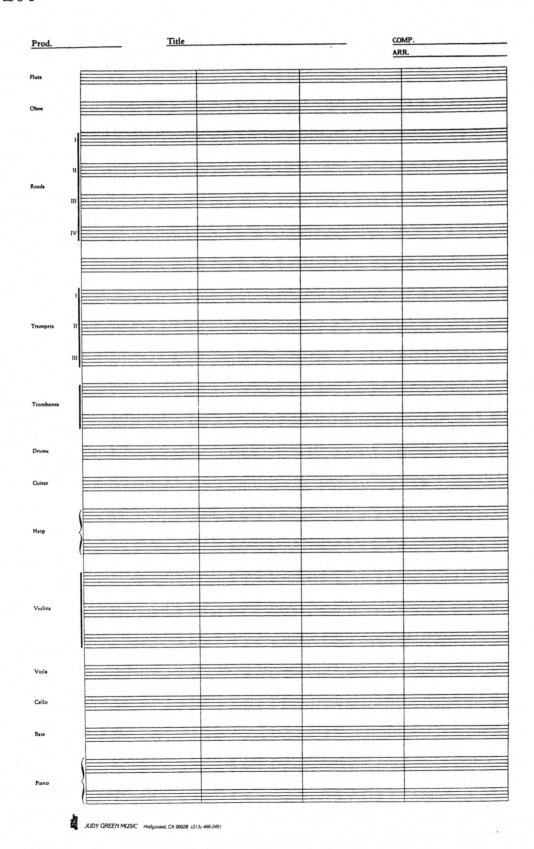

JUDY GREEN MUSIC   Hollywood, CA 90028   (213) 466-2491

EXAMPLE 8-5

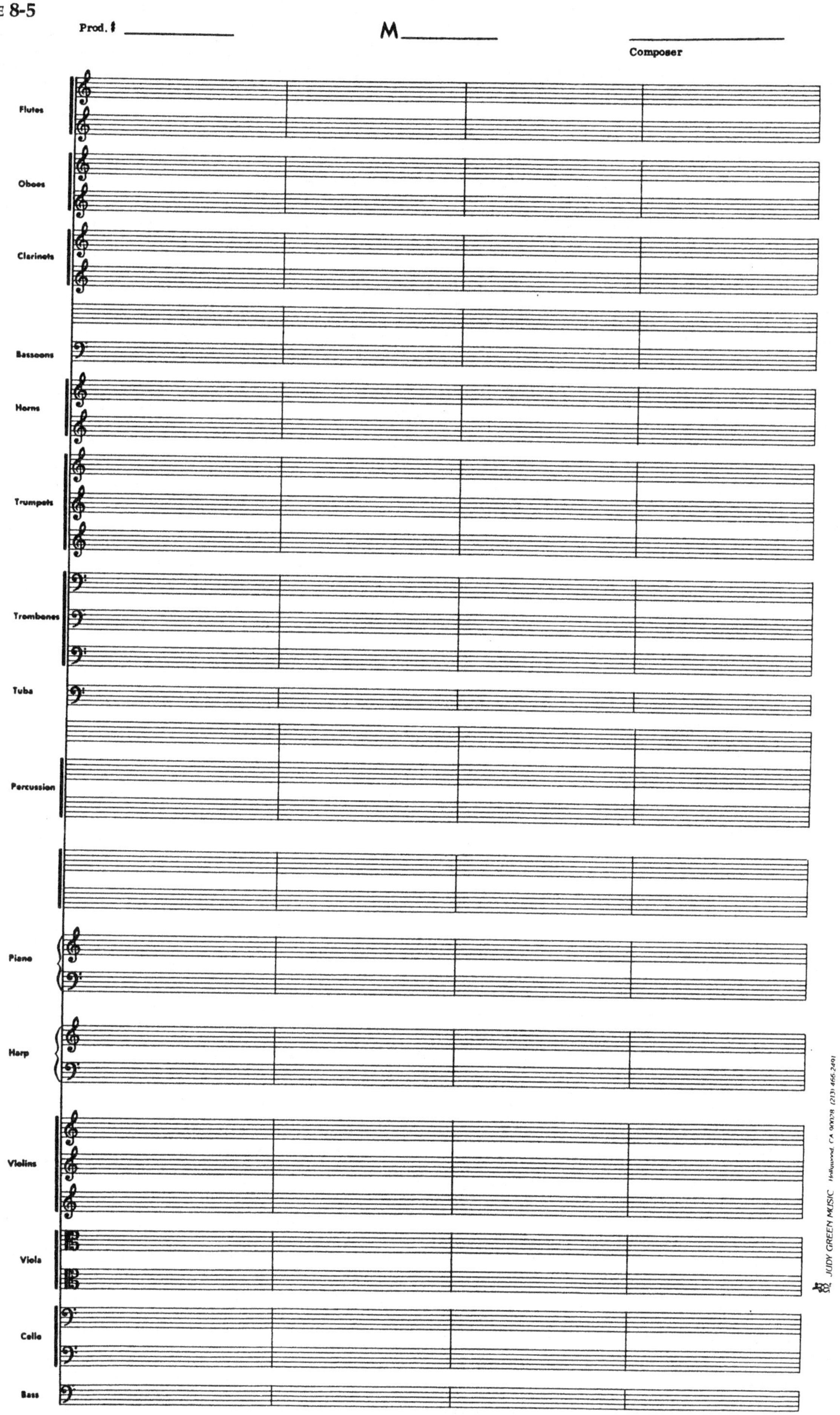
Prod. #
M
Composer
Flutes
Oboes
Clarinets
Bassoons
Horns
Trumpets
Trombones
Tuba
Percussion
Piano
Harp
Violins
Viola
Cello
Bass
JUDY GREEN MUSIC Hollywood, CA 90028 (213) 466-2491

In a more academic setting, score preparation is really treated as a work of art with each page laid out for a specific number of bars. However, this is not an acceptable practice for daily work since no working composer would ever make a deadline.

Doubling Divided Strings With Woodwinds

At p, it's generally considered that 1 woodwind = 4 violins. This means that the woodwind sound will shade the strings, but not predominate. When 2 woodwinds are placed in unison with 4 violins, the woodwind color begins to predominate. When 3 woodwinds are placed in unison with 4 violins, the woodwind sound definitely predominates over the strings. In Ravel's orchestrations, you'll frequently find only 1 woodwind per harmony part when the strings and woods are doubled. By contrast, Debussy's sound is frequently driven by woodwind colors predominating over the divided strings.

The score examples on the following pages give examples of several forms of divisi.

Score Example 8-6 Violin 1 *Div a 2* Ravel *Rapsodie Espagnole, Malaguena*

Score Example 8-6 Violin 1 *Div a 2* Ravel *Rapsodie Espagnole, Malaguena*

Score Example 8-7 Violas *Div a 2* Strauss, *Til Eulenspiegel's Merry Pranks*

Score Example 8-8 Cellos *Div a 2* Mahler *Symphony #1, 1st Movement*

Score Example 8-8 Cellos *Div a 2* Mahler *Symphony #1, 1st Movement*

Score Example 8-9 Violins 1 and 2 *Div a 2* **Strauss** *Til Eulenspiegel's Merry Pranks*

Score Example 8-10 Violins 1 and 2 *Div a 2* In Pizzicato
Ravel *Mother Goose Suite, Laideronnette*

Score Example 8-10 Violins 1 and 2 *Div a 2* **In Pizzicato**
Ravel *Mother Goose Suite, Laideronnette*

Score Example 8-10 Violins 1 and 2 *Div a 2* In Pizzicato
Ravel *Mother Goose Suite, Laideronnette*

Score Example 8-11 Violins 1 and 2 *Div a 3* **Ravel** *Rapsodie Espagnole, Malaguena*

Score Example 8-11 Violins 1 and 2 *Div a 3* **Ravel** *Rapsodie Espagnole, Malaguena*

Score Example 8-12 Violins 1 and 2 *Div a 4*   Wagner *Overture to Lohengrin*

Score Example 8-12 Violins 1 and 2 *Div a 4* Wagner *Overture to Lohengrin*

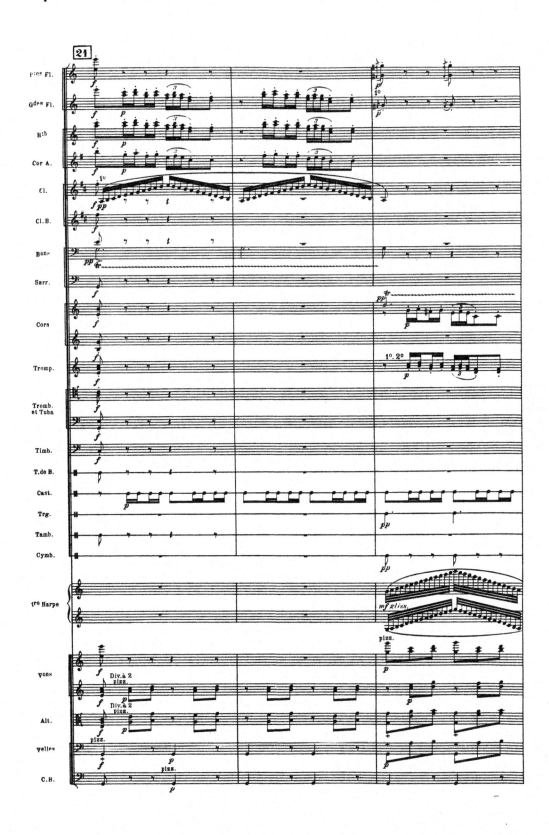

Score Example 8-13 *Div a 2*, **Sectional Pizzicato   Ravel** *Rapsodie Espagnole, Feria*

Score Example 8-13 *Div a 2,* **Sectional Pizzicato** **Ravel** *Rapsodie Espagnole, Feria*

Score Example 8-14 Viola and Cello Divisi With Double Stops   Strauss *Don Juan*

Score Example 8-15 Cellos *Div a 4* Doubled by French Horns   Debussy *La Mer*

Score Example 8-16 Basses *Div a 4* Strauss *Til Eulenspiegel's Merry Pranks*

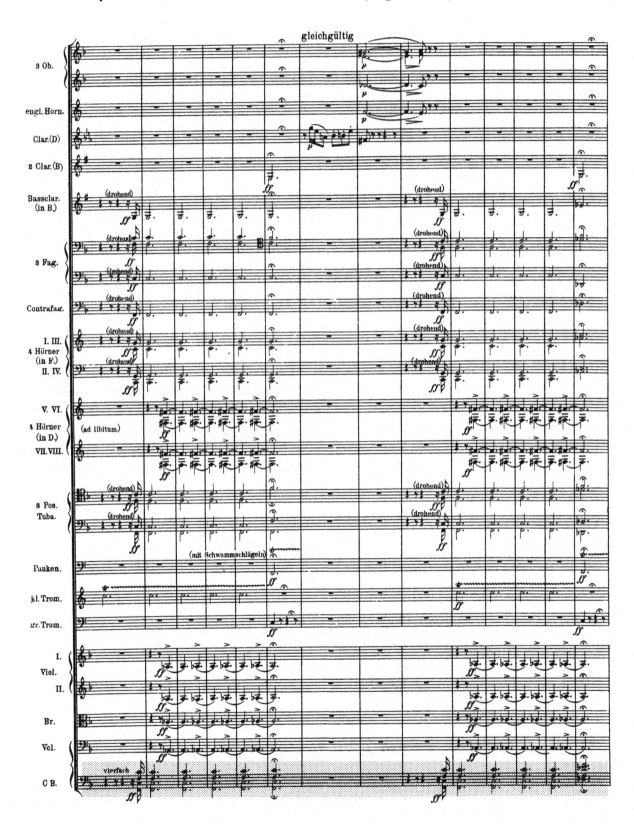

Score Example 8-16 Basses *Div a 4* Strauss *Til Eulenspiegel's Merry Pranks*

Score Example 8-16 Basses *Div a 4* Strauss *Til Eulenspiegel's Merry Pranks*

Score Example 8-17 Basses *Div a 4* Strauss *Don Juan*

Score Example 8-17 Basses *Div a 4* Strauss *Don Juan*

Score Example 8-17 Basses *Div a 4* Strauss *Don Juan*

Score Example 8-17 Basses *Div a 4* **Strauss** *Don Juan*

Score Example 8-17 Basses *Div a 4* Strauss *Don Juan*

Score Example 8-18 Divisi At the End of A Climactic Phrase
Ravel *Mother Goose Suite, The Fairy Garden*

Score Example 8-18 Divisi At the End of A Climactic Phrase
Ravel *Mother Goose Suite, The Fairy Garden*

Chapter 9

Muted Strings

Strings are muted, creating a "veiled" effect when the mute is attached to the bridge. All the strings, including the basses, can be muted. For studio work, violinists, violists, and cellists keep the mute next to the tailpiece floating between the middle two strings so the mutes can be added in seconds. Basses need a few extra seconds to attach the mute. Some earlier orchestration books have suggested that basses are not generally muted. This in not true today, especially in studio writing.

There are about eight different mutes from which string players select. The composer does not specify the mute to use, leaving that to the player instead. Since many score examples in this book contain muted strings, only one example of a sectional muting is being given.

To indicate strings are muted, write: *con sord.*

To indicate when mutes are to be removed, write: *senza sorda.*

The score reference on the following pages gives an example of muted strings.

Score Reference 9-1   Ravel *Mother Goose Suite, Petit Poucet*

Score Reference 9-1   Ravel *Mother Goose Suite, Petit Poucet*

Score Reference 9-1 Ravel *Mother Goose Suite, Petit Poucet*

Pizzicato

This chapter first examines basic pizzicato technique and then examines the 9 basic uses of pizzicato in string writing. Because there are four different string instruments in the string section, there are four different pizzicato sounds. Besides the 9 basic uses of pizzicato, this chapter also provides examples of how pizzicato differs from one string instrument to another.

Violin Pizzicato

The following guidelines should be considered for violin pizzicato.

1. The most effective strings for pizzicato are G, D and A. Of these, G and D are the strongest.

2. Depending on the rhythmic figure, several beats should be given between going from the bow to the pizzicato. In general, more time is required to take the bow again *after* a pizzicato.

3. The quality of the pizzicato is fairly uniform from low G to E in the very high range. However G above that is obtainable with the understanding that in proportion as the string becomes shorter, the tone becomes poorer.

4. The maximum speed possible for the professional in performing pizzicati in 16th notes is quarter note = 120. The passage should not be too long. For school or community ensembles, MM104 would be safer. (See example 10-1 on next page).

EXAMPLE 10-1

5. The speed of Pizzicati can be considered as unlimited when players are plucking the notes of a chord that could be played as a struck chord, e.g.

EXAMPLE 10-2

Appeggios
Only up and pizzicato arpeggios are possible on the violin and viola.

EXAMPLE 10-3

* The slur is necessary, this effect corresponding to the glissando on the Harp.

6. Descending arpeggios are *not* possible on the violin.

EXAMPLE 10-4

7. All the stopped chords listed in Chapter 7 can be arpeggioed:

EXAMPLE 10-5

8. They can also be subdivided into two or more groups (best bowed or pizzicatoed in *Divisi*):

EXAMPLE 10-6

9. *f* is the loudest pizzicato dynamic possible.

Viola Pizzicato

The same basic guidelines for the violin apply to the viola, too.

1. The most effective strings for pizzicato are C, G, and D. Of these, C and G are the strongest.

2. Depending on the rhythmic figure, several beats should be given between going from the bow to the pizzicato. In general, more time is required to take the bow again after a pizzicato.

3. The quality of the pizzicato is fairly uniform from low C to A in the very high range. However C above that is obtainable with the understanding that in proportion as the string becomes shorter, the tone becomes poorer.

4. The maximum speed possible for professional in performing pizzicati in 16th notes is quarter note = 120. The passage should not be too long. For school or community ensembles, MM104 would be safer.

5. The speed of pizzicati can be considered as unlimited when players are plucking the notes of a chord that could be played as a struck chord.

6. Descending arpeggios are *not* possible on the viola.

7. All the stopped viola chords listed in Chapter 7 can be arpeggiated.

8. They can also be subdivided into two or more groups as shown with the violins.

9. *f* is the loudest pizzicato dynamic possible.

Cello Pizzicato

1. A an octave above the A string should be considered the highest note that's safe to write pizzicato.

2. The maximum speed attainable in a pizzicato passage in 16th notes should not exceed quarter note = 120, but 104 is safe for school and community orchestras.

3. Descending arpeggios *are possible* on the cello. They *aren't frequently used,* but they can be done.

EXAMPLE 10-7

4. All the stopped cello chords listed in Chapter 7 can be arpeggioed.

5. They may also be subdivided into two or more groups as illustrated with the violins.

6. *f* is the loudest pizzicato dynamic possible.

7. Open broken chord arpeggios as a bass line, similar to what might be performed on the piano, are simple and highly effective. Here, the basses are either absent or they perform a light pizzicato to accent key rhythmic points in the bass line.

Double-Bass Pizzicato

1. The Pizzicato can be used in any part of the instrument's range, but the most sonorous register lies between:

EXAMPLE 10-8

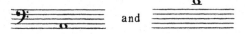

2. Pizzicati are frequently written up to A and even Bb:

EXAMPLE 10-9

but in that range the tone can become dry and unattractive.

3. Pizzicato playing should be avoided in very quick tempo, because of the fatigue it causes the performer. The result can be a lackluster performance. When writing bass pizzicato in a fast tempo, and depending on the number of basses available, the composer might consider writing the basses *divisi*, giving a few bars to each group alternatively:

EXAMPLE 10-10

4. Because bass pizzicato rings out, pizzicato parts shouldn't be written too low, otherwise the notes will appear to drag.

5. Depending on the line and the number of basses available, half the basses can play the line arco, while the other perform the line pizzicato.

Special Types of Pizzicato

This section briefly discusses Snap Pizzicato, Fingernail and Left Hand Pizzicato.

Snap Pizzicato

Although unable to be quoted in the current edition of this book, Snap Pizzicato first appeared in Bartok's *Music for String Instruments Percussion and Celesta* which the student should make every effort to get and study (Boosey and Hawkes HPS 609). The effect is achieved by physically lifting the string with the finger over the fingerboard. The result is a snapping sound that is quite commonly used in film scoring and other 20th Century works. The effect is used throughout the second movement of the Bartok piece beginning at *200*. The note to be plucked in this manner is noted with this symbol:

EXAMPLE 10-11

On hand copied parts for recording work, write "Snap Pizzicato." At the end of its use, write *ordinario*.

Lower strings work the best for this device. On the first string of each instrument, it's not practical to use this device a fifth above the open string. This device is only possible for accented notes and not consecutive notes in a passage.

The maximum dynamic possible is *ff*.

EXAMPLE 10-12

How Snap Pizzicato Works

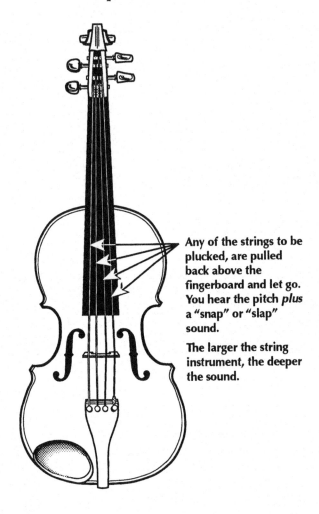

Any of the strings to be plucked, are pulled back above the fingerboard and let go. You hear the pitch *plus* a "snap" or "slap" sound.

The larger the string instrument, the deeper the sound.

Finger Nail Pizzicato

Similar to snap pizzicato in its execution, except that here the finger nail and not the finger plucks the string. The actual instructions are: "pizzicato with the fingernail at the extreme upper end of the string drawn below the finger which touches it."[1] See Bartok's *Music for String Instruments Percussion and Celesta* page 24 at 157. Like snap pizzicato, a symbol must

---

[1] Gardner Read, *Thesaurus of Orchestral Devices*, page 130, Pitman Publishing Corporation, 1953.

be put over the note the device is used on. The symbol is:

EXAMPLE 10-13

Indicating snap & fingernail pizzicato on hand-copied parts:

On a hand-copied score for studio work, it's not always practical to use the fingernail and snap pizzacato symbols. Instead, mark the part in English where the effect is to begin. Where the effect ends, write *ordinario*. Also, prior to rundown alert the Concertmaster as to which measures use snap or fingernail pizzicato.

Left-Hand Pizzicato

This device is mostly used in the solo literature. It has the left hand on the fingerboard doing the pizzicato rather than having the performer put the bow down, strike with the right hand, and then move back to the bow position. Observe how Rimsky-Korsakov used this technique in Score Reference 10-27. *This is not often used in practical playing.*

Other Pizzicato Effects

1. Pizzicato can be written on harmonics. Write *pizz. on Harmonics* on the note to be plucked.

2. Slap pizzicato is the term used to indicate a jazz style of playing. Write *slap (ala jazz)*.

3. For the pizzicato to ring out, write *Let vibrate* above the desired note(s). This device is most often used in the cellos and basses.

4. For a glissando with a pizzicato write *Pizz. on one finger*, and show the note to be plucked and the gliss destination note. This is not a widely used technique. Can only be used on accented notes not consecutive notes.

Compositional Uses of Pizzicato

This section, with full score examples, demonstrates the compositional uses of pizzicato.

Score Reference 10-14 One Pizzicato String Section Accompanying a Solo Instrument
Prokofiev *Peter and The Wolf*

Score Reference 10-15 Whole Pizzicato String Section Accompanying a Solo Instrument
Bizet, *Carmen*

Score Reference 10-15 Whole Pizzicato String Section Accompanying a Solo Instrument
Bizet, *Carmen*

Score Reference 10-16 Pizzicato Double and Triple Stops Accompanying a Solo Instrument
Prokofiev *Peter and The Wolf*

Кошка подумала: „Птичка занята спором?
Сейчас я ее сцапаю." И неслышно, на бархатных лапках подбиралась к ней.

Score Reference 10-16 Pizzicato Double and Triple Stops Accompanying a Solo Instrument
Prokofiev *Peter and The Wolf*

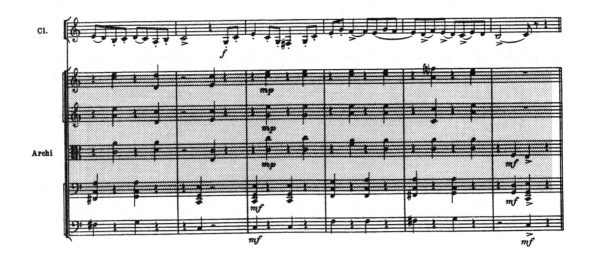

Score Reference 10-17 Reinforcing Key Rhythmic Points in the Melodic Line
Prokofiev *Peter and The Wolf*

Птичка почти задевала крыльями морду волка, и волк сердито прыгал за ней во все стороны.

Score Reference 10-17 Reinforcing Key Rhythmic Points in the Melodic Line
Prokofiev *Peter and The Wolf*

Score Reference 10-18 Dance Rhythm Doubled by Low Brass
Rimsky-Korsakov *Capriccio Espagnole*

Score Reference 10-18 Dance Rhythm Doubled by Low Brass
Rimsky-Korsakov *Capriccio Espagnole*

Score Reference 10-18 Dance Rhythm Doubled by Low Brass
Rimsky-Korsakov *Capriccio Espagnole*

Score Reference 10-19 Pizzicato Rhythmic Line in Basses Later Doubled by Cellos in Octaves
Ravel *Rapsodie Espagnole, Malaguena*

Score Reference 10-19 Pizzicato Rhythmic Line in Basses Later Doubled by Cellos in Octaves
Ravel *Rapsodie Espagnole, Malaguena*

Score Reference 10-19 Pizzicato Rhythmic Line in Basses Later Doubled by Cellos in Octaves
Ravel *Rapsodie Espagnole, Malaguena*

Score Reference 10-19 Pizzicato Rhythmic Line in Basses Later Doubled by Cellos in Octaves
Ravel *Rapsodie Espagnole, Malaguena*

Score Reference 10-19 Pizzicato Rhythmic Line in Basses Later Doubled by Cellos in Octaves
Ravel *Rapsodie Espagnole, Malaguena*

Score Reference 10-20 Pizzicato Bass on the Tonic and Dominant Later Dividing
Mahler *Symphony #1, 3rd Movement*

Score Reference 10-20 Pizzicato Bass on the Tonic and Dominant Later Dividing
Mahler *Symphony #1, 3rd Movement*

Score Reference 10-20 Pizzicato Bass on the Tonic and Dominant Later Dividing
Mahler *Symphony #1, 3rd Movement*

Score Reference 10-21 Pizzicato Cellos on Piano-like Accompaniment Rhythm Doubled by Harp **Mahler** *Symphony #1, 3rd Movement*

Score Reference 10-21 Pizzicato Cellos on Piano-like Accompaniment Rhythm
Doubled by Harp   Mahler *Symphony #1, 3rd Movement*

**Score Reference 10-21 Pizzicato Cellos on Piano-like Accompaniment Rhythm
Doubled by Harp   Mahler** *Symphony #1, 3rd Movement*

Score Reference 10-21 Pizzicato Cellos on Piano-like Accompaniment Rhythm
Doubled by Harp   Mahler *Symphony #1, 3rd Movement*

Score Reference 10-22 Pizzicato and Arco Combined in the Same Register
Sibelius *Swan of Tuonela*

Score Reference 10-22 Pizzicato and Arco Combined in the Same Register
Sibelius *Swan of Tuonela*

Score Reference 10-22 Pizzicato and Arco Combined in the Same Register
Sibelius *Swan of Tuonela*

Score Reference 10-23 Creating a Walking or March-like Feel   Prokofiev *Peter and The Wolf*

Score Reference 10-24 Simulating a Guitar   Bizet *Carmen*

Score Reference 10-24 Simulating a Guitar Bizet *Carmen*

Score Reference 10-24 Simulating a Guitar Bizet *Carmen*

Score Reference 10-24 Simulating a Guitar   Bizet *Carmen*

Score Reference 10-24 Simulating a Guitar   **Bizet** *Carmen*

Score Reference 10-25 Simulating a Guitar   Rimsky-Korsakov *Capriccio Espagnole*

To indicate this technique on the score, write, *Held like a guitar*. Use either arrows, up bow/down bow markings, break the rhythmic pattern, or use a combination of the two as Rimsky-Korsakov did to communicate what he wanted.

Score Reference 10-25 Simulating a Guitar   Rimsky-Korsakov *Capriccio Espagnole*

Score Reference 10-25 Simulating a Guitar Rimsky-Korsakov *Capriccio Espagnole*

Score Reference 10-25 Simulating a Guitar   Rimsky-Korsakov *Capriccio Espagnole*

Score Reference 10-25 Simulating a Guitar   Rimsky-Korsakov *Capriccio Espagnole*

$^{1)}$ T. 110. B автографе: V. II

Score Reference 10-26 Whole String Pizzicato on the Melody
Tchaikovsky *Symphony #4, 3rd Movement*

Score Reference 10-26 Whole String Pizzicato on the Melody
Tchaikovsky *Symphony #4, 3rd Movement*

Score Reference 10-26 Whole String Pizzicato on the Melody
Tchaikovsky *Symphony #4, 3rd Movement*

Score Reference 10-26 Whole String Pizzicato on the Melody
Tchaikovsky *Symphony #4, 3rd Movement*

Score Reference 10-26 Whole String Pizzicato on the Melody
Tchaikovsky *Symphony #4, 3rd Movement*

Score Reference 10-27 Left Hand Pizzicato in the Second Violin
Rimsky-Korsakov *Capriccio Espagnole*

Score Reference 10-27 Left Hand Pizzicato in the Second Violin
Rimsky-Korsakov *Capriccio Espagnole*

Score Reference 10-27 Left Hand Pizzicato in the Second Violin
Rimsky-Korsakov *Capriccio Espagnole*

Natural and Artificial Harmonics

There are two types of harmonics: natural and artificial. Natural harmonics are overtones produced on the open notes of each string by positioning the fingers at specific points on the fingerboard. These points are called nodes. Artificial harmonics are those overtones created on any note *other* than the open note of each string. Harmonics have five basic compositional uses:

◆   to provide a pedal point

◆   to create an animal-like effect (bird call, meowing cat, etc.)

◆   to create a hair raising emotional effect

◆   to fill in a chord tone or reach a chord tone that would be an
     awkward leap in the passage

◆   to perform a melodic theme or background.

Of the five, four can be found in the examples listed in this book. The fifth technique is from the world of film scoring. Two notable examples of this technique are by John Williams in *E.T.*, and *Hook*. With careful listening in *Hook*, you can hear the violins in harmonics perform the *Hook* theme in the first confrontation between *Hook* (Dustin Hoffman) and Peter Pan (Robin Williams) where Hook cannot believe that the grown up before him is the great Pan.

Almost no setup time is required for either natural or artificial harmonics. The maximum dynamic possible for natural harmonics (depending on the section size) is *mf* to *f*. For artificial harmonics, the loudest dynamic possible (again, depending on section size) is *mf*. On all the stringed instruments, harmonics built from the lower three strings offer the most sonority. The least sonority is on the I string.

Labeling Notes for Natural Harmonics

To indicate a natural harmonic, a circle is put above the note that's the harmonic.

EXAMPLE 11-1

A diamond can also be used to indicate which note is to be fingered to produce the harmonic. However since the same note can be reproduced on different strings, the composer should clearly state which string is to be used (Sul G, Sul A, etc.)

EXAMPLE 11-2

The Overtone Series

Below is a chart of the overtone series beginning on C.

EXAMPLE 11-3

Up to the first 8 notes (partials) of the overtone series (excluding the fundamental) are reproducible as natural harmonics. However, it's generally agreed that excluding the fundamental, partials 2-6 are the most successful.

The quickest way to remember the overtone series for natural harmonics is to recognize that its notes create an open voiced major triad. The formula is this: R-R-5-R-3-5. The first R (root) is the fundamental, or the note of the open string. With this in mind, the following tables show the available partials (natural harmonics) for each stringed instrument.

The Violin

Here are the natural overtones for the Violin.

EXAMPLE 11-4

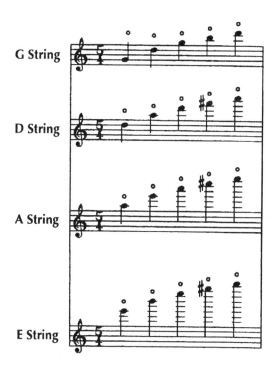

Viola

Here are the natural overtones for the Viola.

EXAMPLE 11-5

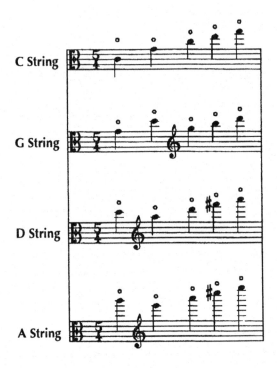

Cello

Cello harmonics are the same as the viola but down an octave.

EXAMPLE 11-6

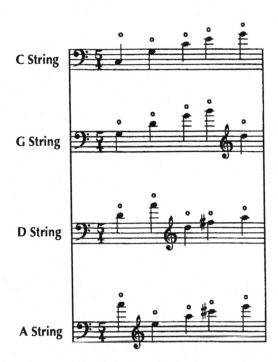

Bass Harmonics

Some minimum discussion about bass harmonics is needed. Prior to the development of the modern bass and the use of steel strings, only natural harmonics were considered possible. It was also considered that on the E-string, only partials 4-5 were available, the rest not being practical to perform. However, this is no longer true. All the natural harmonics are available on the Bass E-String. With artificial harmonics, however, these are practical today with this warning: *artificial harmonics are more difficult for a novice, but are easily playable by professionals.*

When writing bass harmonics, write them where the part should be written, *not* where it sounds. Example 11-7 below accurately reflects where each of the partials are written (remember, they'll *sound an octave below*). Make sure the score and the bass parts are marked: *Play Where Written.*

EXAMPLE 11-7

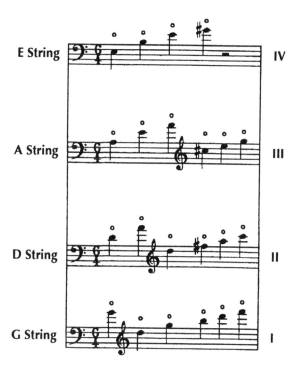

Writing Chords With Bass Harmonics

By dividing the basses, chords of an interesting tone are available:

EXAMPLE 11-8

Fingering and Notating Natural Harmonics

Now that you're aware of which natural harmonics are available per string per instrument, it's necessary to understand how these harmonics are fingered and notated. Earlier, it was mentioned that for natural harmonics, the composer need only put a circle above the note that's the natural harmonic. But there is also an alternate method which is more precise. This uses the *diamond* symbol to demonstrate to the string player *exactly* which note and fingering the composer wants. The *procedure* below, explained using the G string of the Violin, is replicated on each string on each of the stringed instruments. At the end of this section, are charts for the violins, violas, and cellos with each procedure marked out.

To repeat, taking as a fundamental tone the note produced by each of the open strings, the 2nd, 3rd, 4th, 5th, and 6th upper partials are obtained with a single finger lightly touching the string.

Fingering the Second Partial
The 2nd partial is obtained by touching the string at the point where the depressed finger would produce the same note. Simply put the circle above the note that's the harmonic.

EXAMPLE 11-9

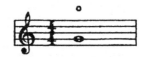

Fingering the Third Partial: Two Ways
The 3rd partial is obtained in two different ways:

Third Partial Fingering #1
by touching the string at the point where the depressed finger would produce the perfect fifth. The diamond is placed at the perfect fifth position and above it is shown the note achieved:

EXAMPLE 11-10

Third Partial Fingering #2
by touching the string at the point where the depressed finger would produce the same note.

Here you put the circle above the note to be the harmonic and the name of the string.

EXAMPLE 11-11

Fingering the Fourth Partial: Two Ways
The 4th partial can also be obtained in two different ways:

Fourth Partial Fingering #1
by touching the string at the point where the depressed finger would produce the perfect fourth. The diamond sign is placed at the perfect fourth position and above it is shown the note achieved:

EXAMPLE 11-12

Fourth Partial Fingering #2
by touching the string at the point where the depressed finger would produce the same note:

EXAMPLE 11-13

Fingering the Fifth Partial: 4 Ways
The 5th partial can be obtained in four different ways:

Fifth Partial Fingering #1
at the point where the depressed finger would produce the major third. The diamond sign is placed at the major third position and the note above it achieved:

EXAMPLE 11-14

Fifth Partial Fingering #2

by touching the string at the point where the depressed finger would sound the major sixth. The diamond sign is placed at the major sixth position and the note above it achieved:

EXAMPLE 11-15

Fifth Partial Fingering #3

by touching the string at the point where the depressed finger would produce the major tenth. The diamond sign is placed at the major tenth position and the note above it achieved:

EXAMPLE 11-16

Fifth Partial Fingering #4

by touching the string at the point where the depressed finger would produce the same note. The circle is simply put over the note that's the harmonic:

EXAMPLE 11-17

Note on Fingering the Fifth Partial

The first two ways of fingering the 5th partial are the only ones used in the orchestra. With the 3rd way the harmonic is strangled and does not come out immediately. With the 4th way the tone is very pure, but it requires considerable stretching to reach this position, which would be still more difficult on the Viola, because of its larger dimensions.

Fingering the Sixth Partial: Two Ways

The 6th partial can be obtained in two ways:

Sixth Partial Fingering #1

by touching the string at the point where the depressed finger would produce the minor third. The diamond sign is placed at the minor third position and the note above it achieved:

EXAMPLE 11-18

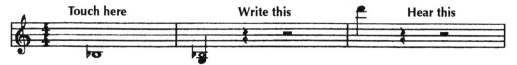

Sixth Partial Fingering #2

by touching the string at the point where the depressed finger would produce the same note. Simply put the circle above the note that's the natural harmonic and define the string that should be used:

EXAMPLE 11-19

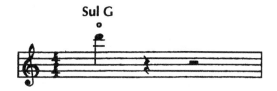

Note on the Sixth Partial

If the first method is used, the harmonic comes out with difficulty, without beauty or charm. The second method involves a painful stretch. So it's wise to use the same note coming out as the 4th partial of the neighboring string, a fifth above.

Tables of Natural Harmonics
For Violins, Violas, Cellos, and Basses

Violins

EXAMPLE 11-20

Violas

EXAMPLE 11-21

Cellos

EXAMPLE 11-22

Basses

It's not always practical to use all the natural harmonics available on the Bass. On the III string, consider staying with only partials 2-6. On the II string, partials 2-7. And on the I string, partials 2-7. Above this, check with the bass players to see what their capabilities are. It never hurts to ask.

Artificial Harmonics

Artificial Harmonics are those tones produced where the fundamental tone is *not* a note sounded by an open string. These artificial harmonics can only be produced by means of two fingers, the fore-finger serving as an artificial nut, the other finger lightly touching the string at a given point.

For these tones, no circle is used above the note to be the harmonic. Instead, the composer must work out for the string player which harmonic he specifically wants. There are four partials above the artificial fundamental that are achievable.

The procedure below has been worked out for the violin only. You replicate this procedure for each string instrument to determine the appropriate harmonic to be notated.

Artificial Harmonics for the Basses

Artificial harmonics are copied where the fingering is written not where it sounds. Therefore, clearly mark the score over bass harmonics: *Play Where Written.*

The Fourth Partial

The diamond sign is placed a perfect fourth above the artificial fundamental. The tone produced is the artificial fundamental sounded two octaves above.

EXAMPLE 11-23

The Third Partial

The diamond sign is placed a perfect fifth above the artificial fundamental. The tone produced is an octave and a fifth above the artificial fundamental.

EXAMPLE 11-24

The Fifth Partial

The diamond sign is placed a major third above the artificial fundamental. The tone produced is a tone two octaves and a major third above the artificial fundamental.

EXAMPLE 11-25

The Sixth Partial

The diamond sign is placed a minor third above the artificial fundamental. The tone produced is a tone two octaves and a perfect fifth above the artificial fundamental.

EXAMPLE 11-26

Which To Use in Practical Daily Writing

Of the four partials listed for artificial harmonics, the fourth partial (diamond sign a perfect fourth above the artificial fundamental) is the one most commonly used. A much richer sound is achieved with the third partial than the fourth. However, outside professional orchestra and studio players, the third partial is considered a little too difficult to perform. The fifth and sixth partials are not common, they are risky to produce, and they don't sound as strong as the third and fourth partials.

The following pages contain score examples of natural harmonics and artificial harmonics.

Score Examples of Natural Harmonics

Score Reference 11-27 Pedal Point Full Section   **Mahler** *Symphony #1, 1st Movement*

Score Reference 11-27 Pedal Point Full Section Mahler *Symphony #1, 1st Movement*

Score Reference 11-27 Pedal Point Full Section   Mahler *Symphony #1, 1st Movement*

Score Reference 11-27 Pedal Point Full Section Mahler *Symphony #1, 1st Movement*

Score Reference 11-27 Pedal Point Full Section   Mahler *Symphony #1, 1st Movement*

Score Reference 11-28 Hair Raising Effect **Stravinsky** *Firebird*

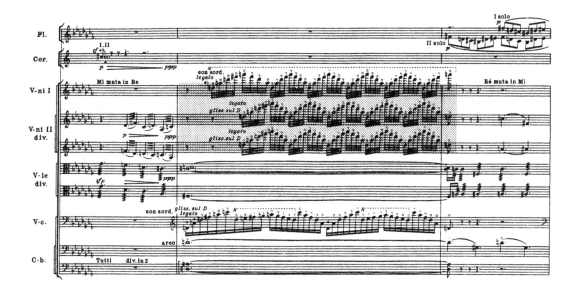

Score Reference 11-29 Pedal Point Mixed With Stops   Rimsky-Korsakov *Capriccio Espagnole*

Score Reference 11-29 Pedal Point Mixed With Stops   Rimsky-Korsakov *Capriccio Espagnole*

1) Тт. 136-155. В автографе у Cast. вторая четверть: 𝄽

Score Reference 11-29 Pedal Point Mixed With Stops   Rimsky-Korsakov *Capriccio Espagnole*

Score Reference 11-29 Pedal Point Mixed With Stops   Rimsky-Korsakov *Capriccio Espagnole*

Score Reference 11-30 Melodic Figure in Cellos   Prokofiev *Peter and the Wolf*

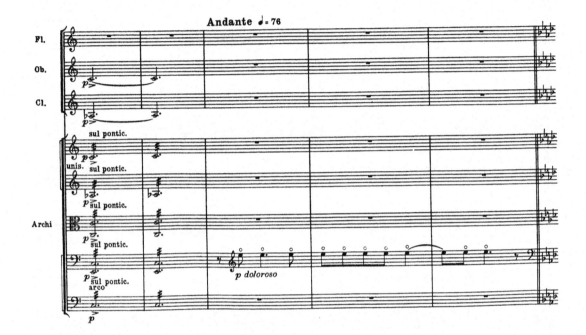

Score Reference 11-31 Basses and Violas Creating Chord Tones
Ravel *Mother Goose Suite, Pavanne*

Score Examples of Artificial Harmonics

Score Reference 11-32 Pedal Point in Violin 1
Debussy *La Mer, Dialogue of the Wind and the Sea*

Score Reference 11-32 Pedal Point in Violin 1
Debussy *La Mer, Dialogue of the Wind and the Sea*

Score Reference 11-32 Pedal Point in Violin 1
Debussy *La Mer, Dialogue of the Wind and the Sea*

Score Reference 11-32 Pedal Point in Violin 1
Debussy *La Mer, Dialogue of the Wind and the Sea*

Score Reference 11-32 Pedal Point in Violin 1
Debussy *La Mer, Dialogue of the Wind and the Sea*

Score Reference 11-32 Pedal Point in Violin 1
Debussy *La Mer, Dialogue of the Wind and the Sea*

Score Reference 11-33 Creating an Animal-like Effect (Bird Calls) With Glissandi
Ravel *Mother Goose Suite, Petit Poucet*

Score Reference 11-34 In the Cellos & Violas   Ravel *Mother Goose Suite, Petit Poucet*

Woodwind Basics

The first discussion is about the organization of the woodwind section and doubles from the major symphony orchestra to the studio session player.

Orchestra Woodwinds: Seating and Doubles

There are three sized woodwind sections per instrument, depending on the importance and size of the orchestra. These are 4, 3 and the minimum of 2 players per instrument.

General Seating Arrangements for Orchestra and Studio Sessions
The woodwinds sit directly behind the violas. Behind the woodwinds sit the French horns.

EXAMPLE 12-1

French Horns	
Clarinets	**Bassoons**
4 3 2 1	1 2 3 4
Flutes	**Oboes**
4 3 2 1	1 2 3 4

The numbers below the instrument name designate the seating position of the lead player (1). The number of players within each section also dictates who doubles what.

Doubles in a Four Player Symphonic Section

In a four player section, the following doubles can be planned for:

Flutes	Oboes	Clarinets	Bassoons
3 Flutes I-III	3 Oboes I-III	3 Clarinets I-III	3 Bassoons I-III
Bass Flute (III)	Eng. Horn (IV)	Small Clarinet (III)	Contrabassoon (IV)
Piccolo (IV)		Bass Clarinet (IV)	

In a major orchestra, the third chair player (if there's no part written for him) can, at the conductor's discretion, double the lead player's part or spell him so that the lead player has a break.

Doubles in a Two or Three Player Symphonic Section

The minimum symphonic woodwind section consists of one pair of each of the following instruments, especially with smaller orchestras: Flutes, Oboes, Clarinets, and Bassoons. The last symphonic player in each section most often doubles these instruments:

Flute II or III	*doubles*	Piccolo
Oboe II or III	*doubles*	English Horn
Clarinet II or III	*doubles*	Bass Clarinet
Bassoon II or III	*doubles*	Contrabassoon

Doubles in the Studio Orchestra

Flute players are generally expected to double piccolo, alto flute and bass flute regardless of their "chair." Oboe players are expected to double the English horn. Bassoon players are expected to double the Contrabassoon. Clarinet players will double the A-Clarinet, the Bass Clarinet, and when available, the Small Clarinet and the Bassett horn.

Asking for Doubles

For a standard orchestra, it's assumed that the second or third player of each section will have these doubles (as already illustrated). For a studio orchestra, it's best to assume *nothing*. When doubles are required, the orchestra contractor must be told up front what your needs are. Waiting until the session begins is too late.

To make themselves more valuable as studio players, sax players often learn other woodwinds that they double. The most common sax doubling is the clarinet. The second most common doublings are the flute and alto flute. Some baritone sax players also learn bass clarinet and bassoon.

Labeling Part Numbers and Marking the Score

In symphonic writing, parts are labeled with Roman numerals for all instruments. In studio writing, Arabic numbers are used.

When a player is to move to a doubled instrument, the score and parts are marked *To xxxxxx.* On the average, a few bars in moderate tempo are needed to change to a double. When the player is to go back to the original instrument, the score and parts are marked *To xxxxxxx.*

Oboe 2 Doubling the English Horn

When Oboe 2 is doubling the English horn, there is a key change going to the English horn and then going back to the Oboe 2 part.

Clarinet 2 Doubling the Bass Clarinet

There is not a key change for Clarinet 2 moving to the Bass Clarinet since both are in the key of Bb. However, if Clarinet 2 is playing an A-Clarinet, there will be a key change.

When to Use the A-Clarinet

With a complicated key signature, say three sharps or three flats and up, using the A-Clarinet simplifies the key signature for the player.

Octave Changes for Piccolo and Contrabassoon

There are no key changes for the Piccolo and Contrabassoon, but it should be remembered that the Piccolo sounds an octave higher than written and the Contrabassoon an octave lower.

The Alto Flute

Discussed later in this chapter, the Alto flute (which is a transposing instrument) is considered a *must* double for studio flutists. However, when booking a recording session, be sure to mention to the orchestra contractor what you want. For semi-professional and academic symphonic organizations, check first to see if one of the flute players doubles the alto flute. If not, then the orchestra may have to contract out and hire a player just to perform your score.

Use of Woodwind Doubles

The following remarks by Rimsky-Korsakov suggest the characteristics, timbre, and use of special instruments. These remarks are *completely subjective* and are *not* law.

The Piccolo

The piccolo's duty is principally to extend the range of the flute in the high register. The whistling piercing quality of the piccolo in its highest range is extraordinarily powerful, but doesn't lend itself to more moderate shades of expression. The low and middle register of the piccolo correspond to the same register in the normal flute, but the tone is so much weaker that it's of little service in those regions.

The Small Clarinet

The small clarinet in its highest register is more penetrating than the ordinary clarinet. The low and middle register of the small clarinet correspond to the same register in the normal clarinet, but the tone is so much weaker that it's of little service in those regions.

The Contrabassoon

The contrabassoon extends the range of the ordinary bassoon in the low register. The characteristic of the bassoon's low range are still further accentuated in the corresponding range of the contrabassoon, but the middle and upper registers of the latter are by no means so useful. The very deep notes of the double bassoon are remarkably thick and dense in quality, very powerful in *p* passages.

The English Horn

The English horn is similar in tone to the ordinary oboe, the listless dreamy quality of its timbre being sweet in the extreme. In the low register it's fairly penetrating.

The Bass Clarinet

Though strongly resembling the ordinary clarinet, the bass clarinet is of darker color in the low register and lacks the silvery quality in the upper notes; it's incapable of joyful expression. Often used to double low basses. Mixes well with the Contrabassoon and Bassoons when doubling extremely low bass lines.

Rimsky-Korsakov Woodwind Color Chart

The chart in Example 12-2 on the following page, created by Rimsky-Korsakov, breaks each of the woodwind ranges into four registers: low, medium, high and very high. With each register, Rimsky-Korsakov has given adjectives to describe the color of each register. Limits to each register aren't defined absolutely because of instrument design changes and the quality of players available.

In the very high range, only those notes are given that per Rimsky-Korsakov, "could really be used." Consider these as safe limits. The signs > < are used by Rimsky-Korsakov to show how an instrument's resonance increases or diminishes in relation to the characteristic quality of its timbre. The extent of greatest expression is marked with a bracket under the notes.

EXAMPLE 12-1

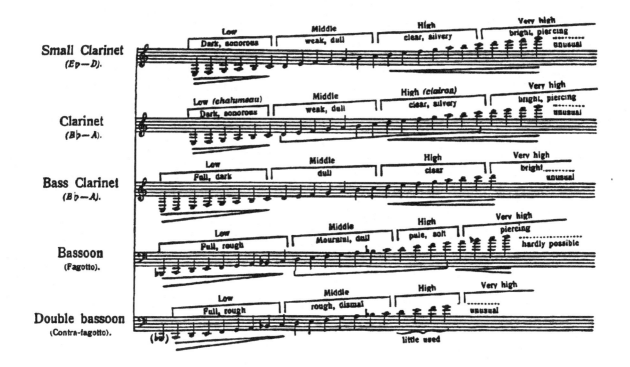

These instruments give all chromatic intervals.

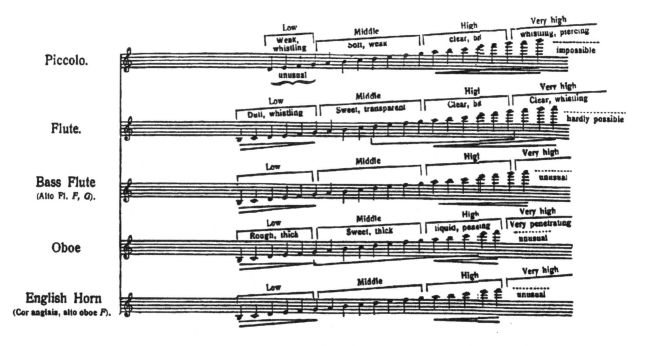

Dynamics, *p - pppp*, Within the Range Breaks

The following breakdown in example 12-3 on the following page gives an *approximation* of the difficulty of dynamics *p-ppp* of the woodwinds within each range break. With this chart, keep in mind that the Strings can easily play at virtually any dynamic level in any range break depending on the technique and bowing used. Use this information with the chart in example 12-2.

EXAMPLE 12-3

	Low	**Medium**	**High**	**Very High**
Piccolo				*pp* most difficult
Flute	*pp* very easy	*pp & ppp* very easy	*p* hard, but poss.	*pp* most difficult
Oboe	*pp* most difficult (Bb toC#)	*p* hard in first half (above D) not hard in 2nd half	*p* and even *pp* possible	
English horn	*p* hard, but poss.	*p* not hard	*pp* possible	
Clarinet	*pppp* very easy	*ppp1/2* very easy	*pp1/2 - ppp* not difficult	*p1/2 - pp* most difficult
Bass clarinet	*p* and even *pp* very easy	*p* and even *pp* very easy	*p* not difficult	
Bassoon	*pp* most difficult	*p* not hard	*pp* possible	*p* hard, but poss.
Saxes	*p* hard, but poss.	*p* and even *pp* easy	*p* not difficult	
French horn	*p* hard, but poss.	*p* not difficult	*pp* very difficult	
Trumpets	*pp* possible	*p* not difficult	*pp* most difficult	
Trombone	*pp* possible	*p* and even *pp* not difficult	*pp* most difficult	

Dynamic Balance Chart

Use this chart as a starting point for learning how to mix instruments from other sections. The information is general and subject to what registers the instruments are written in.

EXAMPLE 12-4

at *f* or *ff*   1 Trumpet = 1 Trombone = 2 Fr. horns = 2 or 3 Saxes

1 Fr. horn = 2 Flutes = 2 Oboes = 2 Clarinets = 2 Bassoon

Thus,   1 Trumpet = 1 Trombone = 2 French horns = 4 Woodwinds

at *p*   1 Fr. horn = 1 Flute = 1 Oboe = 1 Clarinet = 1 Bassoon = 1 Sax

at *pp*   1 Trumpet = 1 Trombone = 1 Fr. horn = 1 Sax = 1 Flute = 1 Oboe = 1Clarinet = 1 Bassoon

Psychological Characterization of Their Sound

In the effort to characterize from a psychological point of view the timbre of each of the four families, the following observations by Rimsky-Korsakov apply to the middle and upper registers:

Flute
Cold in quality, specially suitable in the major key to melodies of light and graceful character. In the minor key, to slight touches of transient sorrow.

Oboe
Simple and cheerful in the major, pathetic and sad in the minor.

Clarinet
Pliable and expressive, suitable in the major to melodies of a joyful or contemplative character, or to outbursts of mirth. In the minor, to sad and reflective melodies or impassioned and dramatic passages.

Bassoon
In the major, an atmosphere of senile mockery. In the minor, a sad ailing quality.

In the extreme registers, the instruments conveyed the following impressions to Rimsky-Korsakov's mind:

	Low Register	Very High Register
Flute	*Dull, Cold*	*Brilliant*
Oboe	*Wild*	*Hard, Dry*
Clarinet	*Ringing, threatening*	*Piercing*
Bassoon	*Sinister*	*Tense*

Tone Color and Expression

"It's true that no mood or frame of mind, whether it be joyful or sad, meditative or lively, careless or reflective, mocking or distressed can be aroused by one single isolated timbre.

"It depends more on the general melodic line, the harmony, rhythm, and dynamic shades of expression on the whole formation of a given piece of music. The choice of instruments and timbre to be adopted depends on the position that melody and harmony occupy in the seven octave scale of the orchestra. For example, a melody of light character in the tenor register could not be given to the flutes, or a sad, plaintive phrase in the high soprano register confided to the bassoons.

"But the ease with which tone color can be adapted to expression must not be forgotten. In the first of these two cases, it can be conceded that the mocking character of the bassoon could easily and quite naturally assume a light-hearted aspect. In the second case, the slightly melancholy timbre of the flute is somewhat related to the feeling of sorrow and distress that the passage is to be saturated. The case of a melody coinciding in character with the instrument on which it's played is of special importance, since the effect produced cannot fail to be successful.

"There are also moments when a composer's artistic feeling prompts him to use instruments, the character of which is at variance with the written melody (for eccentric, grotesque effects, etc.." RIMSKY-KORSAKOV

Comprehensive Range Chart

The range chart on the following page shows where each instrument is written, where it sounds, and which clefs are used. Whole notes denote the practical range. Black notes show the extreme range as performed by professional studio players and virtuosi.

EXAMPLE 12-5

(1) Non-transposing.

Muting the Woodwinds

Of late years, the habit of muting woodwinds has come into fashion. This is done by inserting a soft pad, or a piece of rolled up cloth into the bell of the instrument. Mutes deadened the tone of the oboes, English horns, and bassoons to such an extent that it's possible for these instruments to attain the extreme limit of *pp* playing. The lowest note on the bassoon, English horn and oboe are impossible when the instruments are muted. Mutes have no effect in the highest register of woodwind instruments.

The Other Flutes: Alto and Bass

There are two other flutes available, however, these are most often used in studio work. The first is the Alto flute. The Alto flute is in G and transposes up a perfect fourth. The first octave and a half for ensemble work is considered the most effective.

Alto Flute Range

EXAMPLE 12-6

The Bass Flute is in C and it's written an octave above where it sounds. The Bass flute is rarely used except in recording work.

Bass Flute Range

EXAMPLE 12-7

Writing for Alto and Bass Flute

The source for learning to write for these instruments that also includes recorded examples is Henry Mancini's *Sounds and Scores* available from Alexander Publishing.

The Saxes

Saxes are not frequently used in symphonic writing, but they are heavily used in pop and film scoring. There are four saxes most commonly used: soprano, alto, tenor, and baritone sax. There's also a bass sax, but this is rarely used. The comprehensive range chart in example 12-8 on the following page shows where each sax is written and where each sounds.

EXAMPLE 12-8

- ◆ The Soprano sax transposes up a major second.

- ◆ The Tenor sax transposes up a major ninth.

- ◆ The Alto sax transposes up a major sixth.

- ◆ The Baritone sax transposes up a major sixth plus an octave.

- ◆ The Bass sax transposes up a major second plus two octaves.

Standard Combinations of Woodwinds on the Melody

The following are the most successful combinations. Please note that these combinations are covered in depth in Volume 2, *Orchestrating the Melody Within Each Section.*

Most Common Unison Woodwind Combinations

Flute + Oboe

Flute + Clarinet

Flute + Bassoon

Flute + French horn

Oboe + French horn

Oboe + Clarinet

Oboe + Bassoon

Clarinet +French horn

Bassoon + French horn

Three Woodwinds to a Unison Line

Flute + Oboe + Clarinet

Flute + Clarinet + Bassoon

Oboe + Clarinet + Bassoon

Oboe + Clarinet + French horn

Clarinet + Bassoon + French horn

Most Common Octave Combinations

Flute - Clarinet

Flute - Oboe

Flute -Bassoon (often a 2-octave spread)

Oboe - Clarinet

Oboe - Bassoon

Oboe - French horn

Clarinet - French horn

French horn - Bassoon

Flute + Oboe - Clarinet + Bassoon

Flute + Oboe - Clarinet + French horn

Flute + Clarinet - Oboe + Bassoon

Flute + Clarinet - Oboe + French horn

Flute + Clarinet - French horn + Bassoon

Oboe + Clarinet - French horn + Bassoon

Woodwind Ensembles

Flute, Oboe, Clarinet, French horn, Bassoon

2 oboes, 2 clarinets, 2 horns, 2 bassoons

2 oboes, 2 clarinets, 4 horns, 2 bassoons, 1 bass, 2 bassett horns.

Most Common Sax Sections

With 3 or 4-part harmony:

      Alto-Tenor-Baritone Sax

      Tenor-Tenor-Tenor-Baritone Sax (Woody Herman Four Brothers sound)

With 4-part harmony and the melody doubled an octave below:

      Clarinet-Alto-Alto-Tenor-Tenor (Glenn Miller sound)

      Alto-Alto-Tenor-Tenor-Baritone Sax (most common sax section)

Multiphonics

Multiphonics are a special technique typically available from only the top players. It's the simultaneous performance of two or more notes. These are rarely used in practical writing. For a detailed discussion, please see *New Sounds for Woodwinds* by Bertolozzi, Oxford University Press.

Chapter 13

The Flute

Italian, Flauto

German, Flöte

French, Flûte

The range of the flute depends on whether it's a European or American model. The European range is from Middle C (C3) to D above C6. The American flute extends the range down a half step to B natural. For practical writing purposes however, the range illustrated below is the safest.

EXAMPLE 13-1

Note that the final notes at the end of the range should be written with a dynamic of *f* or louder. The C and B below are difficult to produce and should only be written for top players.

In fact, for safety, it's wise not to write the flute above A5.

EXAMPLE 13-2

Impossible *piano*  excellent *forte*

Dynamics and Flute Writing

In the upcoming score examples, the following principles will be observed:

1. Most flute solos are written in the medium and high registers, and that frequently, the solos are across the two registers vs. being written exclusively in one register.

2. For the flute to be heard, the supporting orchestral ensembles are usually written two dynamic levels *below* the flute part, but sometimes only one dynamic level less. So if the flute solo is at *f*, the supporting ensemble will either be written at *mf* (one dynamic level less) or *mp* (two dynamic levels less).

3. When the flute is written in lower registers for a live performance, the bass line in traditional symphonic literature is usually handled by the cellos, since the overtones from the basses tend to cover the flute in the lower register. Note, however, that this situation is avoided all the time in modern recording since the flute can be isolated on tape.

4. Notes in the extreme high register are best reached in scale passages and not leaps.

5. Two flutes playing the melody and background line respectively in different registers create a unique coloristic sound.

6. In ensemble writing, the flute frequently reinforces the first harmonic of the Oboe (by playing an octave above), or the Clarinet. If, in a group of wind instruments, the Flutes doubling the upper parts in the octave are suddenly concealed or removed, the quality of the music changes and can become dull or dark. Yet from the score, the Flutes seem to be acting as fillers.

The following pages contain score examples of flute registers.

Score Reference 13-3 Low Register   **Mahler** *Symphony #1, 1st Movement*

Score Reference 13-4 Low to Medium Register   Dvorak *New World Symphony*

Score Reference 13-5 Low Register
Ravel *Mother Goose Suite, Pavanne for a Sleeping Princess*

Score Reference 13-6 Medium Register   Dvorak *New World Symphony*

Score Reference 13-7 Medium Register **Debussy** *Prelude to the Afternoon of a Faun*

Score Reference 13-8 Medium Register   Ravel *Daphnis and Chloe*

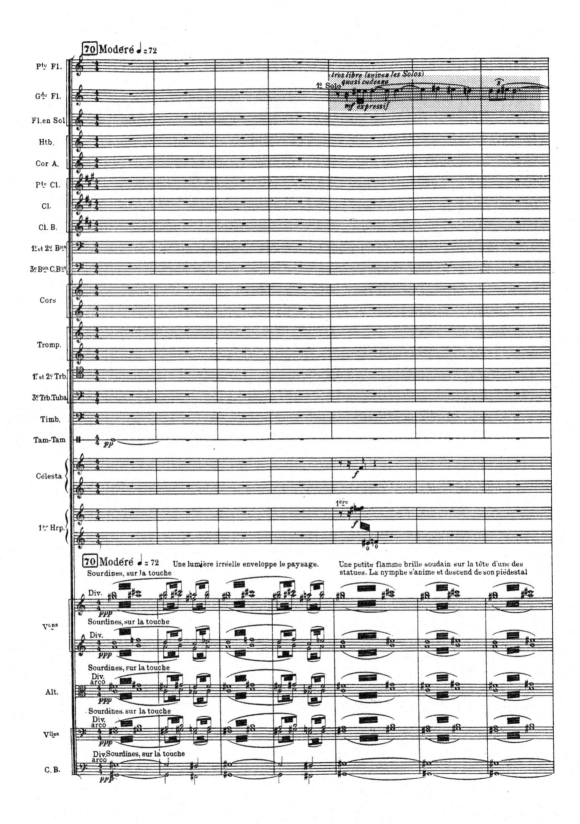

Score Reference 13-8 Medium Register   **Ravel** *Daphnis and Chloe*

Score Reference 13-9 High Flute   Bizet *Carmen, Intermezzo*

Score Reference 13-9 High Flute   Bizet *Carmen, Intermezzo*

Score Reference 13-10 High Flute **Prokofiev** *Peter and the Wolf*

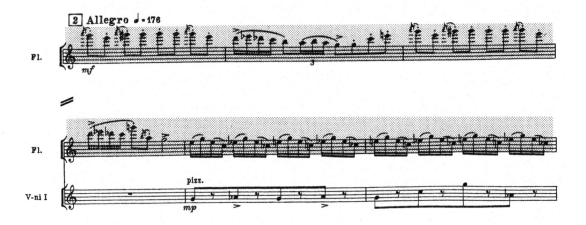

Score Reference 13-10 High Flute   **Prokofiev** *Peter and the Wolf*

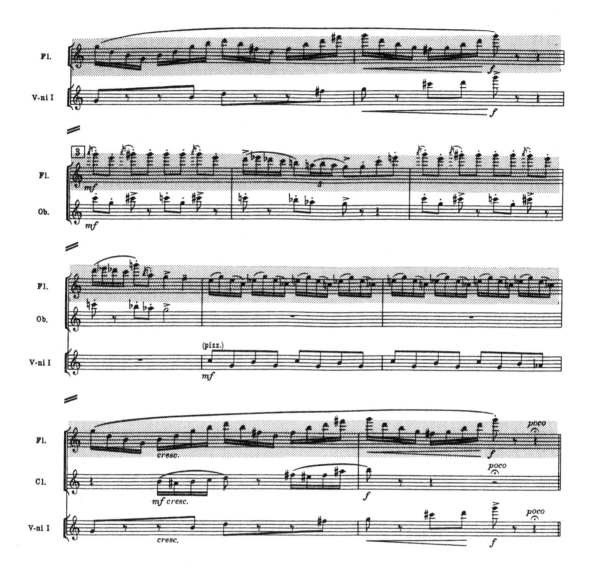

Score Reference 13-11 Very High Flute Tchaikovsky *Nutcracker Suite, Danse Chinois*

Score Reference 13-11 Very High Flute   Tchaikovsky *Nutcracker Suite, Danse Chinois*

13-12 Very High Flute   Rimsky-Korsakov *Scheherazade*

13-12 Very High Flute Rimsky-Korsakov *Scheherazade*

Harmonics

Harmonics are a special pale flute coloring produced by overblowing the funadmental with the resultant pitch an octave and a fifth higher. Harmonics are indicated, like the strings, by putting a circle above the note. The harmonics used are the following:

EXAMPLE 13-13

The fundamentals used for harmonics are the first 14 degrees of the scale:

Example 13-14

Score Reference 13-15 Flute Harmonics Ravel *Rapsodie Espagnole, Feria*

Articulation

Tonguing is to wind instruments what bowing is to stringed instruments. Flute-players make use of three kinds of tonguing: single, double, and triple articulation. Slurred notes are played in one breath as *legato*.

Single Articulation

Single-articulation is produced by pronouncing the consonant *t* (as in *tut*). It's with this tonguing that the maximum strength of tone and greatest intensity of color is obtained. It corresponds to detached bowing on the Violin:

EXAMPLE 13-16

However, great speed isn't possible with single tonguing. In florid passages, the flautist uses double-tonguing (see below), that alternately articulates the consonants *t* and *k*, or to triple-tonguing, which involves the use of the three letter *t k t*, as in t(u), c(u), t(u), (i.e. t and k are pronounced according to the phonetic system).

Speed of Articulation Low Register

With single-articulation the maximum safe speeds attainable in the low register are:

EXAMPLE 13-17

The passage shouldn't be too long, because of the fatigue experienced by the player.

Speed of Articulation High Register

In the high register, the speed of articulation may, of course, increase. However, the top Bb isn't usually articulated in a quicker tempo than quarter note = 120.

EXAMPLE 13-18

As a comparison, with double tonguing, the passage below could be executed at quarter note = 160 or better.

EXAMPLE 13-19

Score Reference 13-20 Single Tonguing and Legato
Tchaikovsky *Nutcracker Suite, Danse of the Mirlitons*

Score Reference 13-20 Single Tonguing and Legato
Tchaikovsky *Nutcracker Suite, Danse of the Mirlitons*

Score Reference 13-20 Single Tonguing and Legato
Tchaikovsky *Nutcracker Suite, Danse of the Mirlitons*

Score Reference 13-20 Single Tonguing and Legato
Tchaikovsky *Nutcracker Suite, Danse of the Mirlitons*

Double Tonguing

To repeat, in florid passages double-tonguing alternately articulates the consonants *t* and *k*,

EXAMPLE 13-21

EXAMPLE 13-22

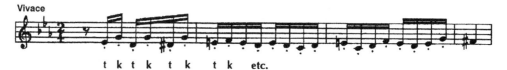

Double-tonguing allows for easy and rapid performance of repeated notes:

EXAMPLE 13-23

EXAMPLE 13-24

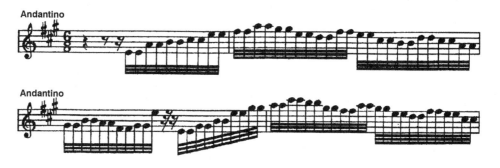

In the medium register with double-tonguing, Flutes can manage to compete with Strings in point of speed, being able to produce a true tremolo as used by Rimsky-Korsakov in *Grande Paque Russe*:

EXAMPLE 13-25

13-26 Double Tonguing   **Ravel** *Rapsodie Espagnole, Malaguena*

13-26 Double Tonguing   Ravel *Rapsodie Espagnole, Malaguena*

13-26 Double Tonguing Ravel *Rapsodie Espagnole, Malaguena*

13-27 Double & Single Tonguing Mixed   Mendelssohn *Midsummer Night's Dream*

13-27 Double & Single Tonguing Mixed **Mendelssohn** *Midsummer Night's Dream*

Puck. He Geist! Wo geht die Reise hin? *attacca*

Triple Tonguing

When triplet groups are written, triple-tonguing is used. It's nearly as rapid as double-tonguing. With triple tonguing, there's always a slight risk of inequality of tone, because of the natural tendency to accent the last of three consonants. Triple tonguing uses the three letters *t k t*, as in t(u), c(u), t(u).

Passages like the following are easy, becasue of the likeness of the figure and the absence of any kind of melodic feeling. They're played mechanically:

EXAMPLE 13-28

Here's a more difficult figure that calls for the utmost care in execution:

EXAMPLE 13-29

13-30 Triple Tonguing **Mendelssohn** *Symphony #4, Presto*

13-30 Triple Tonguing Mendelssohn *Symphony #4, Presto*

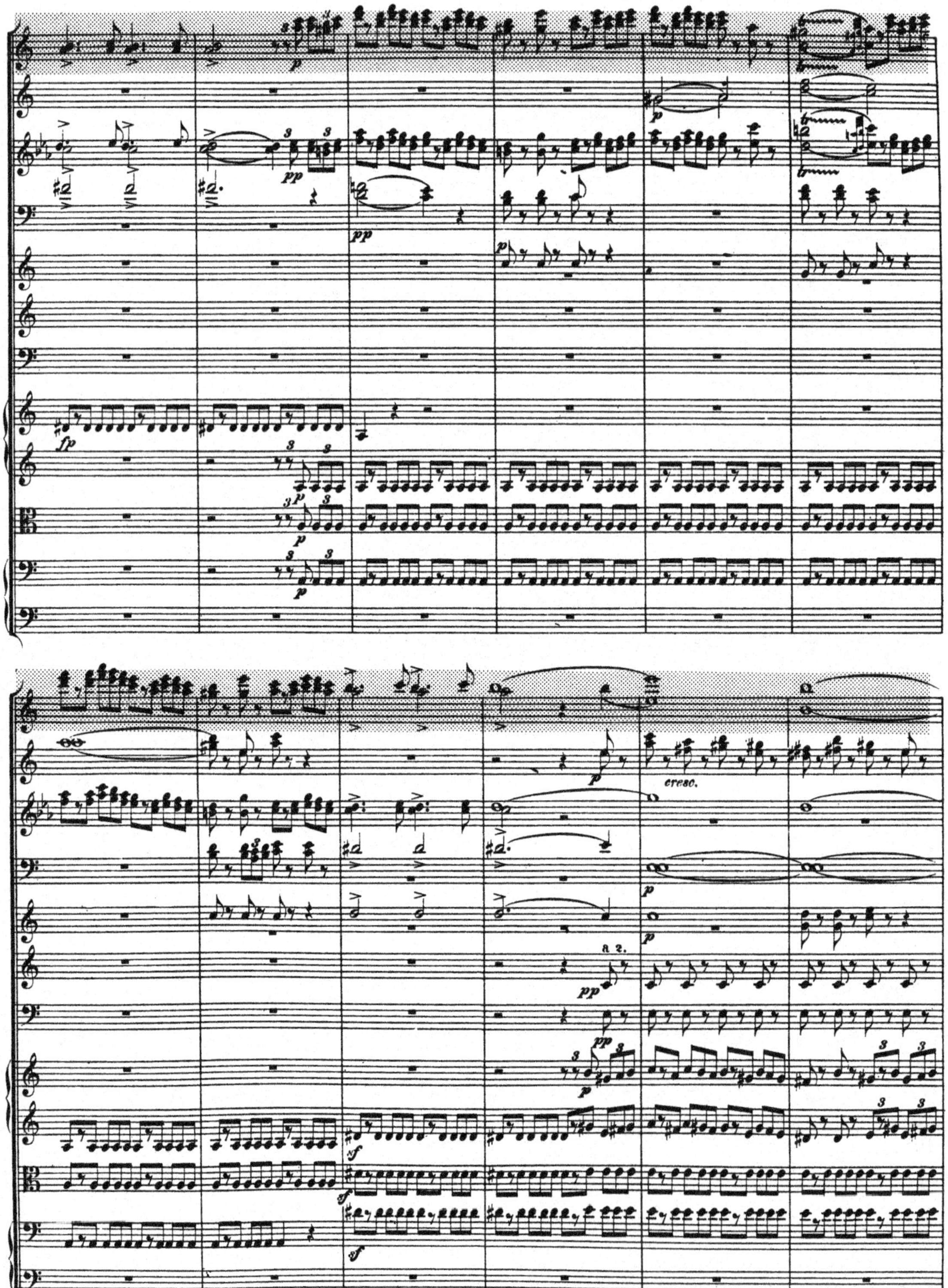

13-30 Triple Tonguing   Mendelssohn *Symphony #4, Presto*

13-30 Triple Tonguing   Mendelssohn *Symphony #4, Presto*

13-31 Triple Tonguing   **Ravel** *Rapsodie Espagnole, Feria*

13-32 Triple Tonguing   **Debussy** *La Mer, Jeax de vagues*

13-32 Triple Tonguing   Debussy *La Mer, Jeax de vagues*

13-32 Triple Tonguing **Debussy** *La Mer, Jeax de vagues*

Shakes and Tremolos

In the first octave, it's wise not to exceed the interval of a fifth. Above the second octave, it's wise not to exceed a third.

Score Reference 13-33 Shakes   Debussy *Nocturnes, Sirenes*

Score Reference 13-34 Shakes   Debussy *La Mer, Jeux de vagues*

The Piccolo

Italian, Flauto Piccolo

German, Kleine Flöte

French, Petite Flûte

All the remarks made in the preceding chapter about the fingering and articulation of the Flute, apply equally to the Piccolo. All that was said about the shakes and tremolos holds true with the Piccolo with two exceptions: the two highest shakes on the Flute,

EXAMPLE 14-1

aren't practical on the Piccolo. If the first of these two shakes were written, it would be played in the lower octave—such is the practice of orchestral performers when a composer has been too daring.

Of the four registers, the piccolo is most often written for in the medium, high , and very high registers. In the very high register, it's frequently used to double high violins and flutes. Piccolos are used on the melody to create an American patriotic or military feel, or to create a pixiesh, puckish or childlike feel.

EXAMPLE 14-2

Sounding an octave higher

14-3 Piccolo on the Melody, Low - Medium Register   Ravel *Mother Goose Suite, Laideronnette*

14-3 Piccolo on the Melody, Low -Medium Register   Ravel *Mother Goose Suite, Laideronnette*

14-4 Piccolo on the Melody, Low-Medium Register   **Ravel** *Mother Goose Suite, Petit Poucet*

14-5 Solo Piccolo on the Melody, High Register Ravel *Daphnis & Chloe*

14-5 Solo Piccolo on the Melody, High Register   Ravel *Daphnis & Chloe*

14-5 Solo Piccolo on the Melody, High Register   Ravel *Daphnis & Chloe*

14-5 Solo Piccolo on the Melody, High Register   Ravel *Daphnis & Chloe*

14-6 Reinforcing Violins Playing Natural Harmonics, High Register
Rimsky-Korsakov *Scheherazade*

14-6 Reinforcing Violins Playing Natural Harmonics, High Register
Rimsky-Korsakov *Scheherazade*

14-6 Reinforcing Violins Playing Natural Harmonics, High Register
Rimsky-Korsakov *Scheherazade*

14-6 Reinforcing Violins Playing Natural Harmonics, High Register
Rimsky-Korsakov *Scheherazade*

14-7 Piccolos Reinforcing the High Strings, Very High Register
Mahler *Symphony #1, 4th Movement*

14-8 Piccolos Double Tonguing Ravel *Rapsodie Espagnole, Feria*

14-8 Piccolos Double Tonguing   Ravel *Rapsodie Espagnole, Feria*

(★) Glissez en effleurant la corde *du côté du chevalet*

14-9 Piccolos Triple Tonguing   Ravel *Rapsodie Espagnole* [23]

14-10 Piccolos Flutter Tongue Ravel *Mother Goose Suite, Petit Poucet*

14-11 Arpeggios Reinforcing Violin 2   **Ravel** *Daphnis and Chloe*

14-11 Arpeggios Reinforcing Violin 2   Ravel *Daphnis and Chloe*

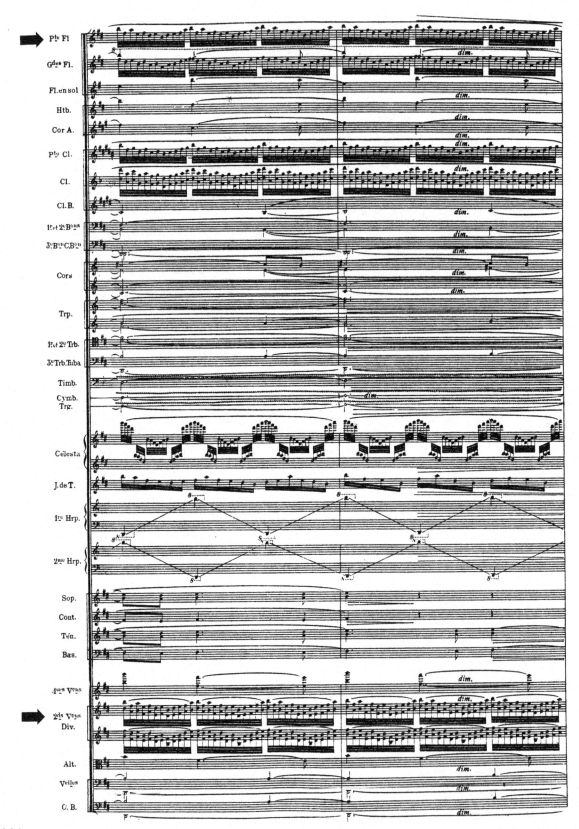

14-12 Arpeggios Against Violins Doing Fingered Tremolo   Ravel *Daphnis and Chloe*

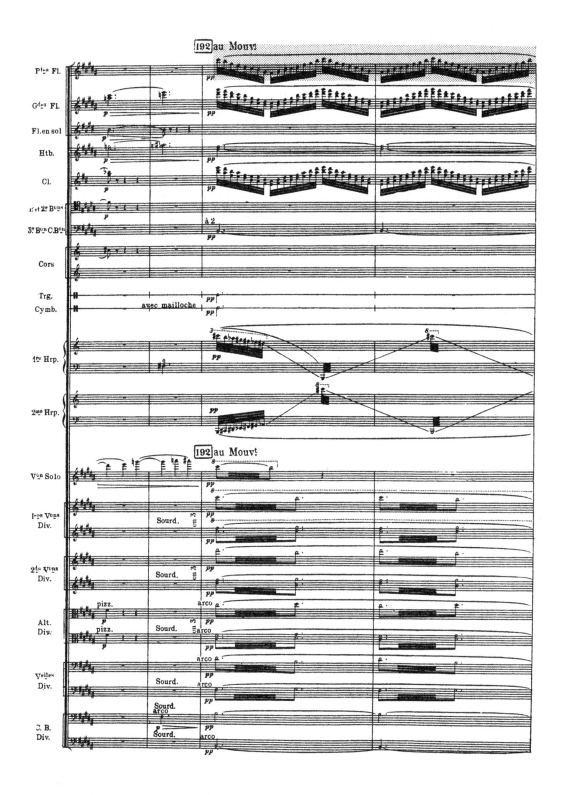

14-12 Arpeggios Against Violins Doing Fingered Tremolo   Ravel *Daphnis and Chloe*

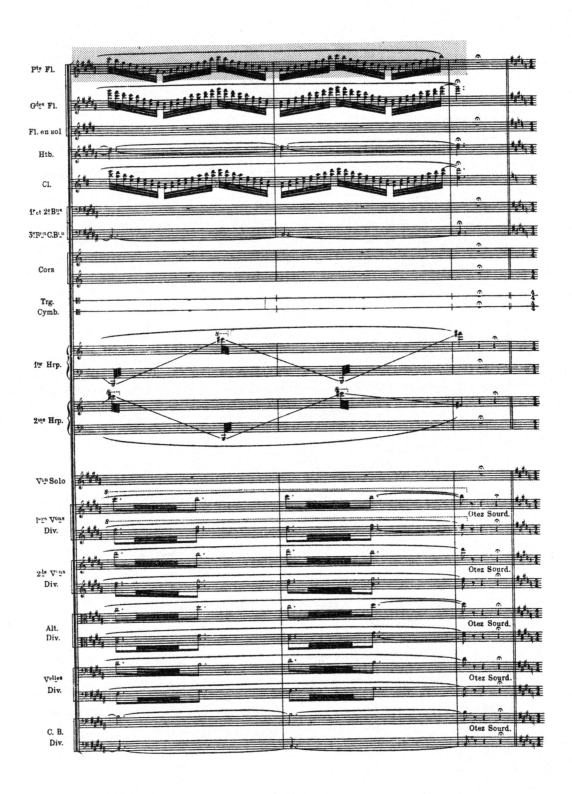

14-13 Piccolos Doing Shakes   Ravel *Daphnis and Chloe*

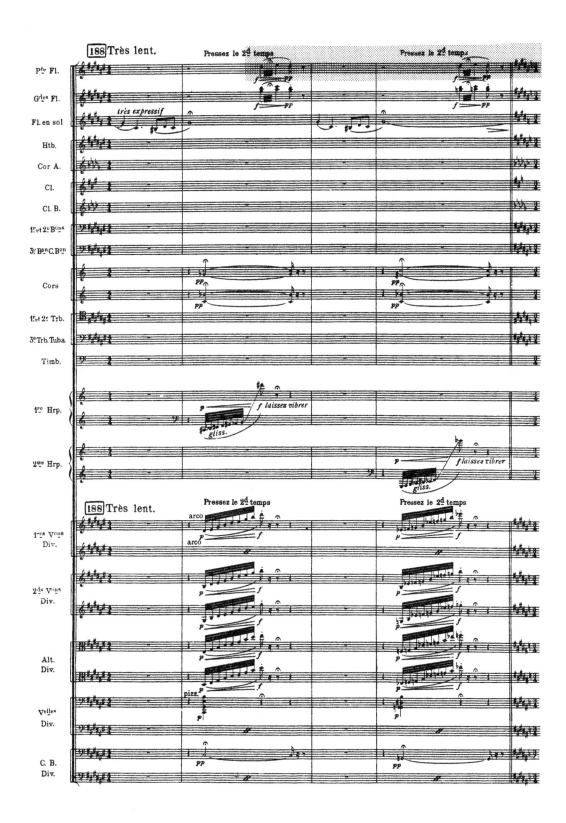

The Oboe

Italian, Oboe

German, Oboe

French, Hautbois

The Oboe differs from the Flute in not being capable of double or triple tonguing. It's a melodic instrument, the reed being slower of speech than the mouthpiece of the Flute. It's safe range is:

EXAMPLE 15-1

Writing for Oboe

1. Most oboe solos are written in the medium, and medium-high registers.

2. As with the flute, the ensemble is usually written below the oboe dynamic marking. However, with the oboe, you can write one dynamic level below the actual oboe part.

3. When strings are muted, they can be written at the same dynamic level as the oboe.

4. The harp can also be written at the same dynamic as the oboe.

5. At the bottom of the register, the oboe has a coarse thick sound that's best used for special circumstances like its use by Prokofiev in *Peter and the Wolf* to mimic the waddling duck.

15-2 Low Register Oboe   Prokofiev *Peter and the Wolf*

15-2 Low Register Oboe   Prokofiev *Peter and the Wolf*

15-3 Medium Register Oboe   **Ravel** *Mother Goose Suite, Petit Poucet*

15-4 Medium Register Oboe   Bizet *Carmen*

15-4 Medium Register Oboe   Bizet *Carmen*

15-5 Medium Register Oboe   **Dvorak** *New World Symphony*

15-6 High Register Oboe   Rimsky-Korsakov *Scheherazade*

15-6 High Register Oboe   Rimsky-Korsakov *Scheherazade*

15-7 High Register Oboe   Beethoven *Symphony #6, 3rd Movement*

15-7 High Register Oboe   Beethoven *Symphony #6, 3rd Movement*

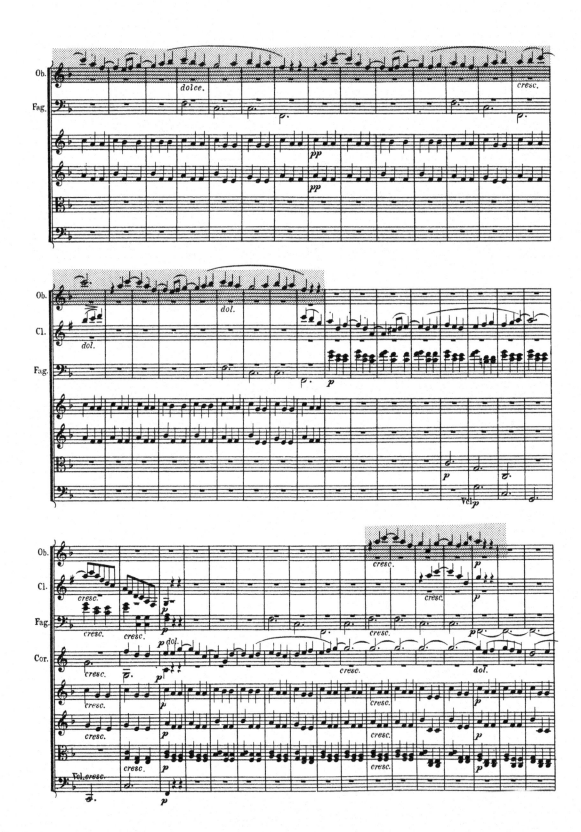

15-7 High Register Oboe   Beethoven *Symphony #6, 3rd Movement*

15-8 Very High Oboe   Ravel *Rapsodie Espagnole*

15-8 Very High Oboe   **Ravel** *Rapsodie Espagnole*

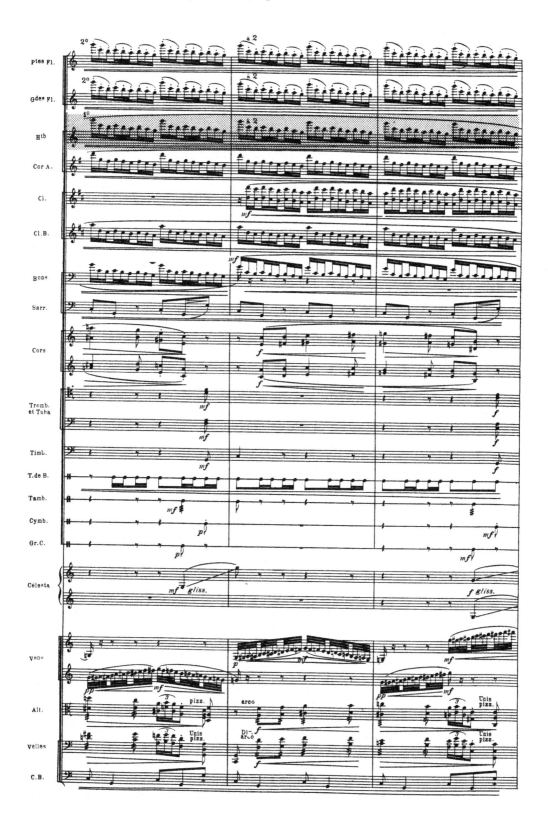

15-8 Very High Oboe   **Ravel** *Rapsodie Espagnole*

Articulation

The Oboe only uses single-articulation (the letter t as in "tu"). Double-tonguing is not used for the Oboe, nor is triple-tonguing. So, any rapid repeating of the same note is simply not idiomatic for the instrument.

It's wise not to articulate the oboe faster than:

EXAMPLE 15-9

 to  regardless of the register.

Slurred Notes

Ascending intervals are, generally speaking, more easily slurred than descending ones, the lips being more easily contracted than distended.

So, all octave skips can be slurred from middle C to E, a tenth above.

EXAMPLE 15-10

The same slurs would be much more awkward descending, as in the following passage, which is dangerous beyond mm 120:

EXAMPLE 15-11

Or this one, impossible beyond mm 112:

EXAMPLE 15-12

On the other hand, here is a perfectly practicable passage, with a very expressive concluding cadence. Despite the quick rate of movement, the difficulty of execution here isn't very great since the cadence allows the lips time to prepare for the wide skip:

EXAMPLE 15-13

Length of Breath

The Oboe consumes far less wind that the Flute. If a competition were started between oboists and flautists, the flautists would soon be compelled to acknowledge themselves defeated, their wind-supply being exhausted long before that of their rivals. There are few examples more convincing, in this connection, than the Largo of Handel's "Second Concerto," and the Prelude to the 3rd act of "Tannhauser," so difficult of performance, on account of the length of the phrase and the impossibility of taking breath. The Oboe alone, among the woodwind instruments, is equal to the task.

Transposing Oboes

To the Oboe family belong three transposing instruments: the Oboe d'amore, the Cor Anglais (covered in it's own chapter), and the Barytone Oboe.

The Oboe d'amore
This instrument is a minor third lower in pitch than the standard instrument. Its compass is from:

EXAMPLE 15-14

To the Oboe d'amore Bach assigns his most pathetic cantilenas; for *mf* effects nothing can equal the charm of the upper register:

EXAMPLE 15-15

(Qui sedes. *Mass in B minor.*)

Each time the instrument skips by a sixth to the accented beat, in the last three bars of the example quoted above, the effect is truly exquisite.

> See also, in the same Mass, the Bass air: *Et in spiritum sanctum*, accompanied by two Oboi d'amore. In this connection too, the *Passion according to St. Matthew,* the *Christmas Oratorio,* the *Cantatas,* the *Magnificat,* etc. should be studied.

The Oboe d'amore is played in the same manner as the ordinary Oboe. It has the same mechanism and can execute the same shakes, save two:

EXAMPLE 15-16

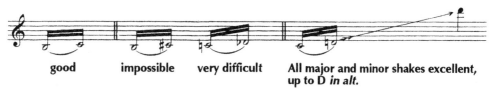

good   impossible   very difficult   All major and minor shakes excellent, up to D *in alt.*

These two shakes (x,y) will be rendered possible by means of a special key, easily fitted on to the instrument, if ever it comes to be used in the orchestra.

The Barytone Oboe
An octave below the standard instrument, with the following compass:

EXAMPLE 15-17

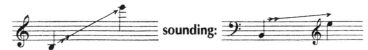

sounding:

The fingering and mechanism are those of the ordinary Oboe. The Barytone Oboe will form an admirable bass when all the instruments of the same family are concentrated into a focus of intense, almost aggressive quality.

Other Oboes

There's the Musette and the Pastoral Oboe (in Ab), two varieties of the same kind of instrument, only differing in the reed. Neither is used in the orchestra.

The Soprano Oboe in Eb is used together with the Small Clarinet in Eb in military bands. This is a very sonorous instrument with an extremely piercing upper register. Its compass is from

EXAMPLE 15-18

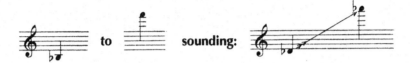

The fingering and mechanism are the same as for the other instruments of the Oboe family. So far, the Soprano has only been used once in the orchestra: by Vidal in *La Burgonde*.

The English Horn

Italian, Corno Inglese

German, Englisch Horn

French, Cor Anglais

The English horn is simply the Alto of the Oboe – (the old Oboe da caccia, so much used in former times (– and it's a fifth lower in pitch than the oboe.

EXAMPLE 16-1

The English horn has three distinct timbres. The lower register is very powerful, the upper register weak and thin. The best register is between:

EXAMPLE 16-2

All figures around the highest C#:

EXAMPLE 16-3

are very troublesome for the performer, this being one of the worst notes on the instrument.

Formerly this shake:

EXAMPLE 16-4

was impossible on the English Horn. Nowadays, thanks to a special key, all shakes from low B natural to high D natural can be executed:

EXAMPLE 16-5

(All possible, both major and minor).

Writing For English Horn

1. The English Horn is most often written for in the medium and high registers.

2. The ensemble should be written at least one dynamic level below the solo English Horn.

3. Muted strings can be written at the same dynamic level as the solo English Horn.

16-6 Low to Medium High English Horn   Sibelius *Swan of Tuonela*

16-6 Low to Medium High English Horn Sibelius *Swan of Tuonela*

16-6 Low to Medium High English Horn Sibelius *Swan of Tuonela*

16-6 Low to Medium High English Horn   Sibelius *Swan of Tuonela*

16-7 Medium English Horn   Dvorak *New World Symphony, 2nd Movement*

16-7 Medium English Horn   Dvorak *New World Symphony, 2nd Movement*

16-8 HIgh English Horn   Ravel *Mother Goose Suite, Petit Poucet*

The Clarinet

Italian, Clarinetto
German, Klarinette
French, Clarinette

Except for the Alto and Bass flutes, and the English horn, the clarinets are the remaining transposing instruments in the woodwinds. There are four clarinets most commonly used in the orchestra. These are the Bb and A-Clarinets, the Bb Bass Clarinet, and the Small Clarinet in Eb.

Transposition Chart

Bb Clarinet	Transpose up a whole step from concert
A Clarinet	Transpose up a minor third from concert
Bb Bass Clarinet	Transpose up a major ninth from concert
Bassett Horn	In F transpose up a perfect 5th
Alto Clarinet	In Eb transpose up a major 6th
Eb Clarinet	Transpose up a major sixth from concert
EEb Contraalto Clarinet	Up an octave and a 6th
BBb Contrabass Clarinet	Up an octave and a 9th

Writing for Clarinet

The clarinet is considered to be the most sociable of the woodwind instruments because of its blending quality.

1. Although advisable to write the ensemble at least one dynamic level less than that of the solo clarinet, a number of the examples in this chapter show that both the ensemble and the clarinet can be written at *p*.

2. The lowest register of the clarinet, called the *chalameau* register, has a very dark sonorous sound capable of outstanding solo work (see *Peter and The Wolf* example in this chapter) or for mixing with the French horns in unison or harmony.

3. In arpeggios, it's used to create a bubbly almost sea-like feeling.

4. It's used to great advantage in scale passages (especially chromatic ones). However, when the Clarinet is required to play bravura passages, care must be taken *not* to increase the difficulty by writing in extreme keys. With E major and Eb major difficulties begin. To solve this problem, almost all clarinetists carry both the Bb and A clarinets. With extreme keys they simply switch clarinets and transpose on sight. With the Bb-Clarinet, the keys C, F, G, Bb and their relative minor keys are excellent, because they're easy.

5. The pianissimo of the Clarinets (in the low and medium registers) represents the *minimum* of sound obtainable from wind instruments. Compared with Clarinets, Flutes in their lower register seem as intense and metallic as Trumpets would be in a mezzo forte. It's hardly even a *pp*. The instrument has almost lost its timbre: 'tis but a whiff of air.

6. The Clarinet can have a neutral tone-color in the medium register that lets it blend with almost every group in the orchestra. While the Oboe can be mistaken for no other instrument, the Clarinet can, without attracting notice, take the place of a Second Flute, or of a Second Horn, or even of a bassoon, its full, rich quality of tone possessing an unrivaled power of blending with that of any other instrument.

7. While it can be done, leaps of an octave, especially across registers (see below), are impractical.

Clarinet Writing Insight

In his Piano Concertos, Mozart frequently wrote a single Flute part and two Clarinet parts, treating all three instruments in the same manner, as if they were three Flutes.

In the *Egmont Overture*, Beethoven assigned the dissonant note of the chord to a single Clarinet, treated as if it were a second Horn, the only instance of want of balance in the whole of his orchestral writing, for this one Gb against one Eb, four C's and two Ab's is really very weak:

EXAMPLE 17-1

Clarinet Range by Registers

The Woodwind Basics chapter gave both the range and the color breaks for the Clarinet in the Low to Very High Registers. Clarinetists, however, take a different view as to the registers. For the clarinetist, a change in register isn't a change in color, but rather in a change based on which notes are within the same set of partials. Observe the chart below:

EXAMPLE 17-2

For the clarinetist, his low register is from E below middle C to Bb above middle C. The medium register is B above middle C to C two octaves above middle C (C5). The high register is from C# up to the A. Trills, shakes and tremolos that are written across these breaks are extremely difficult for the clarinetist and should be avoided.

Fingerings
Clarinetists use a system called the Boehm system for fingering the clarinet. The Boehm system is also used on the Bass Clarinet, and all the saxes.

Score Reference 17-3 Low Register Clarinet **Prokofiev** *Peter and the Wolf,* [11]

Score Reference 17-3 Low Register Clarinet   Prokofiev *Peter and the Wolf*

Score Reference 17-4 Low to Medium Register Clarinet   Ravel *Daphnis and Chloe*

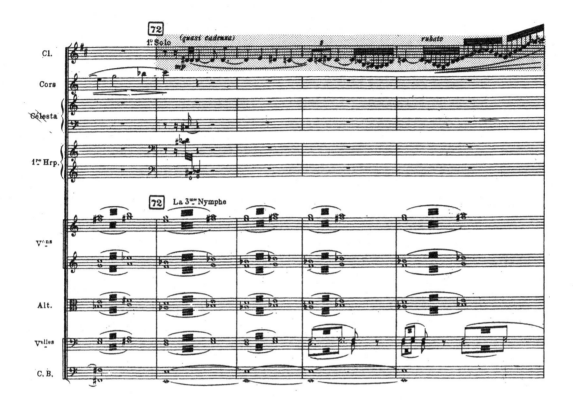

Score Reference 17-5 Medium Register Clarinet
Ravel *Mother Goose Suite, Beauty and the Beast*

Score Reference 17-5 Medium Register Clarinet
Ravel *Mother Goose Suite, Beauty and the Beast*

Score Reference 17-5 Medium Register Clarinet
Ravel *Mother Goose Suite, Beauty and the Beast*

Score Reference 17-6 High Register Clarinet Ravel *Mother Goose Suite, Pavanne*

Score Reference 17-7 Very High Register Clarinet   Prokofiev *Peter and the Wolf*

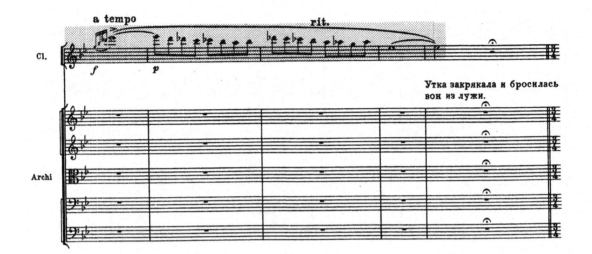

Articulations

The maximum speed for articulated notes and staccato passages should hardly exceed

EXAMPLE 17-8

EXAMPLE 17-9

Many composers treat Clarinets as if they were Flutes, causing them to articulate as rapidly as these latter instruments in very quick tempo like the opening of the *Italian Symphony* (see below). Clarinet-players admit that, in this passage, although they do their best to keep pace with the Flutes, their execution is not really satisfactory. If they stood in the foreground, they'd attract unfavorable notice.

EXAMPLE 17-10

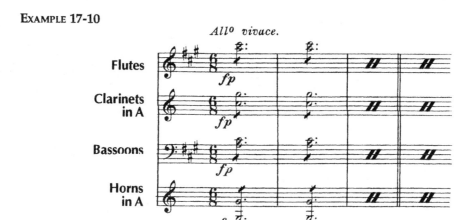

Clarinetists deal with this articulation issue by breaking such rhythmic figures into patterns of slurred and staccato notes. See Example 17-11 on the following page.

EXAMPLE **17-11**

Accomplished clarinetists can also double-tongue a passage when quarter note = 180mm. But not all clarinetists can do this. Check with the musicians who will perform your work before writing it.

Guidelines for Shakes and Tremolos

Before writing a shake or tremolo, it's wise to first call a clarinetist and have him read it over it to see if this is what you have in mind.

1. Avoid ALL shakes and tremolos across the register breaks. (Example 17-2)

2. In the lower register, anything from E up to G above middle C is possible.

However, alternate fingerings on on some notes can cause intonation problems.

3.   In the middle register, intervals over a perfect 4th can become more awkward.

4.   In the high register, intervals over a 3rd are the most difficult. Anything over high F# should be avoided.

The Alto Clarinet

The Alto Clarinet is tuned in G, a fourth below the standard instrument (if Bb be considered the normal key). This member of the Clarinet family is not much in use nowadays. Its range is:

EXAMPLE 17-12

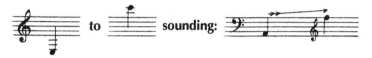

No higher notes can be obtained.

Mendelssohn has written two duets for Alto Clarinet and Bb Clarinet.

The Small Clarinet

This is also an instrument rarely used, except in military bands, for which it is tuned in Eb. It sounds a minor third higher than written.

Berlioz has used it in the *Nuit de Sabbat* of his *Symphonie Fantastique*, and Wagner in the *Finale* of the *Walkure*. In this latter work, the Small Clarinet is tuned in D, but the performer frequently transposes his part, playing on the ordinary instrument in Eb.

EXAMPLE 17-13

For extended solo use of the D clarinet, see also Strauss' *Till Eulenspiegel's Merry Pranks*.

Jazz and Pop Uses of the Clarinet

The clarinet is a vital element of jazz for both early big band and Dixieland. For jazz uses of the clarinet you're referred to these sources: Gershwin: *An American in Paris*, and *Together Again: The Benny Goodman Quartet* now available on CD.

Score Reference 17-14 Clarinet Cadenza   **Ravel** *Rapsodie Espagnole, Prélude à la nuit*

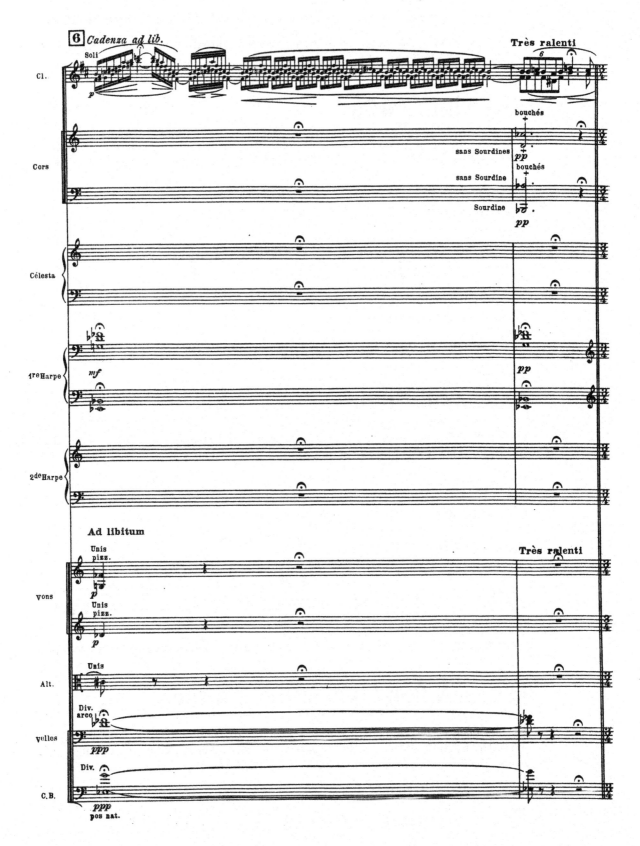

Score Reference 17-15 Arpeggios Ravel *Daphnis and Chloe*

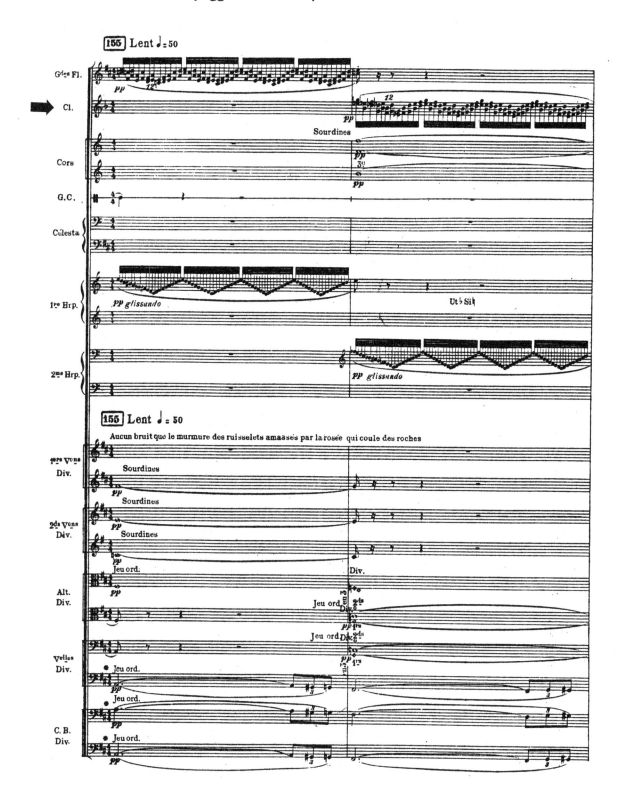

Score Reference 17-15 Arpeggios Ravel *Daphnis and Chloe*

Score Reference 17-15 Arpeggios Ravel *Daphnis and Chloe*

Score Reference 17-15 Arpeggios **Ravel** *Daphnis and Chloe*

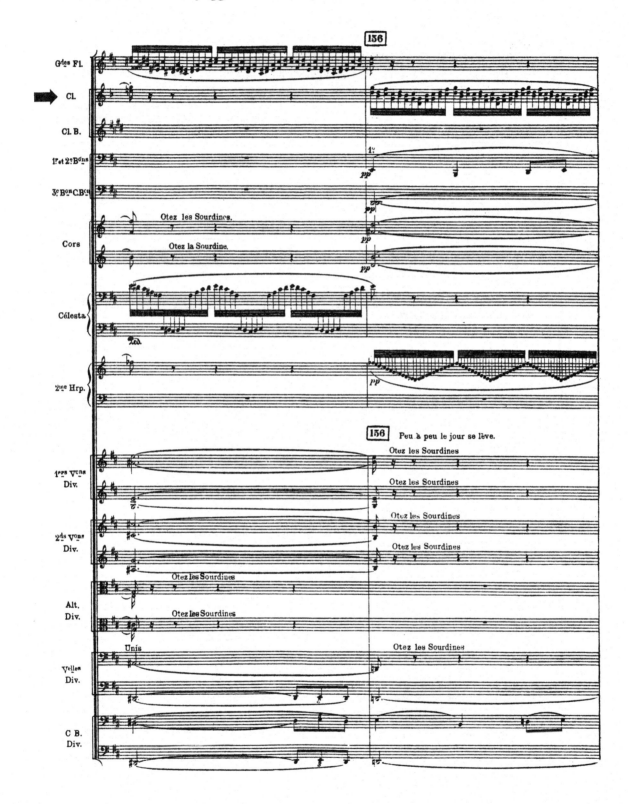

Score Reference 17-15 Arpeggios Ravel *Daphnis and Chloe*

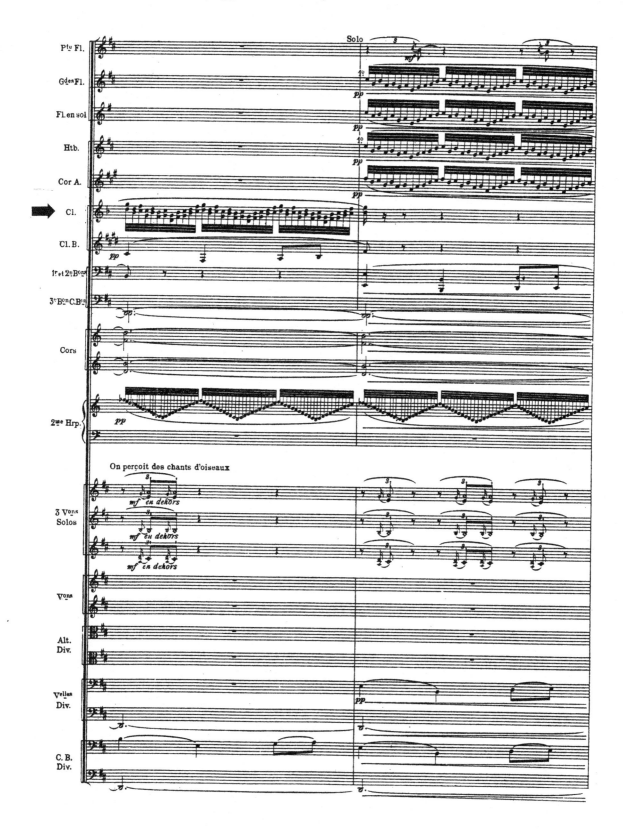

Score Reference 17-16 Shakes   Stravinsky *The Firebird*

Score Reference 17-16 Shakes   Stravinsky *The Firebird*

*Joué par deux exécutants.

The Bass Clarinet

The Bass Clarinet is written like the Bb Clarinet, but sounds an octave lower. It's range is from:

EXAMPLE 18-1

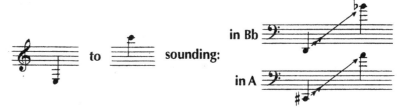

About the A Bass Clarinet

For completeness, the range of this instrument is given. However, please note that it's *no longer used today.* All bass clarinet part are for the Bb Bass Clarinet.

However, some have been outfitted with additional keys that let it go down to Bb below C#, but this isn't a standard for all the instruments.

The lower register, which contains the richest and fullest notes, is, of course, the most valuable. The mechanism of the Bass Clarinet is identical with that of the standard instrument.

There are two methods for notating the Bass Clarinet. The French method, transposes the sound up an major ninth so that the part reads in treble clef. *This is the method used today.*

The second method is the German school where the part is only transposed up a major second from where it sounds and written in the bass clef. (Wagner uses this method). This is not used today. *Don't use it.*

The Bass Clarinet can go from an *f* to a *pp* as easily as the standard instrument itself, especially in the bottom register. Thus for very quiet passages in the bottom register, the bass clarinet can be an effective substitute for the bassoon which at the bottom of its range cannot play that softly. If it were necessary to have a phrase repeated in slow-dying echoes, the effect required could probably be obtained by employing the three following wind instruments in succession:

EXAMPLE 18-2

Composers and compositions using the bass clarinet include:

◆   *The Nutcracker* by Tchaikovsky

◆   All Wagner works

◆   All Strauss works

◆   All Mahler works

◆   *3rd Symphony* by Schumann

◆   *Grand Canyon Suite* by Grofé

Bassett Horn Example

Please see Mozart Grand Partita in Bb, K361.

Writing for the Bass Clarinet

1.   Shakes and tremolos are possible, but be aware that they don't speak as fast the regular clarinet.

2.   In modern 20th century scoring, the Bass Clarinet is frequently mixed with Bassoons and Contrabassoons to either double the Basses or to create an independent line of exceedingly dark quality. It can also be to create a rich ensemble that mixes a Cello lead on the melody supported by winds. The bass clarinet is not frequently used on the melody.

When it is however, depending on the harmony, the effect can range from sinister to mysterious. For recorded examples of the bass clarinet on the melody see *The Ghost and Mrs. Muir* soundtrack by Bernard Hermann.

Mixing the Bass Clarinet with The Bassoon and Contrabassoon

The following combination was used by Ralph Vaughn Williams in *Sinfonia Anartica*. All parts written where sounding.

EXAMPLE 18-3

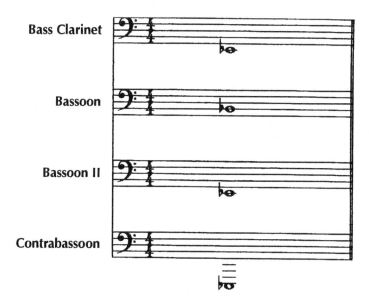

This combination mixed with the strings was used by Ravel, *Pictures at Exhibition, Gnomus*.

EXAMPLE 18-4

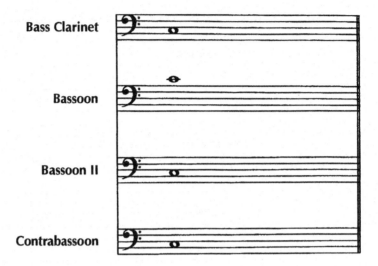

The Bass Clarinet can be the third voice in a Clarinet choir ala Ravel, *Pictures at an Exhibition, Promenade*.

EXAMPLE 18-5

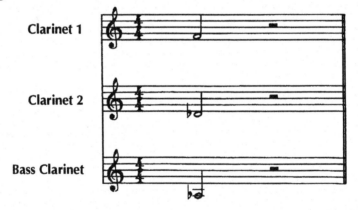

Score Reference 18-6   To Create an Ensemble With Cello Lead a la Wagner in *Overture to Tristan and Isolde*

Note that the Bass Clarinet is written with the German Method in this example.

Score Reference 18-6   To Create an Ensemble With Cello Lead a la Wagner in
Overture to Tristan and Isolde

Score Reference 18-7 Bass Clarinet
Tchaikovsky, *Nutcracker Suite, Dance of the Sugar Plum Fairies*

Score Reference 18-7 Bass Clarinet
Tchaikovsky, *Nutcracker Suite, Dance of the Sugar Plum Fairies*

Chapter 19

The Bassoon

Italian, Fagotto
German, Fagott
French, Basson

The Bassoon has a range of:

EXAMPLE 19-1

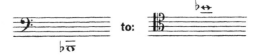

In writing for the orchestra, it's dangerous to exceed the top limit, but in a solo piece, the performer can be asked to play up to D, a third higher:

EXAMPLE 19-2

Wagner once even wrote E, but he was justified in doing so in that special case, first because his theme was such that the high E was necessary, and second, because the intensity of the Cellos and Violas, playing in unison and doubling the Bassoon part, was likely to neutralize any mistake made at such a height.

EXAMPLE 19-3

The following pages contain score examples of the bassoon playing the melody.

Score Reference 19-4 Low Register Bassoon   Tchaikovsky *Symphony #6, 1st Movement*

Score Reference 19-4 Low Register Bassoon   Tchaikovsky *Symphony #6, 1st Movement*

Score Reference 19-5 Low Register Bassoon   Prokofiev *Peter and the Wolf*

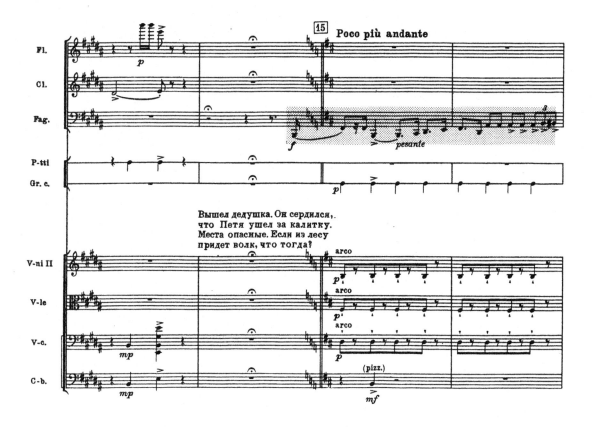

Score Reference 19-5 Low Register Bassoon   Prokofiev *Peter and the Wolf*

Score Reference 19-5 Low Register Bassoon   Prokofiev *Peter and the Wolf*

Петя не придал никакого значения словам дедушки
и заявил, что пионеры не боятся волков.

Score Reference 19-6 Medium Register Bassoon   Bizet *Carmen*

Score Reference 19-6 Medium Register Bassoon   Bizet *Carmen*

Score Reference 19-7 High Register Bassoon   Rimsky-Korsakov *Scheherazade*

Score Reference 19-8 Very High Register Bassoon   Stravinsky *Rite of Spring*

The bottom fifth can compete with the Brass in tone-power. The Bb can even form the bottom of the trombones. However, in that case, the strain on the bassoonist's lungs involved in the production of such intense sounds must be taken into account, and the part written to not completely exhaust the performer.

Writing for the Bassoon

It's astonishing that an instrument descending lower even than the horn, and able to sound deep notes of such intensity, should also be capable of acrobatic feats that none of its neighbors can do. It's available for every combination. It blends with every group—woodwind, brass, and strings alike. It can be put to all kinds of work.

Reinforcing an Accent of the Strings
It can reinforce an accent of the strings, and not stick out.

EXAMPLE 19-9

Completing the Horn Section
It can complete the horn group, blending so perfectly that it cannot be distinguished from the brass.

EXAMPLE 19-10

Handling the Bass Line

It can handle the whole weight of the harmony when put on the bass line:

Score Reference 19-11   Tchaikovsky *Nutcracker Suite, Danse Chinois*

Score Reference 19-11   Tchaikovsky *Nutcracker Suite, Danse Chinois*

Score Reference 19-11 Tchaikovsky *Nutcracker Suite, Danse Chinois*

Score Reference 19-11 Tchaikovsky *Nutcracker Suite, Danse Chinois*

Score Reference 19-11 Tchaikovsky *Nutcracker Suite, Danse Chinois*

Score Reference 19-11   Tchaikovsky *Nutcracker Suite, Danse Chinois*

Adding Energy to the Strings

Figures played by the Cellos and Basses, or even by the whole String section, can gain in energy and intensity when doubled by the Bassoon:

EXAMPLE 19-12

Mixing With Pizzicato Strings

The staccato of the Bassoon can, when necessary, be as light as the String pizzicato:

EXAMPLE 19-13

This staccato of the Bassoon, in the *Serenade of Mephistopheles* is as flexible as a pizzicato.

EXAMPLE 19-14

Mixing With the Flute

By combining the Bassoon with the Flute, at a distance of two octaves, Mozart obtained the sweetest and richest timbre in the orchestra.

EXAMPLE 19-15

Sometimes Mozart even writes the Bassoon two octaves below the Violin:

EXAMPLE 19-16

As Part of a Woodwind Ensemble With Cello Lead
Score Reference 19-17   Borodin *Symphony #1, 3rd Movement*

Score Reference 19-17 **Borodin** *Symphony #1, 3rd Movement*

Articulations

Like the Oboe and the Clarinet, the Bassoon uses only *single-articulation*. From the lowest Bb to the highest Bb, all notes can be repeated or detached, either *f* or *p*, almost as easily as on the Cello.

For instance, in the low register:

EXAMPLE 19-18

In the medium and high registers:

EXAMPLE 19-19

For slurred notes, the Bassoon, like the Oboe and the Clarinet, can go up more easily than it can go down:

EXAMPLE 19-20

However, descending slurs are practicable in slow tempo, and even in quick tempo when the intervals are small:

EXAMPLE 19-21

Staccato notes, skips of an octave, a tenth, a twelfth, a fifteenth, etc., can be played on the Bassoon with ease and rapidity:

EXAMPLE 19-22

Descending slurs to be avoided:

EXAMPLE 19-23

plus all slurred intervals starting downwards from Gb, Eb, D, C#, and C natural in the lowest register:

EXAMPLE 19-24

In slow tempo, descending slurs can be played (except the intervals mentioned above), provided they're used in an ensemble, and not in a solo:

EXAMPLE 19-25

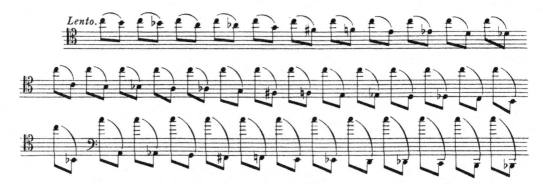

Taking any one of its notes as a starting point, the Bassoon can descend the scale chromatically, but this is somewhat dangerous, and speed is checked.

Length of Breath

General rule: The lower the pitch of the instrument, the more breath that's needed to play it. So, the sustaining-power of a Bassoon, playing in the lower and upper registers, is limited—according to an experiment made with the assistance of Mr. Eugene Bourdeau, Professor at the Conservatoire—respectively as follows:

EXAMPLE **19-26**

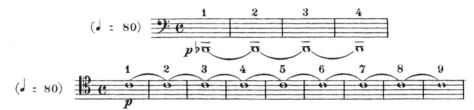

Even in the higher register, this maximum is seldom exceeded, and, of course, when playing *f*, it's greatly lessened, since the duration of the sound is in inverse proportion to its intensity.

Shakes and Tremolos

Because each shake or tremolo must be handled on an individual basis (due to the way the bassoon is constructed), it's best to first consult with a bassoonist to see how mechanically feasible the shake is. As a general rule however, shakes over the internal of a fourth are not advised.

The Contrabassoon

French, Contre-Bassoon
Italian, Contrafagotto
German, Kontrafagott

The Double-Bassoon sounds an octave below where written. Its range (where sounding) is:

EXAMPLE 20-1

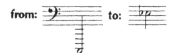

A major use of the Contrabassoon is to double the string basses since its lowest note is a whole step lower than the lowest note on a five string bass. It can also be used as the foundation for the brass section, especially when only two trombones may be available. When used on the melody the contrabassoon provides a dark sinister quality.

The following pages contain score examples of the contrabassoon.

Other writing uses have already been shown in Chapter 18, *The Bass Clarinet*.

Score Example 20-2 Contrabassoon On Melodic Theme
Ravel *Mother Goose Suite, Beauty and The Beast*

Score Example 20-2 Contrabassoon On Melodic Theme
Ravel *Mother Goose Suite, Beauty and The Beast*

Score Example 20-2 Contrabassoon On Melodic Theme
Ravel *Mother Goose Suite, Beauty and The Beast*

Score Example 20-2 Contrabassoon On Melodic Theme
Ravel *Mother Goose Suite, Beauty and The Beast*

Score Example 20-2 Contrabassoon On Melodic Theme
Ravel *Mother Goose Suite, Beauty and The Beast*

Score Example 20-2 Contrabassoon On Melodic Theme
Ravel *Mother Goose Suite, Beauty and The Beast*

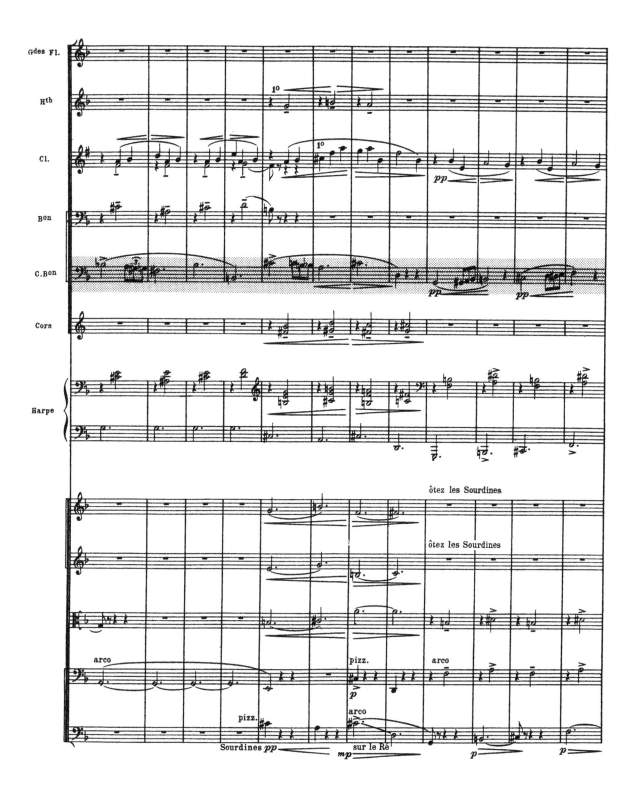

Score Example 20-2 Contrabassoon On Melodic Theme
Ravel *Mother Goose Suite, Beauty and The Beast*

Score Example 20-2 Contrabassoon On Melodic Theme
Ravel *Mother Goose Suite, Beauty and The Beast*

Brass Basics

There are four basic brass instruments used in both the orchestra and studio work. These are the trumpet, the trombone, the tuba, and the French horn. Of the four instruments, only two really have doubles: the trumpet player and the tuba player. Here are the doubles for the trumpet and tuba by type of work.

Instrument	Symphony	Studio
Trumpet	Bb, C	Bb
	Piccolo Trumpet	Piccolo Trumpet
		Flugelhorn
Tuba	small Bb (euphonium) F, CC Tuba	small Bb (euphonium) F, CC Tuba

For either types of work, the tubist may elect to use the Eb Tuba instead of the F tuba. the BBb Tuba, while sometimes used in symphonic and studio work, is most often used in military and school bands.

Trumpet Doubles

For doubles, the trumpet is most often asked to double the C trumpet and piccolo trumpet for symphonic work. The flugelhorn and occasionally the piccolo trumpet are most often used for studio work, jazz and pop sessions. (For examples of flugelhorn playing, you're referred to the music of Chuck Mangione).

Tuba Doubles

Generally, the tuba player will use the C tuba for both symphonic and studio work. When a lighter tuba sound is required, like in the music of Ravel or Debussy, the Euphonium may be used. Often, at either a symphonic session or scoring date, the tuba player will have two tubas available depending on the music to be performed. Since each tuba offers unique sound qualities, it's advisable to call the tuba player to have him play some examples from each instrument to define more clearly the sound you have in mind.

French Horn and Trombone

Neither instrument has doubles. But there are other trombones, notably the Bass Trombone which is used for low work, usually the third or fourth part. The third player in the trombone section is usually the Bass Trombonist. The trombonist may be asked to play a Bass Trumpet part which is handled on an instrument that's basically a valve trombone.

Mutes

All the brass instruments have mutes of one type or another. The instrument with the most number of mutes is the trumpet, followed by the trombone. The French horn and tuba have the least mutes available. In symphonic work, the score is marked *con sord* (with mute) or *muted*. When the mute is to be removed, mark the score *senza sorda* or *open*. Unless otherwise specified, the performer will automatically use a straight mute. All other mutes for all other kinds of sessions must be specified. The chart below shows which mutes are used on which instruments.

Mute	Trumpet	Trombone	Tuba	French Horn
Straight	x	x	x	x
Harmon	x	x		
Wah-Wah	x			
Whisper	x			
Solo Tone	x	x(tenor only)		
Cup	x	x		
Plunger	x	x		
Hat or *Derby*	x	x		
Bucket	x	x		

Unfortunately, only the straight mute is really used in symphonic sessions. So, to hear examples of the other mutes, you'll need to spend time listening to these artists:

Trumpets: *Miles Davis, Dizzy Gillespie, Doc Severinsen, Maynard Ferguson, Clark Terry, Art Farmer, Louis Armstrong.*

Cornet: *Jimmy McPartland*

Trombones: *Stan Kenton Orchestra, J.J. Jackson, Urbie Green, Jack Teagarden.*

Brass Section Sizes: Symphonic and Studio

Depending on the composer and the piece, brass section sizes can vary greatly. However, the chart below shows the basic sizes you can expect to be available for the typical symphony orchestra or what's usually asked for in a standard sized studio orchestra. For studio work, there is this exception: when studio writing, you can have anything you want as long as it's in the budget. It's not necessary that you even have a full brass section, or any brass, if the project or film doesn't require it. If you're going to use a full brass section, most of the time, the instrumentation chart shown below will be more than adequate.

Trumpets	Trombones	Tuba	French Horns
3, sometimes 2	2 Tenor, 1 Bass Trombone	1 (optional in studio work)	4, sometimes 3

Expanding the Brass in The Studio
In the studio, brass section expansion occurs in these situations:

Trumpet
In sessions where four or more harmony parts are wanted, and the budget supports it, the section can be expanded to four players, less often to five. Most big band (also called stage band) writing requires *no less than* four players.

Lead Section Players in Jazz/Studio Ensembles
When doing jazz/studio work with a brass ensemble, you want to be careful to select what's called a *lead trumpet player* vs. looking for someone to play part #1. The lead trumpet player is the Concertmaster of the brass section. His playing shapes the entire ensemble, especially with tutti brass passages. The sound of the band will also take on his sound as well as his phrasing. So it's important that you carefully specify with the contractor exactly what you want. Also, do not assume that the Lead Player is an accomplished soloist. Many times he will be. But most often, the jazz solo part is passed on to the second, third, or fourth player in the section.

Trombones
When a fourth part is needed, most often the tuba is used for another color with the trombones and because it blends well with the French horns. In big bands, the section can be expanded to four players (three tenor trombones and one bass trombone) which is the

standard-sized trombone section. For a more expansive sound, five trombones can be used with the last part or two parts being the Bass Trombone (with a possible Tuba double). Such combinations were used by the late Stan Kenton in his jazz orchestra. For jazz work, the lead player or the second player will often be the soloists.

French Horns

For studio work, there's usually a minimum of 3 French horns used (3-part harmony and unison writing). When a fourth harmony part is required, it can either be played by a bassoon, or by adding a fourth French horn. Otherwise the French horns can expand based on the general principle that at *f*, 2 French horns equal 1 trumpet or 1 trombone. When the section is expanded to six players and a full brass section is present, generally there will be two players to a part for 3-part harmony in *f*. If there are eight French horn players and a full brass section, then there will be two players per part for 4-part harmony in *f*.

Examples of Modern Horn Writing

For some superb examples of French Horn writing, please see the following albums: *The Rocketeer* (James Horner), *Rio Conchos: The Artist Who Did Not Want to Paint* (Jerry Goldsmith, Intrada RVF 6007D), *Star Trek V: The Final Frontier* (Jerry Goldsmith), *Peter Gunn* (Henry Mancini), *Mr. Lucky* (Henry Mancini), *Always* (John Williams), *E.T.* (John Williams) *Indiana Jones and The Last Crusade* (John Williams). For superb score examples to study for pop writing, you're referred to Mr. Mancini's *Sounds and Scores*.

Comprehensive Range Chart

The chart on the following page is given with this understanding: that true professional jazz and studio players can play substantially higher than the charts indicate. However, this is a very personal thing where you should only write that high when you know who's going to be playing the part. Top trumpet jazz and studio players can play G above second line C (C5) all the way up to Double High C (C6) transposed. Top trombone players are regularly called on to play Bb above middle C. Top tuba players, when they've run out of tuba literature to perform, have been known to sight read French horn parts for the *fun* of it.

EXAMPLE 21-1

Seating the Brass: Symphonic and Studio

The seating below is the most common for both the symphony and the full studio orchestra. Please note that the trumpets are often on risers in such a session:

EXAMPLE 21-2

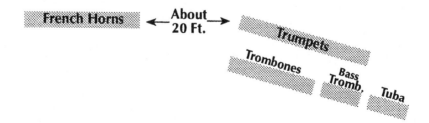

Trumpet and Trombone Seating and Parts

Trumpet and trombone parts are labeled with Arabic numbers for jazz and studio work, and Roman numerals for symphonic work. The Bass Trombone part, for symphonic work, is usually marked III, but to avoid confusion, write Bass Trombone.

Trumpets in a jazz/studio situation mix the seating as follows:

Trumpet 3   **Trumpet 2**   **Trumpet 1**   **Trumpet 4**

Trumpets are almost always seated. But in jazz/studio work, where extremely high trumpet work is required consistently (called *scream trumpet* parts), it's common for the trumpets to stand and physically lean back to get greater use out of the diaphragm for the high work.

If there are three trumpets, the seating will be:

Trumpet 3   **Trumpet 1**   **Trumpet 2**

In symphonic work, the Trumpets are seated left to right, Trumpet 1 to Trumpet 3.

In jazz/studio work, the trombones will generally be seated similar to the trumpets above. This way the lead trombone player can hear the lead trumpet player, and so, work more effectively together for a united sound.

French Horn Parts and Studio Seating

In the symphony, the top two harmony parts (in a 4-part chord) are labeled French Horns I and French Horns III. The lower two harmony parts in a 4-part chord are labeled French Horns II and French Horns IV.

For studio work, the French Horns are labeled in Arabic numbers 1-4 and are usually seated from left to right (1-4) so that the full harmony can be heard left to right.

Working With Older Scores

Before the acceptance of the modern valve horn (French horn) and trumpet, parts were written for various crooks or slides which the brass player inserted to have a range of notes to perform across the harmonic overtone series. The following two charts explain how to transpose these parts from older scores into concert for ease in study.

French Horn Transpositions to Concert for Older Scores

Horn in Bb *alto*	*Transposes Down*	*a step*
Horn in A	*Transposes Down*	*a minor 3rd*
Horn in G	*Transposes Down*	*a perfect 4th*
Horn in F	*Transposes Down*	*a perfect 5th*
Horn in E	*Transposes Down*	*a minor 6th*
Horn in Eb	*Transposes Down*	*a major 6th*

Horn in D	*Transposes Down*	*a minor 7th*
Horn in C	*Transposes Down*	*an octave*
Horn in Bb *basso*	*Transposes Down*	*a major 9th*

Trumpet Transpositions to Concert for Older Score

Trumpet in F	*Transposes Up*	*a perfect 4th*
Trumpet in E	*Transposes Up*	*a major 3rd*
Trumpet in Eb	*Transposes Up*	*a minor 3rd*
Trumpet in D	*Transposes Up*	*a major 2nd*
Trumpet in C	*Sounds as Written*	
Trumpet in Bb	*Transposes Down*	*a whole step*
Trumpet in A	*Transposes Down*	*a minor 3rd*

Special Brass Articulation Markings for Jazz/Studio Work

There are 13 special articulation markings common to jazz/stage band ensemble work only. The definitions on the following pages are *not* standard for the symphony and will create unacceptable results if used with that kind of ensemble.

EXAMPLE 21-3

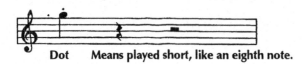

Dot — Means played short, like an eighth note.

Doo — Means played longer, the full value.

Dut — Means played about 2/3 the value.

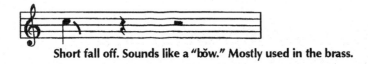

Short fall off. Sounds like a "bŏw." Mostly used in the brass.

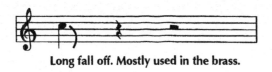

Long fall off. Mostly used in the brass.

Shake. Trumpets only.

Turn. Most always used by trumpets only.

Short gliss up. Brass.

Long gliss up. Brass.

Means the note is to be "swallowed". It's sounded, but not with full value.
Usually found in saxes with extensive eighth and sixteenth note tutti passages.

Means, "ahh." Trumpet and trombones only.

Means, "ooo." Trumpet and trombones only.

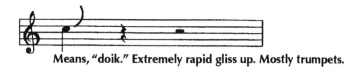

Means, "doik." Extremely rapid gliss up. Mostly trumpets.

Writing for Brass

Because the instruments have changed so much over the years, the writer is compelled to go outside the classics to modern jazz and soundtrack recordings to really hear the possibilities available.

In that sense, writing for brass must be viewed from an historical stylistic perspective based on the types of horns being available to the composer from the 1600s forward and the kinds of parts that were typically written for them during that period.

To that end, and with deference to my friends who are Bass Trombonists, I've deleted the Bass Trombone Chapter in favor of an expanded chapter covering brass, woodwind, and string writing.

The Bb Trumpet

Italian, Tromba
German, Trompete
French, Trompette

There are two basic trumpets in use today. These are the Bb and the C. The Bb Trumpet transposes up a major second from the concert score. The C Trumpet is a concert instrument. For the performance of Baroque music, the D, Eb, and also the Bb Piccolo trumpet are used.

Trumpet Range

There are several ways to consider the trumpet range. The safest range is to generally not write the performer over top line G (transposed A).

EXAMPLE 22-1

For symphonic writing (assuming a top drawer section), it's wise not to write the trumpets over high C (second line C above the staff, transposed D).

EXAMPLE 22-2

But, if you're working with professional players who have abundant experience in performing big band jazz arrangements, you can write up double high G and possibly double high Bb (transposed Double high A and Double High C).

EXAMPLE 22-3

In essence, the trumpet range is highly dependent on the performer and the music he's most likely to perform.

Talking to a Trumpeter About Range

High notes can be a "macho" issue among trumpeters, especially lead trumpeters with a lot of big band, studio, or road experience. When asking a trumpeter about his range, you must be careful to qualify the question this way: "What's the highest notes or notes you can hit consistently throughout a performance?" Otherwise, the player *will* tell you the highest note he can hit, but it may not be the note he can *consistently* hit either all night long or *consistently* throughout a scoring session.

When working with studio and jazz trumpeters, keep these rules of thumb in mind:

1.   The first and second parts usually get the highest notes. The higher you write, the more frequent rest they'll need. When players are concentrating in the high note area, their sound may tend to get a little muddy much below middle C.

2.   The third and fourth players, who aren't always playing the highest notes, may tend to have a more full sound below middle C.

Some orchestration books suggest that the trumpets can sound dull when written below middle C. This is not necessarily so, especially when written in two part or triadic voicings with the trombones in spread harmony which gives the trumpets a low French horn-like quality. For referencing, please see Henry Mancini's *Sounds and Scores*, Example 79, *Session at Pete's Pad*.

> When working with student ensembles, this lower range quality can often be developed by having the student trumpeters practice from the *Herbert L. Clarke Method* as part of a daily practice routine. This particular method meticulously develops consistent tone color using chromatic scale passages from the low to the high range.

Score Examples With Trumpets

The following score examples demonstrate the open trumpet, but not always the Bb trumpet. So some transposition of parts will be necessary. Not all examples were available for the enclosed tapes. Please note that the two Prokofiev examples are written in concert, and so, are *untransposed*.

Score Reference 22-4 Low - High Register Trumpets
Mendelssohn *A Midsummer Night's Dream, The Wedding March*

Score Reference 22-4 Low - High Register Trumpets
Mendelssohn *A Midsummer Night's Dream, The Wedding March*

Score Reference 22-4 Low - High Register Trumpets
Mendelssohn *A Midsummer Night's Dream, The Wedding March*

Score Reference 22-4 Low - High Register Trumpets
Mendelssohn *A Midsummer Night's Dream, The Wedding March*

Score Reference 22-5 Medium Register Trumpet Debussy *Iberia*

Score Reference 22-6 Medium Register Trumpet in Vertical Harmony With Trombones
Bizet *Carmen Overture*

Score Reference 22-7 Medium to High Register Solo Trumpet   Bizet *Street Boy Chorus*

Score Reference 22-8 Medium to High Register Solo Trumpet
Prokofiev *Lt. Kije, Kije's Wedding*

Score Reference 22-8 Medium to High Register Solo Trumpet
Prokofiev *Lt. Kije, Kije's Wedding*

Score Reference 22-8 Medium to High Register Solo Trumpet
Prokofiev *Lt. Kije, Kije's Wedding*

Score Reference 22-9 Medium to High Register Solo Trumpet   Prokofiev *Peter and The Wolf*

Score Reference 22-9 Medium to High Register Solo Trumpet Prokofiev *Peter and The Wolf*

Articulation

The trumpet can single, double, and triple tongue. Passages must not be too long because of performance fatigue and consequent heaviness of articulation.

Single Tonguing

The following are about the maximum speeds attainable in the low and medium registers:

EXAMPLE 22-10

Double Tonguing

For 16th note figures, quarter note = 80 to 100 is safest.

Triple Tonguing

For 16th note triplets, quarter note = 80MM is safest.

Score Reference 22-11 Double Tonguing and Muted C-Trumpets
Ravel *Rapsodie Espagnole, Malaguena*

Score Reference 22-11 Double Tonguing and Muted C-Trumpets
Ravel *Rapsodie Espagnole, Malaguena*

Score Reference 22-11 Double Tonguing and Muted C-Trumpets
Ravel *Rapsodie Espagnole, Malaguena*

Score Reference 22-12 Mixed Double and Triple Tonguing C-Trumpet
Ravel *Rapsodie Espagnole, Feria*

Score Reference 22-12 Mixed Double and Triple Tonguing C-Trumpet
Ravel *Rapsodie Espagnole, Feria*

Length of Breath

At *p*, the Trumpet can, in moderate tempo, sound a holding-note of 8 or 9 bars in the low register:

EXAMPLE 22-13

and with the same rate of movement, it can hold a note in the medium register for 12 or 14 bars:

EXAMPLE 22-14

These numbers are halved in *f* passages, because the expenditure of breath is doubled.

Trumpet Fingerings

The chart on the next page (Example 22-16), laid out as a scale, shows the notes available with the depression of each valve combination on the trumpet. Each note under each of the fingerings is available by blowing up the overtone series. See below.

EXAMPLE 22-15 HARMONIC OVERTONE SERIES IN C

The basic formula for the trumpet is R-5-R-3-5-R. Other partials are available, but these are the most common.

EXAMPLE 22-16

Trills and Shakes

The following are trills and shakes which may be used: (the cross means bad, the double cross impossible). Trills to avoid are low Ab to Bb, low B to C#, and low C to Db (C#).

EXAMPLE 22-17

The Other Trumpets

This section briefly touches on the Bass Trumpet and Cornet.

Bass Trumpet

The bass trumpet is basically a valve trombone, played by trombonists (*not* trumpeters) using a trombone mouthpiece with 3 valves (models in Bb and C). The Eb version has a fourth valve. Today, the bass trumpet is most often used when trumpet parts are so low, that they cannot be performed by the modern Bb trumpet. It can also be used when a more resounding tone is wanted. However, these are special instruments, and you must check ahead to make sure of their availability before writing for them.

EXAMPLE 22-18

Piccolo Trumpets in D, Eb, and Bb

EXAMPLE 22-19

The Cornet

The cornet is a combination sound of a trumpet and a French horn. However, it has not found acceptance in the symphony orchestra, although it's used a lot in European theatre orchestras and in some bands. It was also the instrument of choice for the late jazz cornetist Jimmy McPartland whose recordings are still available.

EXAMPLE 22-20

Score Reference 22-21 Stravinsky *Petruchka*

The Flugelhorn

The Flugelhorn, a Bb instrument, is a very mellow sounding horn whose use, except for rare quotes in the Symphonic literature, is almost exclusively confined to jazz and studio work. For excellent examples of Flugelhorn work, refer to the music and recordings of Chuck Mangione.

EXAMPLE 22-22

The Tenor and Bass Trombones

Italian, Trombone tenore
German, Tenorposaune
French, Trombone tenor

The trombone works very simply: The slide, which can be drawn out to seven different positions, moves the harmonic series down each position by a half-step. Its practical range is:

EXAMPLE 23-1

Here are the notes available in each position. Please note that some notes are common to two or even three positions:

EXAMPLE 23-2

Note

A quick way to remember the note under each position is to use this formula: R5R357R.

About the 7th Position

When possible, avoid the 7th position. This requires the maximum extension of the slide, and so, it's the most difficult of all. The notes E and B, only available in the 7th position, are difficult to get back and forth to from the higher positions. The move B to Bb can only be made from 1st position to 7th position. In *Sounds and Scores*, Henry Mancini cites that the notes in the 7th position can also be difficult to sustain and control. Thus, except for the low E and B, work out tenor trombone slide positions for notes in the 7th position, with alternates from other positions. See the chart below.

EXAMPLE 23-3

Which Clef to Use

For some symphonic pieces, high work is written in the tenor clef which locates middle C on the second line on the staff. However, for almost all jazz and studio work, high work is kept within the bass clef with the highest practical note being 4th line B or Bb above middle C.

Pedal Tones

Pedal tones are the actual fundamental in the overtone series theoretically available within each position. When used, these tones are very powerful and should only be used at a dynamic of *f* or better. For average tenor trombone players, the pedal tones in the I and II positions are the most available. For top studio professionals, pedal tones in the III and IV positions are available. The pedal tones under positions V through VII are not available.

Example 23-4

The Bass Trombone

The Bass Trombone eliminates the struggle of those low areas that the tenor trombone has difficulty with.

Unlike the tenor trombone, it has six positions:

EXAMPLE 23-5

Here are the notes available in each position. Please note that some notes are common to two positions:

EXAMPLE 23-6

With the trigger, the pedal tones in the first three positions are available to the top players, the first two pedal tones for average players.

Trombone Attachments

There are tenor trombones with an F attachments, Bass Trombones with F attachments, and Bass Trombones with F and E attachments. The attachment is extra rotary tubing activated by a *trigger*. Newer bass trombone models have a D-trigger that makes certain glissandos easier and simplifies playing in certain keys. Be sure to consult with the Bass Trombonist to find out which model he has, what it can do, and what he can do with it.

Contrabass Trombone

The Contrabass Trombone is much more a studio instrument than a symphony instrument. It's often used in place of the tuba when a less mellow sound is required. It sounds an octave lower then the tenor trombone. Because this instrument is mostly used for studio work, please consult with the player before writing to make sure the sound you get is what you have in mind.

Avoiding Problems

Some of the greatest writing problems in the orchestra are for trombonists, especially when the parts are worked out at either the piano or the synthesizer without regard to the slide positions. It's imperative that every trombone part be checked with the charts given to assure and insure the absolute playability of the part. Otherwise, it's completely possible, with barely any effort at all, to create a completely unplayable trombone part.

Articulations

The trombone is capable of performing, single, double and triple tonguing. For best results, this type of work is best kept in the medium registers and up. For single tonguing, quarter note equals 120MM for sixteenth notes is safest. Double tonguing for 16th note figures, quarter note = 80 to 100MM is safest. Triple tonguing for 16th note triplets, quarter note = 80MM is safest.

Jazz Scores For Trombones

For examples of big band writing with trombone soli and solo work, you're referred to Henry Mancini's *Sounds and Scores*.

Three Schools of Trombone Writing

How the trombone is used depends on the particular school of writing used for the assignment. The German school of writing, epitomized by Wagner's use of the brass, is to locate the melody in the lower range of the trombones and tubas in either unison or octave for an extremely powerful sound. The French school of writing is the exact opposite and does not use the trombones in the low register on the melody. Outside of Ravel's *Bolero*, there are very few solo trombone parts in the symphonic literature. The third school of writing is the jazz school where the trombones often have the melody, especially above the staff where notes in the 1st through 3rd positions are easily available. The trombones here are often written in close harmony. Trombones are also used to create pads in open voicings. Superb examples of jazz writing for trombones can be found on almost any Stan Kenton album. Some of these include: *Birthday in Britain, Live At Redlands University, Live At Brigham Young University, Journey to Capricorn, Kenton '76, Live at Butler University.*

The following pages contain score examples of the German and French Schools of Writing. In studying the following examples, note how the trombones are used alone and in combination with other brass instruments.

Score Reference 23-8 German School   Wagner *Ride of the Valkyries*

Score Reference 23-8 German School   Wagner *Ride of the Valkyries*

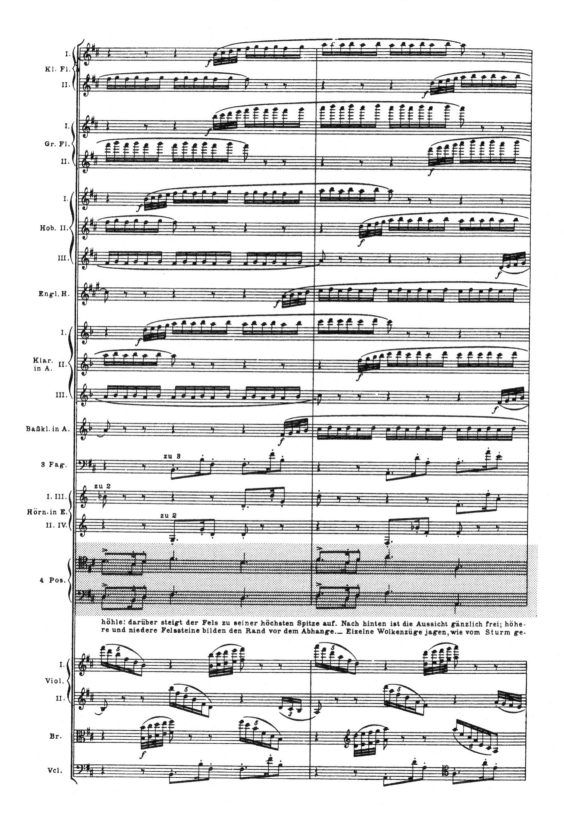

Score Reference 23-8 German School   Wagner *Ride of the Valkyries*

Score Reference 23-8 German School   Wagner *Ride of the Valkyries*

Score Reference 23-8 German School   Wagner *Ride of the Valkyries*

Score Reference 23-9 French School   Stravinsky *Petrushka*

Score Reference 23-10 French School   **Ravel** *Rapsodie Espagnole, Feria*
This example uses C-Trumpets

Score Reference 23-10 French School   Ravel *Rapsodie Espagnole, Feria*

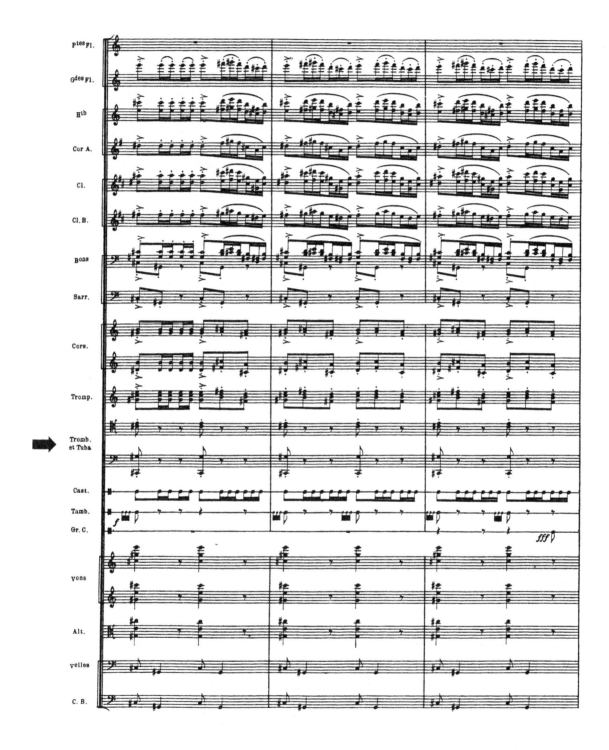

Score Reference 23-10 French School   Ravel *Rapsodie Espagnole, Feria*

Glissando

A standard effect used by the trombones is the glissando where the slide is moved between two notes. Glisses should be no wider than a tritone.

Score Reference 23-11 Trombone Glissando   Debussy *Iberia*

The Tubas

French, Tuba
Italian, Tuba
German, Tuba

While the true bass of the brass section, the tubas are also the mystery instrument of the brass section because there's more to know about them then appears on the surface. The broad range of the tubas is this:

EXAMPLE 24-1

Within this range there are five to six *different* tubas which can be used depending on the melodic needs of the music. That's because some tubas are powerful in the lower range, but not quite as flexible with a melodic figure in the medium to high registers. So, depending on the music, it's not uncommon for a tuba player to use two to three different tubas *within the same movement*. All tubas have at least three valves, some four, others five and six.

All modern tubas are non-transposing and are to be written where they sound (concert). Tubas used are based on the lowness of the writing, and also whether the tuba will be playing the melody, and if so, at what range.

Not Stereotyping the Tuba

The concern of many tuba players is that composers frequently type the tuba as an instrument for comedic work. Tubas add a certain charm when given the melody in their middle and upper registers. The most famous example in the symphonic literature is Ravel's orchestration of *Pictures At An Exhibition, Bydlo*. In contemporary film scoring, composer John Williams has made successful use of the tuba in *Home Alone 1* and *Home Alone 2, Jaws, Close Encounters of The Third Kind*, as has Jerry Goldsmith in *Star Trek V: The Final Frontier* where the tuba is used to play a key motive used throughout the movie. Also, listening to Wagner's use of tubas in the Ring Cycle will give much insight as to the kinds of things tubas can be called on to do.

Of the five or six tubas, the three most commonly used in both symphonic and studio work, in order of range from highest to lowest , are:

◆ the Euphonium (which according to tuba players is *not really* a tuba)

◆ the F Tuba

◆ the Contrabass Tuba in C (also called the CC Tuba or double C Tuba).

Tuba Note

All tuba parts are written in bass clef. The tuba is a nontransposing instrument. Except for pedal tones, tubas can play from *pp* to *ff* at the very bottom of the range. Because the tuba is such a powerful instrument, it's often written one dynamic lower than the rest of the brass section when used. The tuba requires a lot of breath, so be careful not to overwrite. Tubas blend well in unison with bass trombones, bassoons, and the basses. They're superb in sectional work with trumpets, trombones and French horns. They can also be used as a fourth or fifth French horn.

The Euphonium

This tuba is capable of reaching the highest notes. Other names for this instrument (described in the Wagner note below) are *tuba basse* and *tuba ordinaire* (French), *tuba bassa, flicorno basso* (Italian), *Basstuba, Tenortuba* (German). Use the Euphonium when you have the tuba play a melody or a part over Middle C. Here's its range:

EXAMPLE 24-2

F Tuba

It has three names: *bombardon, bass tuba,* or the orchestral *Tuba in F.* It's the middle tuba for high note range. Occasionally, a tuba player may opt for the Eb Tuba, feeling that it handles low range notes a little better. Here's the range of the F-Tuba.

EXAMPLE 24-3

The Contrabass Tuba

This is also called the double C tuba (CC). In Wagner operas, it's labeled as the *Kontrabasstuba.* This is a workhorse tuba. Of the tubas used by Wagner in his operas, this was the bass tuba. Here's its range:

EXAMPLE 24-4

Pedal Tones
Safe pedal tones for the tubas are in this range:

EXAMPLE 24-4A

Real pros can play pedal tones in this range, but as described by one tuba player, "It's a real rumble."

Tubas Used in Wagner's Operas Today

For a complete review of Wagner's tuba section for his operas, please see Forsythe's *Orchestration*. Wagner's objective was to create a tuba sound with a range from the bottom of the CC Tuba to F two octaves above middle C. Today, those *Tenor-Tuben* parts are played by the Euphonium. To be played on the Euphonium, the tenor tuba parts in a Wagner opera, which were written in the treble clef, must be transposed *down* a *major ninth* because the Euphonium is a concert sounding instrument. If the tenor tuba part appears in the bass clef, (notably in the music of Richard Strauss) it's to be transposed *down* a *step*. Euphoniums are also used in military bands. The *Bass-Tuben* parts are played on the Tuba in F (also non-transposing and sounding at concert). And as already stated, the bottom parts are played on the CC Tuba.

The Other Tubas

The other tubas include the BBb Tuba and the Eb Tuba.

The Eb Tuba

Is often used as a substitute for the bass tuba because of its ability to handle notes in the lower region. The range is:

EXAMPLE 24-5

The BBb Tuba

Most often used in military and school bands. Here's its range:

EXAMPLE 24-6

Articulations

Like the other brass, the tuba is capable of doing single, double and triple articulation. Top tuba players can play as rapid articulations as any other brass instruments. For single tonguing, quarter note equals 120MM for sixteenth notes is safest. Double tonguing for 16th note figures, quarter note = 80 to 100MM is safest. Triple tonguing for 16th note triplets, quarter note = 80MM is safest.

However, as with much else in this chapter, a discussion with the tuba player is in order to make sure that the sound you get is what you had in mind.

Mutes and Shakes

Tubas can be muted. But they aren't done so very often because of the uncertainty of tone quality, and because the mutes are so difficult to insert and remove. An example of muted tubas can be found in the introduction to Strauss's *Don Quixote variations*.

The tuba is capable of doing both shakes and trills, however it's almost never written in the symphonic literature. As a general rule, tuba players suggest that you not exceed a whole step for either a shake or a trill. For a trill, a 1/2 step down is considered easier.

The following pages contain score examples for Tubas.

Score Example 24-9 Tuba Shake   **Wagner** *Prelude to Die Meistersinger of Nuremberg*

Score Example 24-9 Tuba Shake   Wagner *Prelude to Die Meistersinger of Nuremberg*

Score Example 24-9 Tuba Shake **Wagner** *Prelude to Die Meistersinger of Nuremberg*

Score Example 24-10 Tuba Mixed With French Horns and Doubled by Contrabassoon
Strauss *Till Eulenspiegel's Merry Pranks* [13]

Score Example 24-11 Tubas + Bass Trombone in Octaves With Tenor Trombones
Strauss *Till Eulenspiegel's Merry Pranks*

Score Example 24-11 Tubas + Bass Trombone in Octaves With Tenor Trombones
Strauss *Till Eulenspiegel's Merry Pranks*

Score Example 24-11 Tubas + Bass Trombone in Octaves With Tenor Trombones
Strauss *Till Eulenspiegel's Merry Pranks*

Score Example 24-12 Tubas + Trombones + Horns   Strauss *Till Eulenspiegel's Merry Pranks*

Score Example 24-13 Tubas + Trombones As a Sustaining Pad
Rimsky-Korsakov *Scheherazade*

Score Example 24-13 Tubas + Trombones As a Sustaining Pad
Rimsky-Korsakov *Scheherazade*

Score Example 24-13 Tubas + Trombones As a Sustaining Pad
Rimsky-Korsakov *Scheherazade*

Score Example 24-14 Tubas Doubling the Strings on the Melody
Rimsky-Korsakov *Scheherazade*

Score Example 24-15 Tubas in a Brass Sectional   Rimsky-Korsakov *Scheherazade*

Score Example 24-15 Tubas in a Brass Sectional   Rimsky-Korsakov *Scheherazade*

Score Example 24-16 Tubas Single Tonguing in Rapid Tempo   Rimsky-Korsakov *Scheherazade*

Score Example 24-16 Tubas Single Tonguing in Rapid Tempo   Rimsky-Korsakov *Scheherazade*

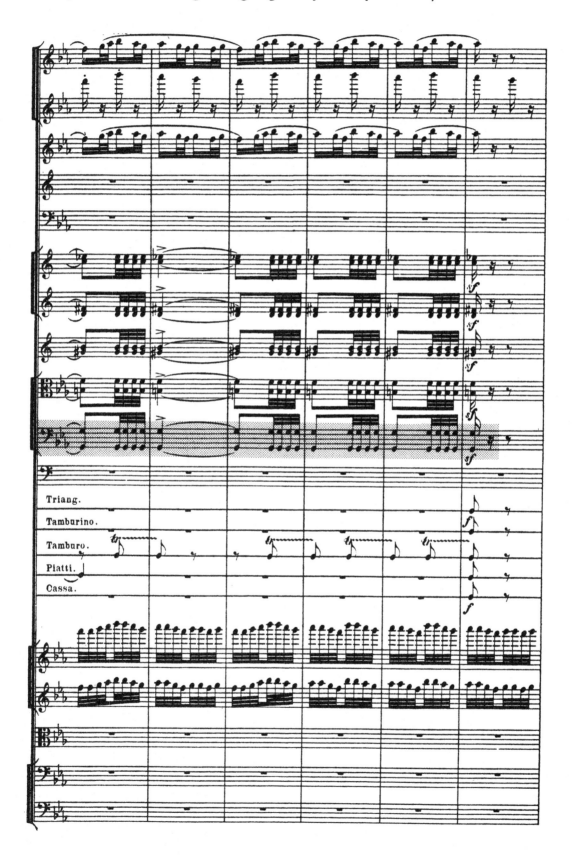

Chapter 25

The French Horn

Italian, Corno cromatico
German, Ventilhorn
French, Cor a pistons

Here's the practical range of the French horns:

EXAMPLE 25-1

In Chapter 21, *Brass Basics*, it was noted that there are four Horns in the symphony orchestra and that the harmony works out as follows:

French Horn I	*Harmony 1*
French Horn II	*Harmony 3*
French Horn III	*Harmony 2*
French Horn IV	*Harmony 4*

It was also noted that the studio orchestra works more like this:

French Horn 1	*Harmony 1*
French Horn 2	*Harmony 2*
French Horn 3	*Harmony 3*
French Horn 4	*Harmony 4*

To these facts must be presented some other information critical to your writing. In the regular symphony orchestra, players I and III have special mouthpieces that permit them to be the *high* horns. Players II and IV use mouthpieces that permit them to be the *low* horns.

But in Hollywood studio work, *no such division exists*. Professional studio French horn players use a different mouthpiece that permits them to perform *both* low and high parts.

Transposing Parts

All French horn parts are written in the treble clef. All French horn parts transpose up a perfect 5th from the concert score. However, there is a trend whereby for symphonic work, key signatures are placed in the score as normal, but in studio work, key signatures are *eliminated* with all accidentals being written *as they appear in the score*. Not all Hollywood composers do this, but it's an option you should be aware of.

Special Transposition Note for the French Horn in F.

Whenever a French horn in F part is written in the bass clef in older scores, transpose the part up a perfect 4th.

On the following pages are French horn score examples.

See Also

Score Example 4-7 **Strauss**, *Don Juan* with French horns doubling the cellos on the theme.

Score Reference 25-2 Low Register French Horns on the Melody
Prokofiev *Peter and The Wolf*
This score example is prepared in concert and is untransposed.

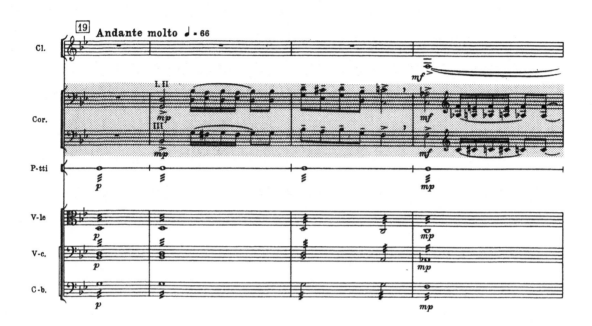

Score Reference 25-2 Low Register French Horns on the Melody
Prokofiev *Peter and The Wolf*

Score Reference 25-2 Low Register French Horns on the Melody
Prokofiev *Peter and The Wolf*

Score Reference 25-3 Low Register French Horns on Repeated Notes
Prokofiev *Peter and The Wolf*

This score example is prepared in concert and is untransposed.

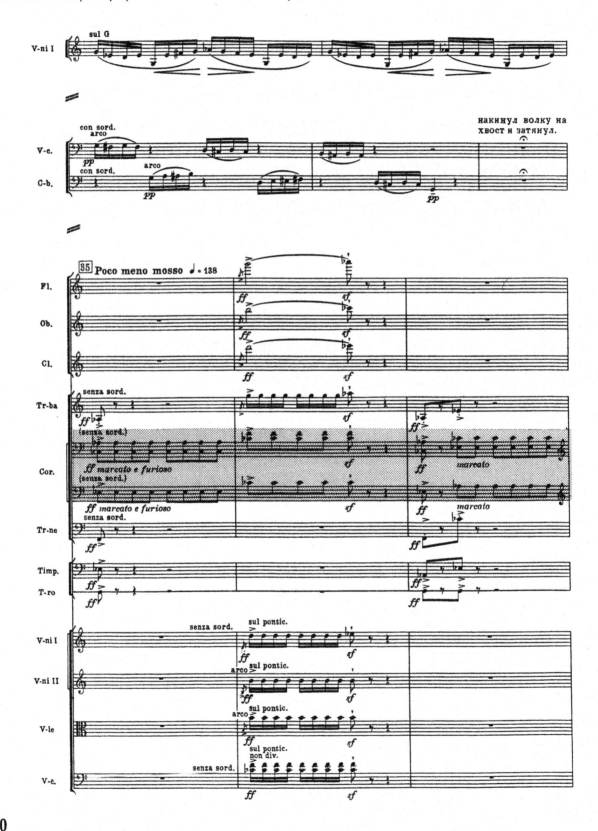

Score Reference 25-3 Low Register French Horns on Repeated Notes
Prokofiev *Peter and The Wolf*

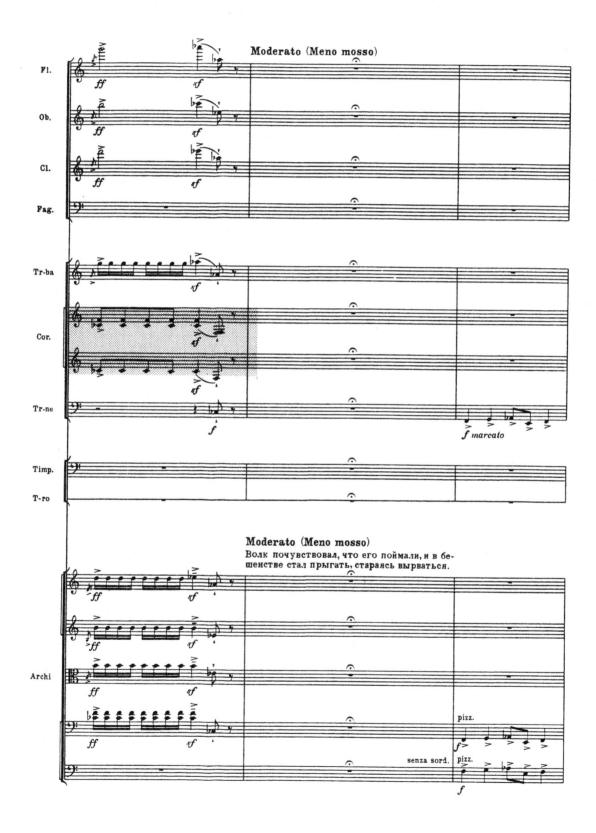

Score Reference 25-4 Medium to High Register French Horns on the Melody

Prokofiev *Peter and The Wolf*

This score example is prepared in concert and is untransposed.

Score Reference 25-4 Medium to High Register French Horns on the Melody
Prokofiev *Peter and The Wolf*

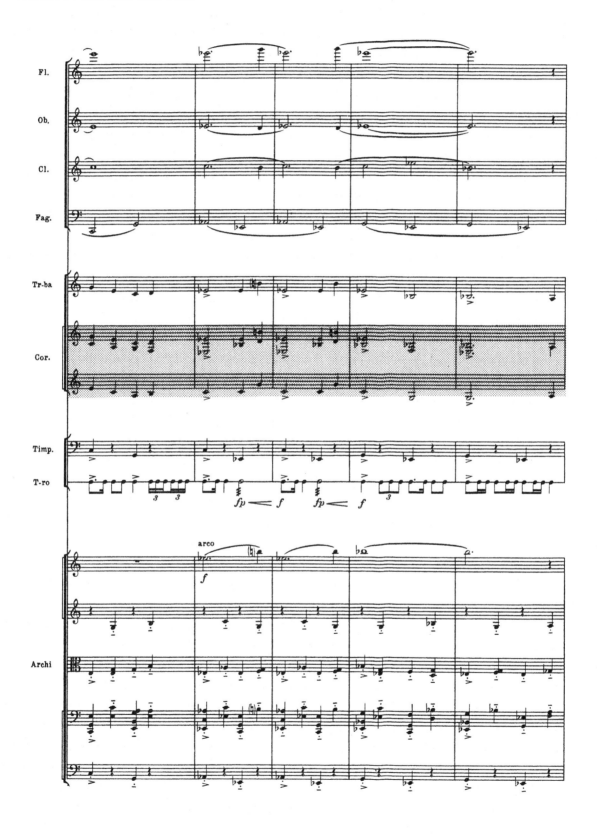

Score Reference 25-4 Medium to High Register French Horns on the Melody
Prokofiev *Peter and The Wolf*

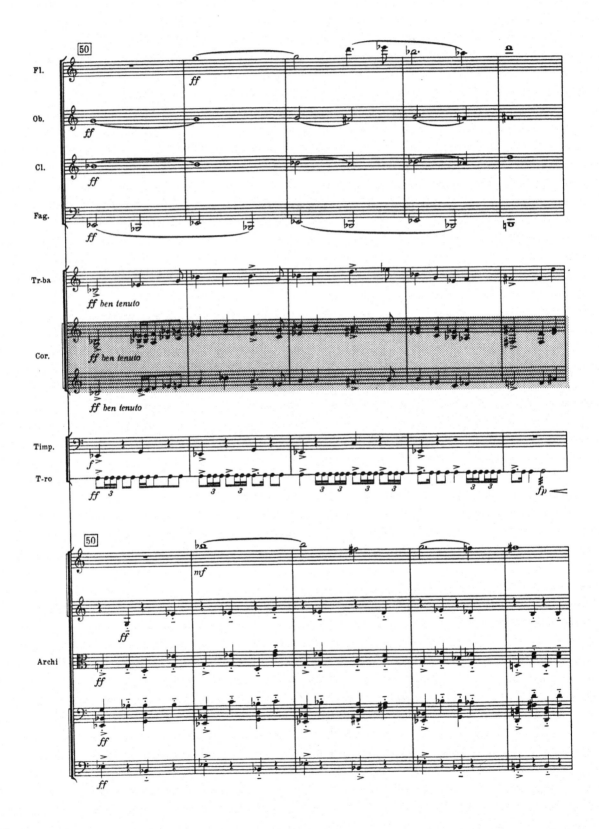

Score Reference 25-4 Medium to High Register French Horns on the Melody
Prokofiev *Peter and The Wolf*

Score Reference 25-5 Medium to High Register French Horns
Tchaikovsky *Nutcracker Suite, Waltz of the Flowers*

Score Reference 25-5 Medium to High Register French Horns
Tchaikovsky *Nutcracker Suite, Waltz of the Flowers*

Score Reference 25-6 High French Horn Solo   Strauss *Till Eulenspeigel's Merry Pranks*

Score Reference 25-6 High French Horn Solo Strauss *Till Eulenspeigel's Merry Pranks*

The Great Blender

Like the Bassoon and Clarinet, the French horn is also a superb blender, especially with woodwinds, thus allowing for many color combinations. A few include:

1. French horn + Clarinet (in unison or in thirds with the clarinets doubled an octave above.)

2. French horn - Clarinet - French horn - clarinet (mixed harmony in 4 parts)

3. French horn - French horn - Bassoon - Bassoon (mixed harmony in 4 parts)

3. French horn - Clarinet - Bassoon (Mixed harmony in 3 parts)

Speed of Articulation

In the low register, only single articulation should be used because the horn doesn't speak as fast. In the middle register, double and triple tonguing can be used successfully.

The maximum safe speed practical in the low register is :

EXAMPLE 25-7

in the medium register (single-articulation):

EXAMPLE 25-8

Register of double and triple articulation, where the speed that can be attained is almost unlimited:

EXAMPLE 25-9

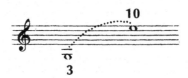

Length of Breath

The following are the results of experiments made with the kind assistance of Mr. Penable, Concert Colonne soloist:

EXAMPLE 25-10

EXAMPLE 25-11

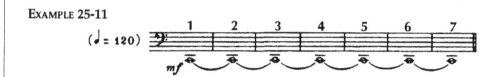

In the medium register, from the 4th to the 8th partial:

EXAMPLE 25-12

Keeping the same metronomic rate of movement, quarter note - 120MM, the lungs can sustain 11 bars *f*, 14 bars *mf* and 25 bars *p*. *However, these are the extremes and should not be applied to an actual piece because the results could be far less than satisfactory. The production of the high notes, because it requires great air-pressure, severely tires the lungs, so that such long holding-notes can hardly be expected above the 8th and 9th harmonics.*

Shakes

The pistons are not used for shakes because air can't travel fast enough through the tubing to do so. Thus, horn-players make use of their lips only.

Major shakes come out well. (They are only possible from the 5th to the 12th, 13th, 14th, and 15th harmonics).

Register in which shakes are practicable:

EXAMPLE 25-13

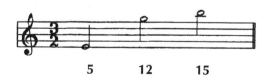

and the best part of this register is:

EXAMPLE 25-14

Shakes between the 12th and 15th upper partials are best avoided in practical writing. They're suitable for virtuosi, but dangerous for most players.

Minor shakes do not come out so well. They are only possible with the hand in the bell, and are really of very doubtful quality.

Score Reference 25-15 French Horn Shake   Strauss *Till Eulenspiegel's Merry Pranks*

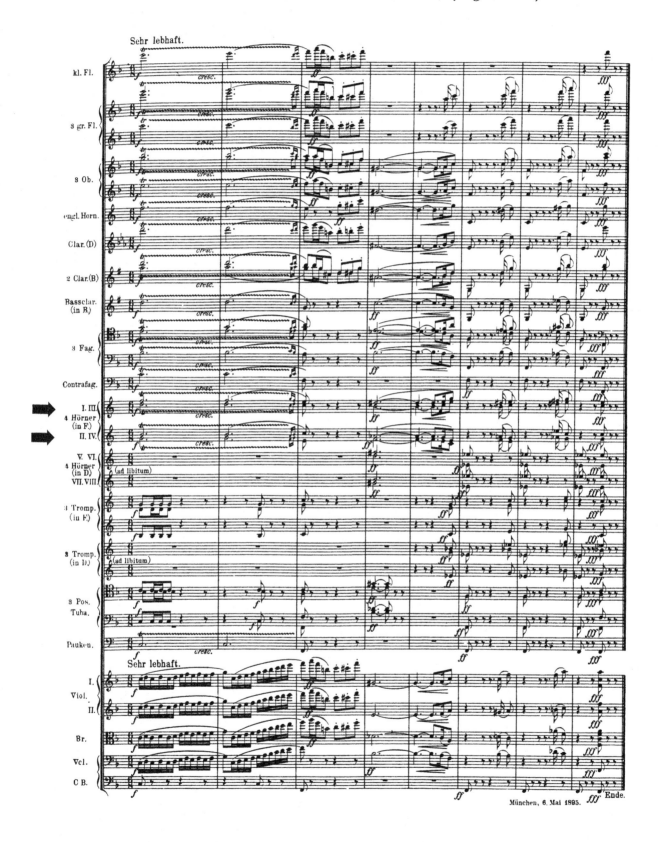

München, 6. Mai 1895.

Muted, Stops and Hand Notes

Besides the rich and poetic quality of the open notes, the Horn possesses three other kinds of very special and characteristic tone-color: these are muted, stopped and hand notes. Muted notes are obtained by means of a mute (*sordino*). Stopped or overblown notes are achieved by the insertion of the right hand in the bell.

Muted Notes

Muted notes are achieved by inserting the mute into the bell of the horn with the right hand. The parts should be marked *con sordino*. When open notes are desired, write either *senza sorda* or *naturale*. The German marking is *mit dampfer* or *gedampft*. When marked *con sordino*, (or *con sord*) the player, unless otherwise and *clearly* directed by the composer, may choose to disregard the use of the mute, and instead mute the note by inserting his right hand into the bell and so, *stopping* the note. Again, this choice occurs because composers have not been specific as to what they really want.

The mute can be inserted at one of three points:

1. before the passage begins;

2. in the break between two phrases (for an echo effect);

3. during the actual performance of a note.

Mutes are made of either cardboard or metal. Neither alters the pitch.

Stopped Notes

The following terms are used for indicating stopped and opened notes.

English	French	Italian	German
stopped	*bouché*	*chiuso*	*gestopf*

English	French	Italian	German
open	*ouvert*	*aperto*	*offen, nicht gestopft*

The sound of a stopped note is like a mildly raspy "ehhhh."

When you want just a few notes stopped, put a + sign over those few notes to be stopped. When stopped notes are concluded, write *naturale*. When notes are mixed between stopped and opened, an "o" is written over the open notes.

Open /Stopped vs. Ooo /Ahh

In the *Brass Basics* chapter, you were instructed that to achieve an *ooo/ahhh* sound in jazz writing, the o is used for the *ooo*, and the + for the *ahhh*. This is not the case for the French horn. The use of + clearly indicates *stopped* while o clearly indicates *open*. Be careful not to confuse the two. Also, in jazz writing, French horns are almost *never* asked to do *ooo/ahhh!* However, all other effects are valid.

Score Reference 25-16 Stopped Horn Going to Open   Ravel *Rapsodie Espagnole, Feria*

Score Reference 25-17 French Horns Muted, Stopped, and Open in the Same Passage
Ravel *Rapsodie Espagnole, Prélude à la nuit*

Analysis: At [1], the French horns are clearly marked *Sourdines* for muted. At [3], the mutes are removed and the note is stopped *(bouche)*. At [4], the horns are playing open *(sons nat.)*. At [5], the horns are back to being muted *(sourdines)*. At [6], the horns are open and stopped. At [8], they're muted again. At [9], they're muted, then opened and stopped.

Score Reference 25-17 French Horns Muted, Stopped, and Open in the Same Passage
Ravel *Rapsodie Espagnole, Prélude à la nuit*

Score Reference 25-17 French Horns Muted, Stopped, and Open in the Same Passage
Ravel *Rapsodie Espagnole, Prélude à la nuit*

Score Reference 25-17 French Horns Muted, Stopped, and Open in the Same Passage
Ravel *Rapsodie Espagnole, Prélude à la nuit*

Score Reference 25-17 French Horns Muted, Stopped, and Open in the Same Passage
Ravel *Rapsodie Espagnole, Prélude à la nuit*

Score Reference 25-17 French Horns Muted, Stopped, and Open in the Same Passage
Ravel *Rapsodie Espagnole, Prélude à la nuit*

Score Reference 25-17 French Horns Muted, Stopped, and Open in the Same Passage
Ravel *Rapsodie Espagnole, Prélude à la nuit*

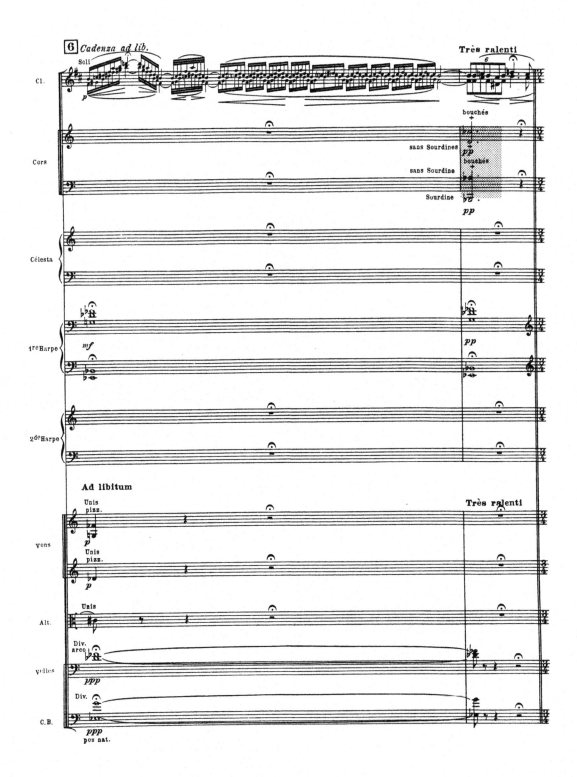

Score Reference 25-17 French Horns Muted, Stopped, and Open in the Same Passage
Ravel *Rapsodie Espagnole, Prélude à la nuit*

Stopped Note Effects at *f*

A more metallic sound, or what Cecil Forsythe in his book *Orchestration* described as varying, "from a savage bark like that of a wild animal to the dull uncertain sound with which a routseat scrapes over a parquet floor." Also, this technique can be done with either an open, stopped, or muted note.

Here the part is marked like this:

EXAMPLE 25-18

German Marking For This Brassy Effect

Germans will mark the score with the term *gestopf -stark anblasen* or the term *Schmetternf* with either a *sfz* or *f* sign. Write *naturale* at the conclusion of the passage.

French Marking for This Brassy Effect

The French will mark *cuivre*, or write *sons bouches* over the passage with either a *sfz* or *f* sign. Write *naturale* at the conclusion of the passage.

English Marking For This Brassy Effect

Write *brassy* over the passage. with either a *sfz* or *f* sign. Write *naturale* at the conclusion of the passage.

Hand Notes

This is a technique that can either raise or lower by half-step, the pitch of the horn by the insertion of the right hand into the bell. This is a unique effect and before writing for it, be sure to have a French horn player demonstrate it for you to make sure this is what you have in mind.

1. If the right hand is inserted into the bell of the horn as the note is being sounded, the pitch is *flattened* in a gradual or portamento manner.

2. If the right hand is inserted hard up into the bell, using significant lip pressure, a completely new series of stopped notes is created a *half-step above* the written pitch. This gives the player a second level of stopped chromatic sounds. These notes are generally labeled as *echo notes*.

Gliss

Although not used as frequently in the classical literature, glisses are quite commonly used in film scoring. This can also be called a *rip*.

Pop Examples of French Horn Gliss

For audio examples, please see Henry Mancini's *Sounds and Scores*:

EX. 74, Peter Gunn   Gliss up

EX. 91 Peter Gunn   Short Fall off (gliss down) and Rip

EX. 176 March of the Cue Balls   Gliss up, Gliss down

Additional French Horn Examples

For additional examples, especially with an expanded section, please see Mahler *Symphonies 1 and 4*. For extended use of the French horn using stopped notes, see the film *The Vanishing*, music composed and conducted by Jerry Goldsmith. For an example of brassy, see Bizet, *L'Arlesienne Suite #1, Carillon* for the bell-like passage.

Score Reference 25-19 Gliss   Stravinsky *Rite of Spring* [36]

Bell Up

This is used for very loud passages. The French hornist lifts the bell of the horn up so it faces the audience. In French, it's marked *pavillons en l'air*. In German, it's marked *Schalltrichter auf*.

Score Reference 25-20 Bells Up Mahler *Symphony #1, 2nd Movement*

Score Reference 25-20 Bells Up Mahler *Symphony #1, 2nd Movement*

The Harp

Italian, Arpa
German, Harfe
French, Harpe

Most major symphony orchestras have two harps. However in the studio, one is usually all that's budgeted. It's tuned in Cb and has 47 diatonic degrees:

EXAMPLE 26-1

By diatonic degrees, it's meant that the notes performed on the harp are set up as a *scale*. Chords within that diatonic scale are available for performance with the understanding that the harpist cannot perform any more than four notes per hand at a time. The modern harp is a double action because of its design with seven pedals. These pedals enable the harp to be completely chromatic and to execute enharmonics, which in turn, permits the harp to execute repeated notes, unique scale possibilities, and chord voicings using enharmonics that would otherwise not be possible.

EXAMPLE 26-2

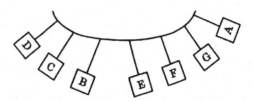

The Harp and Its Pedals

There are three pedals on the left (DCB) and four pedals on the right (EFGA). These pedal positions are represented by a chart used by composers in scores to indicate the scale to be set by the harpist:

EXAMPLE 26-3

There are three notches that each individual pedal can be set in.

1. The top notch is the flat position. This is where the string is the longest and so, vibrates the best.

2. The middle notch is the natural position and is a half-step higher then the flat position.

3. The bottom notch is the sharp position and is a whole step higher than the flat position.

Once the pedal is set, all the strings for that note are set across the seven octaves of the harp. The chart reflects the pedaling.

When a note is to be *flatted*, the chart is marked with a notch mark *above* the line to reflect the pedal position.

EXAMPLE 26-4

When the note is a *natural*, the chart is marked with notch mark vertically *through* the line to reflect the pedal position.

EXAMPLE 26-5

When the note is a *sharp*, the chart is marked with a notch mark *below* the line to reflect the pedal position.

EXAMPLE 26-6

Basic Harp Guidelines

1. The harp part is written on two staves, like the piano part. The best keys for the harp are the flat keys since the harp is tuned in Cb and because of its mechanism, the longer string vibrates more. Thus, the key of Cb Major is preferable to B Major.

EXAMPLE 26-7

2. In a more rapid tempo, it's advisable to write the left hand in octaves, otherwise the music can become thick and heavy.

EXAMPLE 26-8

3. Enharmonics, called *homophones* by harpists, are idiomatic for repeated notes played by both hands since the two strings used are tuned alike.

EXAMPLE 26-9

4. Some composers feel that pentatonic scales formed with harmonics give the most resonance for glissandos, intervals, and/or chords.

5. Unbroken chords should be kept within the octave. However a stretch of a 10th is possible. Some composers feel that the best sounding harp voicings are three-note chords in spread position.

EXAMPLE 26-10

Score Reference 26-11 Chord on Two Hands   Ravel *Mother Goose Suite, The Fairy Garden*

Score Reference 26-11 Chord on Two Hands   Ravel *Mother Goose Suite, The Fairy Garden*

Score Reference 26-11 Chord on Two Hands   Ravel *Mother Goose Suite, The Fairy Garden*

Score Reference 26-12 Arpeggiated Chord on Two Hands
Tchaikovsky *Nutcracker, Waltz of the Flowers*

Score Reference 26-12 Arpeggiated Chord on Two Hands
Tchaikovsky *Nutcracker, Waltz of the Flowers*

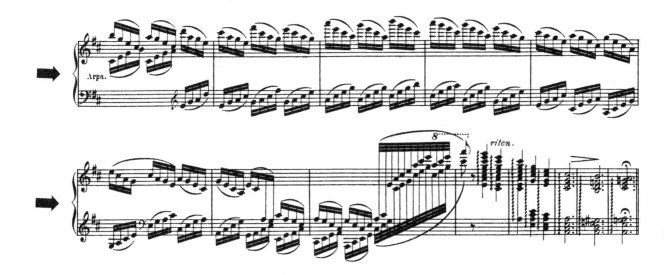

6. The *maximum* stretch of the hand on the harp is a 10th. Broken chord voicings can be planned within that span:

EXAMPLE 26-13A

EXAMPLE 26-13B

7. Unless otherwise noted, chords are rolled or broken slightly in conventional playing and rolled upwards unless otherwise indicated.

8. A bracket, [, is placed before all chords to be performed as a non-arpeggio.

EXAMPLE 26-14

9. Chords can be rolled in opposite directions by adding arrows to the regular wavy lines.

EXAMPLE 26-15A

EXAMPLE 26-15B

10. Chords rolled through with both hands start with either the top or bottom notes.

EXAMPLE 26-16

Score Reference 26-17 Harp Chords Rolled Upward
Ravel *Mother Goose Suite, Laideronnette*

11. Octaves in the lower register work extremely well.

EXAMPLE 26-18

Enharmonics By Pedal Positions

Because of the constant use of enharmonics on the harp, the following information breaks down the enharmonic equivalents for each harp pedal position starting with the actual pitch in Cb. Remember, for two sets of strings to have the same pitch, the pedals must be set enharmonically.

Enharmonic Harp Pedal Charts

Use the charts below with these concepts. The harp is tuned in Cb. Each movement of the pedal alters the pitch by a half-step. Notes in bold reflect the chromatic movement. Notes in italic show the alternate reading. Generally, the first alternate will be the most common.

D Pedal

	Alternate Readings	
Db	*C#*	*Bx*
D	*Cx*	*Ebb*
Eb	*D#*	*Fbb*

C Pedal

	Alternate Readings	
Cb	*B*	*Ax*
C	*B#*	*Dbb*
C#	*Db*	*Bx*

B-Pedal

	Alternate Readings	
Bb	*A#*	*Cbb*
B	*Cb*	*Ax*
C	*B#*	*Dbb*

E-Pedal

Alternate Readings

Eb	*D#*	*Fbb*
E	*Fb*	*Dx*
F	*E#*	*Gbb*

F-Pedal

Alternate Readings

Fb	*E*	*Dx*
F	*E#*	*Gbb*
Gb	*F#*	*Ex*

G-Pedal

Alternate Readings

Gb	*F#*	*Ex*
G	*Fx*	*Abb*
Ab	*G#*	

A-Pedal

Alternate Readings

Ab	*G#*	
A	*Gx*	*Bbb*
Bb	*A#*	*Cbb*

Harp Enharmonics and Some Types of Scales Possible

If you're a jazz writer and familiar with the various modes, you'll readily appreciate that the harp can be set up in specific chord scales (Dorian, Phrygian, Lydian, Mixolydian, Aeolian, Locrian, Ionian) in all the keys.

Synthetic scales can be created:

EXAMPLE 26-19

With enharmonic spellings, scales can be transformed into a succession of minor or major thirds:

EXAMPLE 26-20

Chords can also be created:

EXAMPLE 26-21

Glissandos

Glissandos can be for single notes, intervals, or chords. There are one hand glissandos and two hand glissandos.

There are two basic types of glissando notations.

    1.   The first lists the pitches to be used in the gliss.

EXAMPLE 26-22

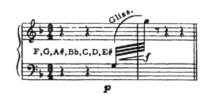

2. The second technique displays the notes usually in 32nd notes.

EXAMPLE 26-23

3. When the gliss is extended over many beats, it's marked on the score like this:

EXAMPLE 26-24

Score Reference 26-25 Glissando in One Hand   Debussy *Prelude to the Afternoon of a Faun*

Score Reference 26-26 Glissando in One Hand   Debussy *Prelude to the Afternoon of a Faun*
Note that this example uses a down arpeggio.

Score Reference 26-27 Glissando in One Hand Ravel *Mother Goose Suite, Laideronnette*

Score Reference 26-27 Glissando in One Hand   Ravel *Mother Goose Suite, Laideronnette*

Score Reference 26-28 Glissando in Two Hands **Ravel** *Mother Goose Suite, The Fairy Garden*

Score Reference 26-28 Glissando in Two Hands   Ravel *Mother Goose Suite, The Fairy Garden*

Score Reference 26-29 Glissando in Two Hands   Debussy *La Mer, De l'aube a midi sur la mer*

Score Reference 26-29 Glissando in Two Hands   Debussy *La Mer, De l'aube a midi sur la mer*

Score Reference 26-30 Glissando Chord in One Hand   Ravel *Rapsodie Espagnole, Malaguena*

Score Reference 26-31 Glissando Chord in Two Hands   Debussy *La Mer, Jeux de vagues*

Score Reference 26-31 Glissando Chord in Two Hands   Debussy *La Mer, Jeux de vagues*

Harp Arpeggios

Harp arpeggios are an extremely effective technique. They can be played with one or two hands, but most often, are played two handed.

Score Reference 26-32 Harp Arpeggio **Debussy** *Prelude to the Afternoon of a Faun*

Score Reference 26-32 Harp Arpeggio   Debussy *Prelude to the Afternoon of a Faun*

Harp Harmonics

The harmonic used by the harpist is the second partial (sounding an octave higher than the fundamental of the open string). Harmonics are most often written in this range:

EXAMPLE 26-33

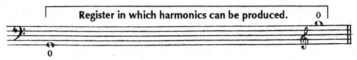

and sounding here an octave higher:

EXAMPLE 26-34

The double action harp permits up to four simultaneous harmonics with the left hand provided the intervals are small, but usually no more than three are written. When writing two or more harmonics for the left hand, do not exceed the interval of the perfect fifth. The right hand can only perform one harmonic at a time. The differences in the number of harmonics available per hand has to do with the position of the hands on the harp.

EXAMPLE 26-35

(The low C is not played as a harmonic.)

Harmonics can only be used in soft passages since they're very, very soft.

Notating Harp Harmonics

Put a circle over the note where it's to be *written*, not sounded. Otherwise, the harpist will play the note(s) an octave higher than that.

EXAMPLE 26-36

Where written   Where sounds

Score Reference 26-37 Single Harp Harmonics in Either Hand
Debussy *Three Noctures, Nuages*

Score Reference 26-38 Single Harp Harmonics in Either Hand
Debussy *Prelude to the Afternoon of a Faun*

Score Reference 26-39 Single Harp Harmonics in Either Hand
Debussy *Prelude to the Afternoon of a Faun*

Score Reference 26-40 Single Harp Harmonics in Either Hand
Ravel *Mother Goose Suite, Laideronnette*

Score Reference 26-40 Single Harp Harmonics in Either Hand
Ravel *Mother Goose Suite, Laideronnette*

Score Reference 26-41 Double Harp Harmonics   Ravel *Mother Goose Suite, Laideronnette*

Score Reference 26-41 Double Harp Harmonics   Ravel *Mother Goose Suite, Laideronnette*

Sons etouffes
English, *dampen*, German, *abdampfen*, French, *pres de la table*

With this technique, the vibrations of the string are stopped once produced creating the effect of violin or viola pizzicato. The passage is played staccato to accommodate the effect.

If the harpist plucks the passage close to the sounding board, the tone produced can easily be mistaken for the metallic timbre of the guitar. This is called *pres de la table*. In German it's called *resonanztisch*.

Score Reference 26-42 Etouffe   **Ravel** *Daphnis and Chloe* [179]

Score Reference 26-43 Pres de la table (*resonanztisch*)   Mahler *Symphony #1, 1st Movement*

Score Reference 26-43 Pres de la table (*resonanztisch*)   Mahler *Symphony #1, 1st Movement*

Shakes and Trills

Trills and tremolos are infrequent in the orchestral literature. They're best notated with both hands.

EXAMPLE 26-44

Tremolos (*bisbigliano*..."whispering") use both hands to keep the strings constantly in motion. Soft dynamics for three or four notes within an octave are playable.

EXAMPLE 26-45

Additional Harp Figures

As follows are sample exercises performed by harpists. Study these examples to see the additional kinds of writing opportunities the harp offers.

EXAMPLE 26-46

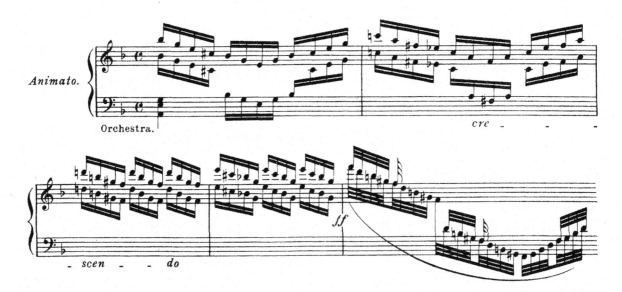

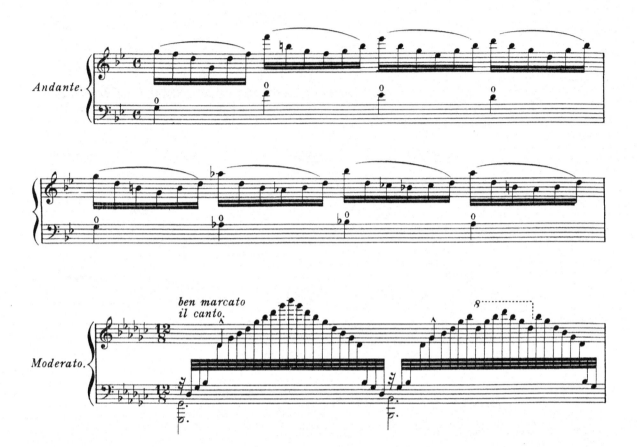

Piano, Organ, Celeste, & the Virtual Orchestra

This chapter covers the three main keyboard instruments used in both the orchestra and studio work, and the *virtual orchestra*. While the organ is not used as frequently in either symphonic or studio work, the piano, celeste and synthesizer are the heavy work-horses of the studio world. There is barely a session where at least a piano or synthesizer isn't used.

Working With Studio Keyboardists

In studio work, the keyboardist will normally play each of the three instruments covered in this chapter. I say normally, because there are occasions when a real specialist is needed, generally for a certain type of sound or style. Otherwise, the top keyboard players, who also usually command double scale, cover all the keyboard tasks with a *verve* unknown elsewhere. These are highly brilliant performers who can literally play or improvise any style at any time. As an example, in one scoring session, this conversation was actually had between the composer and the keyboardist:

"Can you play jazz?" asked the composer.

"Sure, what year?" answered the keyboardist.

"1938."

"Cotton Club or Paul Whiteman?"

"Uhhh, Cotton Club."

"Duke Ellington or Count Basie?"

"@#*%!!!" said the composer.

The keyboardist at the top of the list literally brings a mini-recording studio with him containing on average 15-20 synthesizers and samplers in either keyboard or rack unit form. He'll have a mixing board in his rig that enables him to either mix the sound in stereo on the spot before it's sent into the booth or that allows him to run individual keyboard units directly into the mixing board. The keyboardist charges the session for both rent on the equipment and for cartage fees. Use of synthesizer equipment is not included in the Union fee. The celeste, while considered a percussion instrument, is played by the keyboardist. Many of the top studios will have a celeste. Note, however, that keyboardists *do not provide this unit.* If it's not available at the studio, it will have to be rented.

Studio players can sight read most parts, but if the part is the least "concertized" as in a serious piece, then the parts should be gotten to the keyboardist in advance of the session, at least a minimum of a day so the keyboardist can practice.

If you're looking for a specific type of electronic sound, there are two ways to handle this. The first is to give the keyboardist a broad idea of what you want and let him do the selection at the session (or at least warn him in advance so he can be thinking about it). Studio keyboardists routinely bring with their rig a Macintosh computer which generally handles 50,000 sounds and samples or more. The second option is to write for a specific synthesized sound and either bring it on disk or on a cartridge for the keyboardist, or make sure he has it himself.

When contracting a studio keyboardist do not assume that all either sight read music or read music at all. The top session players all sight read music in a multiplicity of styles. However, if the keyboardist has a rock music background you *cannot assume* prior to the session that he can read music just because he has a lot of keyboards. This is an erroneous assumption that can lead to disaster. Ask the contractor ahead of time.

Also, top keyboardists bring a variety of the top synths and samplers. Some keyboardists not on the A list like a certain style of synthesizers. So when they bring their rig, you get that sound. If you want something other than what's in the rig, you're sunk unless you specify ahead of time what you want.

The Piano

The piano's prototype, the harpsichord, was used in the 17th century for "realizations" of figured bass parts. This specialized form of improvisation was supposed to strengthen bass parts, "fill in" the middle harmonic gaps, and steady the ensemble. In realizations, the left hand doubled the bass part while the right hand moved independently with harmonizations, but *without doubling the top melodic lines.*

By contrast, the piano is often used for doubling, outlining and figure elaboration along with newer musical values that emphasize rhythmical and percussive characteristics. The piano supplies extra tonal strength and emphasis. Sustained cantabile melodies, obvious in earlier periods, are omitted in the symphonic literature.

A superb comparison between the harpsichord and piano usage is found in deFalla's *El Amor Brujo*.

Symphonic Scores With Piano

Samuel Barber, *First Essay for Orchestra*; Aaron Copland, *El Salon Mexico, Rodeo*; Shostakovich, *Symphony #1*; Vaughn Williams, *Sinfonia Anartica*; Stravinsky, *Petrushka*.

Score Example 27-1 Stravinsky *Petruchka*

Score Example 27-1 Stravinsky *Petruchka*

Score Example 27-1 Stravinsky *Petruchka*

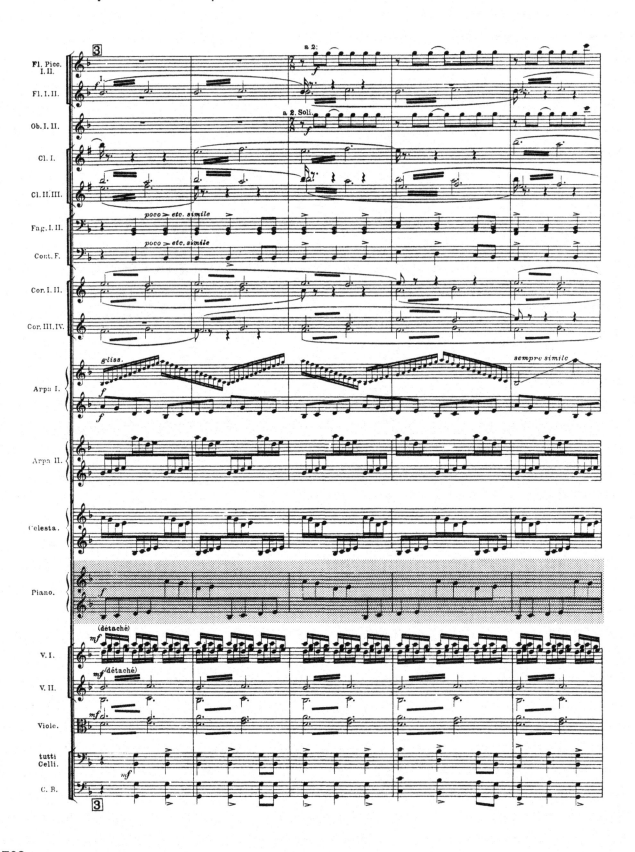

Score Example 27-1 Stravinsky *Petruchka*

In recording work, the piano has many dramatic functions. Melodic or atonal sequences played single line in the octaves drives many an action/adventure scene.

The piano, as part of a smaller studio ensemble, can be used to create an air of somberness or mystery as with John Williams' score to *Presumed Innocent*. It can also state an air of loving simpleness and commitment as used in John Williams' score to *Stanley and Iris*.

For a bluesy feel, Jerry Goldsmith deftly used the piano in *The Russia House*. For a setting of danger, the late Dmitri Tiompkin used the piano in *The Guns of Navarone* in the sea battle scene between the special agents (forces of good) vs. the Nazis (forces of evil). For childlike innocence, see John Williams use of the piano in the opening scenes of *Hook*.

The Organ

When discussing the organ for symphonic and film work, we're talking a great cathedral styled organ vs. more pop organs like a country church with Leslie speakers, Hammond B3's, rock organs of the '60s, etc. The organ's greatest assets are its ability to sustain tone at all dynamics levels with a great variety of timbres, and to project its own power and brilliance.

It has two separate keyboard units. The main one, the manuals for the fingers, vary in number with each instrument. Three banks, or rows, is the average. Each has a standardized range:

EXAMPLE 27-2

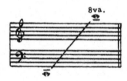

Foot pedals are arranged like the manuals and are tonally augmented from the manuals by couplers. Their range is:

EXAMPLE 27-3

Organ parts have often been included in orchestrations of cantatas, oratorios, and operas with religious connotations since the Baroque period. Solo concertos with orchestral accompaniment are also numerous. However, it was up to the 19th Century composers to bring the organ into the symphony, but with the intent to increase tonal dimensions of timbre and power beyond the extremes achieved with regular instrumentation. This concept is shown in scores with prolonged, sustained pedal tones and the full organ on massive climaxes. The organ can handle these demands since its construction provides for multiple combinations of stops and couplers that insure both timbral variety and tonal strength, along with unlimited capacity for sostenuto. Because it's an instrument distinct from all others, its use orchestrally requires familiarity with its technicalities and tonal characteristics.

The uncertain availability and quality of the organ make it difficult to write for. Although most have good instruments, some concert halls used for orchestral performances aren't so equipped. Be prepared to have an organ part either omitted or perhaps played on an electronic instrument.

These scores are good source material for the study of organ as both a solo and a supplementary orchestral instrument:

- Bach-Respighi, *Passacaglia and Fugue in C Minor*

- Holst, *The Planets*

- Honegger, *Le Roi David*

- Richard Strauss, *Also Sprach Zarathustra*

In film music, the great organ of the 20th Century Fox Studio can be heard in these soundtracks: *Star Trek: The Motion Picture* (Jerry Goldsmith), *Home Alone 1* (John Williams). For a comedy feel, listen to Elmer Bernstein's score for *The Three Amigos* where the organ is used to describe the onscreen heroism in a pre-talkie setting.

The Celeste

The celeste is tonally similar to the glockenspiel, but it's equipped with a keyboard and a damper pedal. It's written on two staves like the piano, but unlike the piano it's *written an octave lower than it sounds*. The range is:

EXAMPLE 27-4

The keyboard action is responsive and lets the player easily execute rapid passages. Its bell-like tones, played *f*, have about half the tonal strength of the glockenspiel when played with hard rubber hammers. The celeste tone, however, is slightly more cutting. The depressed damper pedal increases resonance by the free play of the accumulated vibrations. Since its strongest tone is smothered by heavier orchestral sonorities, expose the significant parts.

The celeste is rarely available in secondary orchestras. A piano played an octave higher than written is the most practical substitute unless a complementing synthesizer sound is available.

The celeste's tone and playing styles are adaptable to musical ornamentation like arabesque figurations, scales, chords, arpeggios, doublings with woodwinds, harp, and muted strings and occasional solo passages.

Score Reference 27-5 Celeste Solo Two Hands   Ravel *Mother Goose Suite, Laideronnette*

Score Reference 27-5 Celeste Solo Two Hands   Ravel *Mother Goose Suite, Laideronnette*

Score Reference 27-5 Celeste Solo Two Hands **Ravel** *Mother Goose Suite, Laideronnette*

Score Reference 27-6 Celeste Doubling Flute, French Horn and Harp in Unison
Then Moving to a Solo   Ravel *Mother Goose Suite, Laideronnette*

Score Reference 27-6 Celeste Doubling Flute, French Horn and Harp in Unison
Then Moving to a Solo   Ravel *Mother Goose Suite, Laideronnette*

Score Reference 27-6 Celeste Doubling Flute, French Horn and Harp in Unison
Then Moving to a Solo   Ravel *Mother Goose Suite, Laideronnette*

Score Reference 27-7 Celeste Doubling Xylophone and Outlining High Flute Parts
Ravel *Mother Goose Suite, Laideronnette*

Score Reference 27-7 Celeste Doubling Xylophone and Outlining High Flute Parts
Ravel *Mother Goose Suite, Laideronnette*

Score Reference 27-8 Celeste on the Melody

Tchiakovsky *The Nutcracker, Dance of the Sugar Plum Fairies*

This passage must be transposed down an octave as its written at pitch for a substitute piano.

Score Reference 27-8 Celeste on the Melody
Tchiakovsky *The Nutcracker, Dance of the Sugar Plum Fairies*

Score Reference 27-8 Celeste on the Melody
Tchiakovsky *The Nutcracker, Dance of the Sugar Plum Fairies*

Score Reference 27-9 Celeste Glissando   Ravel *Mother Goose Suite, The Fairy Garden*

Score Reference 27-9 Celeste Glissando   Ravel *Mother Goose Suite, The Fairy Garden*

Score Reference 27-10 Celeste Doubling Solo Violin and Solo Viola
Ravel *Mother Goose Suite, The Fairy Garden*

Score Reference 27-10 Celeste Doubling Solo Violin and Solo Viola
Ravel *Mother Goose Suite, The Fairy Garden*

Score Reference 27-11 Celeste on Counterline Ravel *Rapsodie Espagnole, Prélude à la nuit*

Score Reference 27-12 Celeste on Rhythmic Accents with Harp, Flutes and Oboe
Ravel *Rapsodie Espagnole, Feria*

Score Reference 27-13 Celeste Playing Arpeggio-like Figures   Stravinsky *The Firebird* (1910)

Score Reference 27-13 Celeste Playing Arpeggio-like Figures   Stravinsky *The Firebird* (1910)

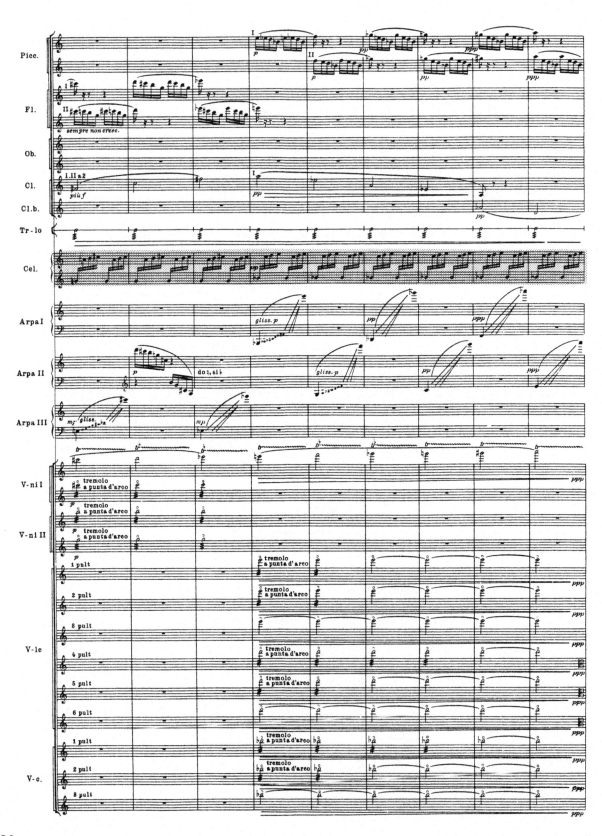

Score Reference 27-14 Celeste Tremolos and Two Hand Broken Chords
Stravinsky *The Firebird* (1910)

Score Reference 27-14 Celeste Tremolos and Two Hand Broken Chords
Stravinsky *The Firebird* (1910)

Score Reference 27-14 Celeste Tremolos and Two Hand Broken Chords
Stravinsky *The Firebird* (1910)

Score Reference 27-14 Celeste Tremolos and Two Hand Broken Chords
Stravinsky *The Firebird* (1910)

Score Reference 27-14 Celeste Tremolos and Two Hand Broken Chords
Stravinsky *The Firebird* (1910)

Score Reference 27-15 Celeste Playing Two Hand Block Chords
Stravinsky *The Firebird* (1910)

Score Reference 27-15 Celeste Playing Two Hand Block Chords
Stravinsky *The Firebird* (1910)

ПОЯВЛЕНИЕ ЖАР–ПТИЦЫ

*Joué par deux exécutants.

The Virtual Orchestra

Since 1988 (the first edition), 1993 (the second edition) and now in the early part of the 21st century (the third edition), we've seen the rise of what can accurately be described as the *virtual orchestra*. Using recording procedures called sampling and special forms of programming called physical modeling, we've reached the point, mid-first decade, of stunning realism with these computer programs. These programs are both angels and devils in one package.

They're angels because they:

1. Guarantee you a performance of your work as long as you have the computing power and a paid electrical bill

2. Empower you to create and produce a more realistic "mock-up" of your work to compete against other compositions in the pile to be premiered by a real orchestra

3. Give you the opportunity to get a lot of work in different styles of music provided you're willing to hustle and not wait for people to discover your talents

4. Don't talk back

5. Work whenever you're available

They're devils because:

1. The better ones are more expensive

2. You need a minimum of two libraries to be successful

3. You do need a computer (or two or three or...)

4. You do need to take the time to learn to record

5. They have a learning curve

6. They aren't real and therefore cannot do exactly what you write, no matter how you wish it so

7. They require that you do financial packages and work for fees that are less than what composers got in the '80s and '90s

8. Learning to use them, called electronic orchestration, is a skill that must be acquired and developed

9. They show what you know and don't know – very quickly

10. They require better than average keyboard skills to create effective parts

Notation Packages and Sample Players

There are four major notation programs three of which come with orchestral sample players. The sample players provide, depending on the work produced, poor to very good representation of what you've written. However, outside academia, the primary work with samplers is done with what's called sequencing/digital audio programs. On the Macintosh there's Digital Performer, Apple Logic, and Cubase SX. On the PC, there's Cubase SX and Sonar.

Recording Production Issues

Virtual orchestras can be purchased by section or by complete orchestra. With companies producing instruments using a programming method called physical modeling, you can purchase individual instruments.

A key issue is knowing whether or not the library has been recorded in the center stage position or with each section recorded in its own onstage seated position.

Onstage Seated Position

There are several virtual orchestras recorded this way. The key advantage is that after recording and editing the parts for phrasing, you then adjust the volume levels for a realistic mix. These libraries are quick to use, sound great, and can be real time savers.

Center Stage Position

When a virtual orchestra is recorded in the center stage position, it means you must learn a procedure called panning and place the instruments yourself where in the stereo spectrum you want to hear them. This sounds hard; but in reality, it only takes a few clicks to set them. In working with these libraries, you'll often need to learn about EQ and stereo imaging to get your best results. Many libraries recorded this way offer stunning realism and great versatility. The advantage of being recorded in the center stage position is that depending on the project, you can place instruments wherever you want in the mix.

Two or More Libraries Needed

Manufacturers hate reading this because they do work hard to give a complete recorded solution, but the reality is that two or more libraries are needed. Here's why.

Avoiding the "Synthy" Faked Sound – Four issues emerge when you try to work exclusively with one library. Depending on the instrumentation, you can get a synthesized sound, no matter how expensive the library. The second issue is also rooted in recording and that's called phasing. When you have a second library to mix parts, you avoid that problem and sound. When stacking parts in vertical harmony with two or more parts, mixing libraries creates a more realistic orchestral sound. Fourth, to compensate for deficiencies in various sounds. For example, one company's violins may sound great in the lower register, but thin in the high and very high registers. By putting two violin programs together from different companies, you solve that problem. In MIDI language, this is called *layering*.

Choice – A friend of mine said it best, "You *are* your sounds."

Time and Convenience

Three Issues in Combining Libraries

While orchestras may have a standard seating arrangement, the placement of mics to record an orchestral sampled section do not have standard placements. As a result, depending on the hall where the orchestra was recorded and the mic positions, they'll all sound different. Let's look at some of the issues.

Mic Position – several sampled orchestras on the market today are recorded with three different mic positions. Generically we could define these three mic positions as *close*, *far* and *distant*. Many others are recorded in the center stage position using one mic position. Even with three mic positions, generally, most composers pick the one in the second position (far) for intimacy and warmth, and to blend other libraries with them. You will find that two or more libraries, aurally, blend well together but their mic positioning isn't as well matched. To match these libraries, you can either use EQ within the sequencing/digital audio recording program or at a hardware mixing board "to move" the mics, or you can use a separate software program with stereo imaging capability to do it for you. Some libraries come in a player format using what's called a "convolution reverb" which has the capabilities of moving both mic and seated positions. Getting virtual orchestras to match up can be a time consuming project, but the end results are often quite stunning.

Seating Positions – Libraries recorded with multiple mic positions match the seating plans taught in this volume. With libraries recorded in the center stage position, you have to use the panning feature to place instruments where you want them on your "virtual stage" or to match instruments already recorded in their seated positions. "Seating" an instrument takes about 2-5 seconds within the computer. A major advantage of the center stage position libraries is that you can set up your own non-orchestral ensembles and set them as needed. For example, using your *Professional Mentor*™, let's say you scored a piece for solo flute and harp. If the orchestra is pre-panned, the flute will be in the center and the harp on the far left. With a center stage position library, you can place either one slightly left and right of center.

Another situation with seating positions is how the strings are seated. There are alternate seating arrangements some of which are useful in electronic scoring. For example, in real life, Vlns 1 and 2 in unison in the high and very high registers is a big sweeping, emotional sound. Most sample libraries can't really duplicate that. Depending on the piece, if you change the seating arrangements to violins 1, violas, cellos, violins 2 with basses in their standard position on the right, you now have unison violins coming out of both the left and right audio speakers.

Another consideration is showmanship. Some scores are intentionally written so that the violins are on the left and right. In live performance this can create a really visually stunning show.

Ambience and Reverb – Some libraries are recorded with the ambience of the hall built into the sound. The benefit of this is that you don't have to worry about adding much reverb. Some libraries are recorded with minimal hall ambience so you can add reverb yourself. This gives you the most control. And once you find a few reverb settings that complement your libraries, it's load and go. The problem comes when you need to mix libraries with different ambiences. Here you have to assign a reverb unit to the library with minimal ambience and adjust it to match the library with the hall ambience. This is very time consuming. To get around this problem, some composers use the library with minimal ambience in a more support role and mix it to take advantage of the natural hall ambience.

Setting Volume Levels

Libraries are recorded using one of these three approaches:

One Dynamic Level - where the strings, for all purpose use, may have been recorded at *mf* only. Volume is used to create a *pp* to *ff* sounding *mf*! Complex to explain, but easiest to use in actual practice. LOTS of libraries, especially older ones, use this approach.

Velocity Cross Switching - where as you play the keyboard, different playing intensities trigger *p*, *mf*, *f*, etc. This is difficult from a keyboard performance perspective, since even professional keyboardists have difficulty consistently playing within a specific velocity range. As a result, dynamics can change depending on how hard you hit the keyboard. The only "cure" for this is to know what velocity rates trigger each dynamic and then edit appropriately inside the sequencer after recording the part. With these libraries, the mod wheel on the master keyboard controller is used to switch between dynamics while live recording. Or, you can go into the sequencing program and draw in the mod wheel changes to alter the dynamic.

Velocity Cross Fading - is a technique that allegedly captures the sound and intensity of the strings as the pitches rise or fall through each dynamic level. Playing lightly gives you *pp*, while "hammering" the keyboard creates *ff*. You see this often with Piano libraries, which is why some have so many velocity layers. This crossfading can take place through performance or, as some prefer, to have the crossfading assigned to the mod wheel on the Master Controller keyboard. This allows for performance, literally on one hand, with dynamics being controlled by the other hand. This means that a Master Controller is needed where the mod wheel is either a separate wheel or slider, where position can be maintained, vs. a spring-loaded action controller similar to that used on Korg keyboards.

With each technique, separate volume at the hardware mixing board, or within the virtual mixing board, is used to set volume levels so that your audio is "hot enough" to record.

Before you start recording, you have to know which technique was used to record the library you're using since this affects your entire recording work process.

The Importance of Planning Dynamics in Your Work

There are certain types of pop music where the musical dynamics are *loud, louder,* and *loudest*. However, there are other types of music where dynamic levels are not just important, but central to the composition and how it's orchestrated. As Rimsky-Korsakov discovered and wrote in his book, when all the instruments are playing at *mp* or *p*, there is an equality of sound where one instrument is not overpowering another. As a result, phenomenal textures and sonorities are possible, as seen in the works of Ravel, Debussy and others.

When working with samples, similar sonorities are possible, however, there is an important issue: getting the signal "hot enough" so that it records properly. This means:

1. Looking over your work and deciding where the softest and loudest dynamics are

2. Seeing how many samples you have actually recorded at that dynamic level(s)

3. Setting the volume levels at the mixing board (virtual or hardware) to be "hot enough" to record, but not so "hot" as to create spiking (resultant clipping) when recording digitally.

This is where score reading and attending live performances pays off, because when listening, you'll know what an instrument at a certain dynamic level sounds like, BUT! You also know what it doesn't sound like.

So even if a sample is labeled *p*, does it sound like the *p* you're looking for? It might not. You can't assume. That's why you have to learn to listen with a discerning, critical ear. And that only comes with score reading and attendance at live performances, score in hand, to set your ears as to how instruments sound at various dynamic levels in live performances, along with how they fit into the "mix" of the live performance.

When planning a mix of your work, realize that recordings, and certainly MP3 files, can lead you down the wrong path in trying to replicate that mix or the EQ. While it seems obsessive/compulsive, since the composer must also be his own recording engineer, it's to your advantage to own different recordings of key works to hear how each was recorded, and then apply the cumulative experience to mixing your own music.

Volume & Intensity

Along with picking samples at the correct dynamic levels, you must also consider *volume* and *intensity*. The higher up the overtone series an instrument plays, the more intense the pitch. The quickest way to hear this is to listen to a tuba playing E3 (E above middle C) and a flute playing the same pitch. With the Tuba, you hear intensity! With the flute, you hear warmth in the lower register. Both are the same pitch, and depending on the player's caliber, can be at the same dynamic level, but the sound and impact is totally different.

Registration and Testing Sounds

In *Professional Orchestration*, I've taught you to listen to how an instrument sounds in the low, medium, high and very high registers.

With a sample library, you need to spend a few minutes with each sound to see how it compares to the actual instrument in the low, medium, high, and very high registers. This is called *career insurance*. One sampled instrument can sound *brilliante* in one register and like a dog in another! So as you go through them, you keep a written notebook of what works best, and where. Don't even try relying on your memory. Write it down so you can look it up. Later, you can experiment with blending orchestral libraries by instrument and comparing the results to audio recordings of live orchestras. The end result is that you end up creating your own orchestral sound.

In Volume 2, *Orchestrating the Melody Within Each Orchestral Section*, I give you nearly a thousand pages of examples with every combination labeled by the low, medium, high, and very high ranges.

Testing a few of these combinations will quickly demonstrate why you need several libraries. Let's say you listen to *L'Arlesienne Suite #1* by Bizet and try to duplicate a string unison. Depending on the library, you could end up with a big fat buzz sounding like a string patch from a synth in the '80s, or it could sound very realistic.

Generally, the way to avoid these problems is to have a second or third library so that the violins come from two different libraries, then the violas plus cellos. With octaves, you have to edit the velocity (the intensity with which you strike the MIDI keyboard) of the lower instrument because it will often sound louder than the instrument in the higher register.

Staying Up to Date

One chapter can't begin to cover all these details. If this is an area you decide to move into, see my *Writing for...Series* for strings, woodwinds, orchestra and brass that dually covers electronic orchestration and editing. I update *How MIDI Works* almost annually to keep you up-to-date. And for up-to-the-minute information, see our online journal, **www.soniccontrol.com** for reviews and other helps.

Print magazines worth reading include *Sound on Sound*, *Electronic Musician*, *Keyboard*, and *Mix*.

Chapter 28

The Percussion Section

When dealing with Percussion, we must think differently between working with the studio player vs. the symphonic player, although both can sometimes be the same person. Before we get to the instruments, we'll talk first about the players.

Types of Studio Percussionists

There are today, three types of studio percussionists.

The Full Serve Studio Percussionist

The first is what I'll define as the "full serve" dedicated percussionist. He's a true artisan in his ability to play all the percussion instruments, plus exotic instruments from around the world. As a studio player, he'll normally bring "everything" to cover whatever the composer may require. Everything includes timpani to timbales to field marching drum to xylophone! However, if you want the drum set, you need to specify that. Many of the top studio percussionists have both symphonic and jazz backgrounds. However, those at the top of the curve do not always have or use electronics.

The Electronic Percussionist

This dedicated percussionist will often be classically trained, but because of the changing demand for electronics, will specialize in drum set, percussion, drum machine programming, electronic drum sets (called KATs), and have samples of the major percussion instruments which he'll have available in samplers. This percussionist gets a lot work from TV dates, movies with a pop oriented soundtrack, and pop music recording.

The Specialty Player

The specialty player is just that, a musician brought into a recording or live performance situation because of the particular musical sound he's created for himself, usually within a specific music style. This could be a rock drummer who only does certain types of rock, or a jazz/fusion drummer, a drummer who specializes in a country groove, a jazz vibist, and so on. The point is, these percussionists are *specialists*. They may not even read music, but they're used because of the brilliance of the style they represent.

The Symphonic Percussionist

There are only two main differences between the symphonic percussionist and the full serve studio percussionist:

1. In a major orchestra, the symphonic percussionist plays the instruments provided by the orchestra whereas the studio percussionist *literally* brings a truck full of stuff! However, there are some situations (as with snare drums or certain Latin instruments) where he may elect to bring his own instruments.

2. Because of the drive to constantly find new sounds for the movies, the studio percussionist will often have a much broader array of instruments available that simply aren't used in symphonic literature.

Recording Studios and Percussion Instrument Availability

It's unwise to assume that a recording studio will have a complete collection of percussion instruments. Prior to booking the date, you must check with the percussionist to see what he has and what he's bringing, and also with the studio to see if any percussion is available *at all*. To avoid an unpleasant surprise, especially if you've never booked that studio before, call ahead to see what they have and then go look at it and play it yourself. Better to know *ahead* of time that the equipment may be inadequate then at the session where it really could be too late to do anything about it.

Kinds of Percussion

Percussion instruments pitch variance and vibrating characteristics differ. Let's review them by their respective categories.

Pitch Variance

1. **Instruments with definite pitch:** timpani, chimes, glockenspiel (orchestra bells), xylophone, marimba, celesta and vibraphone.

2. **Instruments with indefinite pitch:** snare drum (side drum), bass drum, cymbals, tambourine, triangle, wood block, castanets, tom-tom, temple blocks, gong and tam-tam.

Note

The last five were the least common in symphonic orchestration before the mid-1800s and are sometimes referred to as "exotic," because of national associations.

Vibrating Characteristics

Instruments that sound after contact: timpani, concert bass drum, chimes, glockenspiel, cymbals, triangle, gong and tam-tam.

Instruments that don't sound after contact: xylophone, snare drum, drum set bass drum, tambourine, wood block, temple blocks and castanets.

Timbre

A third category is *timbre*, determined by the kind of vibrating surface: membrane, metal or wood.

Membrane: all types of drums, including the tambourine.

Metal: glockenspiel, vibraphone, chimes, cymbals, triangle, gong and tam-tam.

Wood: wood block, temple blocks, xylophone, marimba and castanets.

Instruments with definite pitch need a staff with a suitable clef. Those with indefinite pitch can be written on a staff (usually the bass clef) or on a single line *without* any clef. Some composers have used the treble clef for the triangle and tambourine, a misleading and unnecessary practice.

The percussion instruments, as a section, weren't commonly used until the late 1800s. Exceptions occur in the Haydn *Military Symphony* and the Mozart opera *Abduction from the Seraglio*, where the triangle, cymbals and bass drum are used for color.

Note

The use of the percussion in these two examples shows each composer's intent to add an exotic touch by imitating Turkish military bands. Later, in the *Finale* of Beethoven's *Ninth Symphony*, these instruments increase both the emotional and rhythmic tension. Scoring for the section still aims for this.

Percussion instruments are valuable only when they add unique dimensions of timbre and nuance. Determine their role by their ability to perk up and enrich, something you can't get from other sections of the orchestra. They're supplementary instruments with limited tonal definition that affects their scoring values. This applies especially to those instruments with indefinite pitch. The type of sound and its frequency always affect appropriateness.

Subtleties of percussive timbres are often lost by overwriting and overloading the parts, especially in loud tuttis. The opposite extreme - delicately stroked percussion - is piquant, colorful, and worth investigating. If percussion parts are well-placed and spaced, their timbres add attractive coloristic nuances.

TV/Movie Percussion Note

In the pressures of creating 15-20 minutes worth of music in a single week for a TV show or movie, it's not uncommon to score a rhythmic ostinato with the percussion section over which a long melody is written.

Conventional Uses

Some conventional ways to use percussion instruments at all dynamic levels are:

1. Establishing and maintaining rhythmic ostinatos, best-suited to instruments with indefinite pitch.

2. Outlining melodic ideas and figurations. Definite-pitched instruments are more effective; those with indefinite pitch heighten pulsation and add volume and intensity.

3. Group scoring of mixed-percussion timbres, either separately or in combination with other sections, increases rhythmic vitality or volume while contributing contrast.

4. Coloristic rhythmic effects derived from the design of principal melodic ideas have continuity and interest.

5. Short color splashes, with or without rhythmic pulsation, highlight nuances.

6. As an independent rhythm section with diversified inner rhythmic patterns.

7. For pointing up the apex in tonal climaxes.

8. For long, sustained percussive sound. Rolls on the snare drum, bass drum, cymbal or triangle are most common.

9. For short, quick piling of sound.

10. For carrying out rhythmic patterns not feasible in other sections of the orchestra.

Percussion Vibration

The vibrating characteristics of percussion instruments are totally different from those of the other sections. This is the reason for problems with their notation. Metal instruments continue to sound or ring in varying degrees after contact. Those made of wood and two of the drum group, the snare drum and the tambourine, stop vibrating right after contact. Only the timpani in the percussion group continues to resonate with any effect.

The effect of these vibrating characteristics on the notations of metal percussion instruments is illustrated in example 28-1:

EXAMPLE 28-1

If this notation is used for xylophone or marimba, the sound that results is notated like this:

EXAMPLE 28-2

For instruments with non-vibrating surfaces with indefinite pitch, the sounding notation is shown in example 28-3:

EXAMPLE 28-3

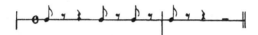

If the effect of continuous tone is required for wooden instruments with definite pitch, the notation reads like this:

EXAMPLE 28-4

Notation for the other instruments in this category, but with indefinite pitch, is shown below:

EXAMPLE 28-5

So, we see that metal percussion instruments don't require any form of tremolo. Those made of wood and the two drum types noted maintain continuous sound only by repeated attacks.

Note:

The notation indicating double strokes in examples 28-4 and 5 is acceptable for tempos of allegro or faster; all slower tempos should have triple flags.

The Drum Group

Timpani

Snare Drum

Bass Drum

Tambourine

Tom-tom

The Timpani
French, *timbales*; Italian, *timpani*; German, *Pauken*

Kettledrums, known by their Italian name, *timpani*, are referred to in the plural because they're always used in pairs. There are two types: copper-kettle-shaped drums with plastic heads hand-tuned, and the pedal-tuned.

The hand-tuned, standard until the early 1900s, has a set of evenly spaced handles around the edges of the rim. One-half turn for each of these handles alters the pitch by about one half-step. This accounts for the need to allow enough time for pitch changes during performance. The hand-tuned type naturally needs longer rest intervals than the pedal timpani, on which pitch changes are made almost instantly. The larger drum is always placed at the player's left. Supplementary larger and smaller timpani are standard with major orchestras, but are rare in school and amateur ensembles.

Studio percussionist and symphonies will usually have four timpani available. The typical sizes are 30", 28", 25" and 23". The combined range of these four timpani is C two octaves below middle C to middle C. The professional timpanist can achieve a range of a major 6th for each drum. But for safety, plan for no more than a perfect fifth range per timpani.

EXAMPLE 28-6

Timpani Sticks
Timpani sticks are wooden with mallet heads ranging from soft to hard. You get considerable variation in sound and attack with different sticks. Stick technique involves single strokes with alternating hands for rolls and common rhythmic patterns. A skilled timpanist is a specialist who performs feats of stick technique on up to four drums. In major symphonies, the timpanist rarely doubles on other percussion instruments.

Timpani Tuning
Classical composers scored for timpani in pairs tuned to the tonic and dominant, always with a C major notation, as for the natural horns and trumpets. Post-Classical composers more accurately notated by writing correct pitches, but omitting accidentals, except tunings, at the beginning of each movement. Not until the late 1800s did composers begin using accidentals in timpani parts. Since then, attempts have been made to include key signatures in order to

standardize. These experiments have, in general, been resolved by writing the exact notation, including accidentals in the parts as they occur, but omitting key signatures. Example 28-7 illustrates this for timpani notation.

EXAMPLE 28-7

In film work, the timpani is often tuned to specific pitches that allow the performance of a melody or a bass ostinato. The part can be a solo or it can be doubled by pizzicato cellos and basses, or even the bassoons.

Notation Styles

Although the timpani's resonance is vibrant, *continuous* tone is possible only with the roll. All rolled notes which aren't tied should theoretically get new attacks, as with other instruments. (This notation occurs in scores before the early 1900s.) Eliminate confusion by indicating clearly the starting and stopping points of all rolls. You can write notation for all rolled notes in either of the ways shown in example 28-8a and b. Rolled intervals for one player are practical if confined to two drums (example 28-8c):

EXAMPLE 28-8

Timpani notation is precise for tone durations and playing styles. Timpani resonance is controlled by applying the finger-tips to the drum head, choking off the tone. Playing styles allow all types of dynamics for accents, *staccato* strokes and rolls.

Orchestral Usage

Timpani parts in early Classic scores were stylized. They were often combined with horns and trumpets as the way to get the most sonority and brilliance. As already noted, this instrumental combination was important for climaxes and strong cadences. Some of the last scores of Haydn and Mozart show deviation from this usage; but it was for Beethoven to boldly use the timpani in new ways. His nine symphonies show a progressive independence of the timpani for significant solo parts.

EXAMPLE 28-9

Note in example 28-9a the use of the timpani as an independent bass part. The following example from Tchaikovsky's *Fourth Symphony* illustrates this use half a century later:

EXAMPLE 28-10

Note another development of Beethoven's approach in example 28-9c in the opening measures of the *Scherzo* movement by Sibelius, where the timpani plays the rhythmic pattern of the main theme.

EXAMPLE 28-11

Berlioz' innovative scoring for four solo timpani in the Pastoral movement of his *Symphonie Fantastique* suggests distant thunder.

EXAMPLE 28-12

Orchestral Uses of the Timpani

1. For building climaxes either with a roll or for the repetition of the rhythmic figure not necessarily doubled by other instruments

2. For emphasis in all forms: melodically, harmonically and rhythmically

3. When played staccato, it's like the *pizzicato* of the cello and bass

4. Effective combined with the brass, either full or in part

5. For solo snatches of thematic bits, often arranged antiphonally

6. For outlining the pulsations of bass *ostinatos*

7. In long, sustained rolls as pedal points for either *crescendos* or *diminuendos*

8. In intervals—played together or broken

9. For creating tension with *ostinatos*, preferably derived from the rhythmic pattern of principal thematic ideas

Since the timpani have been a basic part of the orchestra practically since its inception, consider them musical instruments and not supplementary "noise makers." Although percussive, they don't belong to the percussion category; they're not as limited in their usage as other percussion instruments.

The Snare Drum

French, *caisse claire (or tambour)*; Italian, *cassa (or tamburo)*; German, *Trommel*

Because snare drums aren't standardized (they vary in size and sonority) it can cost the orchestrator, conductor, and player valuable rehearsal time while the conductor/composer listens to hear if the snare drum is giving him the sound he wants. If it's not, the percussionist (especially the studio percussionist) will literally demonstrate the part on various sized snare drums until the conductor/composer "hears" the sound he perceives he wants. Or, he'll play the part with varying size sticks until the conductor hears what he likes.

The model most often used for orchestral work is a chrome metal drum 6" x 14" (or 15") deep with two plastic heads. A set of snares *(wire-covered gut strings)* are attached to a clamping device that regulates their tension and contact with the bottom drum head. The movement of these snares on the bottom head accounts for its bright, *secco (dry, hard and brittle)* tone.

There's a smaller snare drum about 3" deep called a piccolo snare drum. The piccolo snare generally gets a brighter, more cutting sound.

A field snare drum is the kind used in a marching band and it has a much deeper sound to it. All snare drums today use plastic heads on the top and bottom.

When the snares are released, the sound is similar to that of an Indian tom-tom or other folk-type drum.

Rolls: Double and Buzz

Highly trained studio and symphonic percussionists are trained in specific types of rolls. The basic roll is handled as a double stroke (RR LL). Standardized rolls by the National Association of Rudimental Drummers are the 5, 7, 9, 11, and 13 stroke rolls. Rolls placed before the beat act as a group of grace notes attached to a target note (called the *stinger* by drummers). Rolls can start on the beat for added emphasis and often end with an accented note. The snare drum roll, unlike the timpani's, is most often double-stroked. The end of rolls is clearly indicated by tying rolled notes to an unrolled note, as in example 28-13. This method is correct for rolls on all percussion instruments.

EXAMPLE 28-13

Rolls that don't have an accent on the end that are played *mp* to *pppp* are called *buzz* rolls. They're done by the percussionist using controlled multiple bounces per stick vs. a double stroke roll.

Flams and Ruffs

Two styles of stick technique, the "flam" and the "drag," apply only to the snare drum. Both prefix one or more grace notes to basic notations. Typically, the maximum number of grace notes is four, handled like a five stroke double stroke roll. Triplet ruffs, with three grace notes before the accented note, can be handled single stroke, or with a double stroke triplet sticking like this: RRL R or LLR L. Each produces a different sound and feel. The difference between written and sounding notations resulting from these styles is illustrated in the conventional roll-off (below).

EXAMPLE 28-14

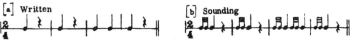

Orchestral Uses of the Snare Drum

The snare drum in both symphonic and film composition is most often used for military music and the afterbeats in dance forms. Notable exceptions occur in the *March to the Scaffold* movement in the *Symphonie Fantastique* by Berlioz and in the final climax of Strauss' symphonic poem *Till Eulenspiegel*. In these passages, both composers called for large military drums to create a mood of impending doom.

Composers since have used the snare drum:

1. to give percussive verve to important rhythmic figurations (Debussy's *Fetes*)

2. to maintain endless *ostinatos* (Ravel's *Bolero*)

3. to build grandiose climaxes (Aaron Copland's *Outdoor Overture*)

4. Other composers have used it uniquely in the softer dynamic levels, fascinating in timbre and design (Ravel's *Rhapsodie espagnole*; Prokofiev's Symphony *No. 5*; Bartok's *Concerto for Orchestra*).

Snare Drum Special Effects

Several special effects have been created to vary the snare drum's normal characteristic timbre. Plus the tom-tom drum with released snares, these include:

◆ muffled head (cloth covering the "batter" head);

◆ playing with wire-spread brushes or timpani sticks and rim shots (striking one stick against a second stick in contact with the batter head and metal rim to produce pistol-like reports);

◆ a cross stick used in Latin music where the stick is laid across the drum and the shank end strikes the rim creating a woodblocky-type sound.

The Bass Drum
French, *grosse caisse;* Italian, *cassa, gran cassa;* German, *grosse trommel*

There are two types of bass drums: symphonic and pop/jazz.

Symphonic
The bass drum is a "noise maker" *par excellence* with a booming resonance of great carrying power proportionate to its size. The symphony model has two plastic or calfskin heads about 30" in diameter and a wood shell with a depth of some 16".

Notation and playing techniques are similar to that for the timpani with one exception: A single bass-drum beater, or stick, with a large, moderately hard head is commonly used. If you substitute timpani sticks, direct the kind of head you want: soft, medium or hard.

Historically, the bass drum is paired with the cymbals. This combination persisted well into the mid-1800s, when composers recognized the value of separation of the two. One advantage is the bass-drum roll, with its ominous thud. Others are short strokes for rhythmic, dynamic and coloristic effects, either alone or combined with other percussion instruments. The symphonic bass drum can create a devastating effect when combined with low strings performing Snap Pizzicato doubled by the low brass.

Pop/Jazz
The pop/jazz is part of the drum set (sometimes called a *kit*). *Occasionally,* some drummers will use a 24" bass drum, but most often, the bass drum in a drum set is standardized between 14" x 18" up to 14' x 22". Often, the front head of the bass drum is removed and a blanket inserted to more effectively muffle the drum. Used in dance music, its purpose is to provide an ongoing rhythmic ostinato while the drummer's left hand clearly defines beats 2 and 4 (called the *backbeat*). The bass drum is notated on the A space in the bass clef.

Tom-Toms are often attached to the top of the bass drum. Most of the time, there will be two tom-toms (usually 8" x 12" and a 9" x 13").

The Tambourine
French, *tambour de Basque;* Italian, *tamburo basco, tamburino;*
German, *Schellentrommel, Tamburin*

The orchestral tambourine has a diameter of about 10", but with only one drum head, equipped with a set of small metal disks called jingles. These jingles are set in pairs and vibrate in response to movement of the instrument.

Playing Styles
Several playing styles are used.

For percussive strokes on the drum head, the player uses either his fist or knuckles. Different kinds of drum sticks are sometimes substituted.

Continuous rolls of the jingles are made either by shaking the instrument or by using a specialized technique of rubbing a moistened thumb around the edges of the drum head. Neither style produces any percussive sound from the drum head. A continuous percussive roll is made only with drum sticks.

Orchestral parts for the tambourine suggest something "exotic"; but this association isn't entirely justified. Actually, its dual percussive characteristics add zest to music that is rhythmic and festive. It's a kind of miniature drum with jingles, capable of splash-color effects at all dynamic levels.

Metal Percussion

Triangle

Cymbals

Glockenspiel

Vibraphone

Chimes

Gong

Tam-tam

Antique Cymbals

The Triangle
French, *triangle*; Italian, *triangolo*; German, *Triangel*

The triangle is a small steel bar shaped like a triangle, but with one open end. The standard orchestra size is about 6 1/2" on a side. A small steel rod is used as a beater. Short rhythmic patterns, ostinatos, and tremolos are common at all dynamic levels. Its bright, high-pitched, bell-like tone is piquant. A few strokes enliven soft dance measures or a powerful tutti. Its brilliance is the key to estimating its effectiveness. You can find representative parts for the triangle, without other percussion instruments in the following symphonies: Schumann *No. 1*, Brahms *No. 4*, Dvorak *No. 5* and Tchaikovsky *No. 4*.

The Cymbals
French, *cymbales*; Italian, *piatti*; German, *Bechen*

Cymbal resonance and tonal strength vary with size and quality. The preferred orchestral sizes for symphonic ensembles range from 15" to 18" in diameter. Turkish cymbals, made of a brass alloy, have been preferred for their vibrating qualities. Matched pairs, played manually, are supplemented by a third, suspended cymbal for use with different kinds of drum sticks. There are four basic cymbal playing techniques.

Paired Cymbals

1. The normal playing style calls for glancing blows of paired cymbals. Can be played *pp* to *ff*. The cymbals can ring for a long period if the percussionist raises his arms and faces the cymbals towards the audience. The cymbals can be choked (creating a "chank" kind of sound) by having them pulled into the percussionists chest after striking. For these types of cymbals, label the part *piatti*.

2. By "rubbing" the cymbals together in what's called a two-plate roll. It must be marked in the score as such.

Suspended Cymbals

3. By striking a suspended cymbal with a regular drum stick or timpani mallet. When using the mallet, a more gong-like sound is achievable.

4. By rolling on a suspended cymbal most often with a pair of mallets, less often symphonically with regular drum sticks. For these kinds of cymbals, label the part *suspended cymbal*.

Mallet Note For Suspended Cymbals

For the suspended cymbal, direct the type of sticks to use: wood, metal or timpani. Omitting this information leads to distortion of the part.

Choke Note

Tone is stopped almost instantly by bringing the cymbals in contact with clothes, indicated by *dampen* or *choke*. A hand *chokes* a suspended cymbal. If the cymbals are to continue vibrating after contact beyond the limits of notation for a given measure, the words *allow to vibrate* or *laisser vibrer* are written in the part.

Notating Cymbal Parts

Notating cymbal parts changes depending on the kind of music being written.

Stage Band and Studio Work

Cymbal parts are marked in published arrangements for stage band as follows:

1. Most of the time in the bass clef.

2. The ride cymbal is notated on the middle C line with an X as the notehead. This line designates a rhythm played on the ride cymbal, at the bell of the cymbal or a crash. The drummer will automatically play the part as a ride part unless marked *Bell* or *Crash*.

3. The hi-hat cymbal is marked on the B line just below middle C also with an *x* as the notehead. When the hi-hat is open, an *o* is put above the rhythm. When it's closed, a + sign is put above the note.

4. When the hi-hat is playing on the back beats (2&4) or on beats 2 & 3 in a jazz waltz, the part is usually notated on the F line below the bass clef, also with an *x*. This tells the drummer the left foot is performing the hi-hat part.

EXAMPLE 28-15

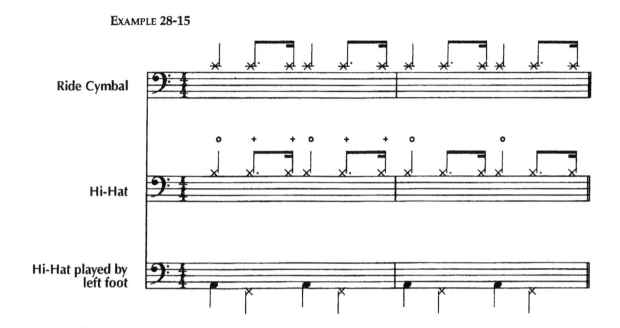

Ride Cymbal

Hi-Hat

Hi-Hat played by
left foot

Symphonic Notation

For symphonic notation, you can use either the x on the notehead for the cymbal, or a regular notehead. What counts is clearly marking the part for the type of cymbal used (suspended vs. crash) and the sound desired. Cymbal players can have their own part, or they can share the part with the bass drum. When sharing the part, you can write the bass drum on the A space in the bass clef and the cymbal part on the B line below middle C as described above.

The Glockenspiel

French, *jeu de timbres, carillon*; Italian, *campanella*; German, *Glockenspiel*

Sounds two octaves higher than written.

EXAMPLE 28-16

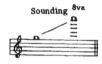

Sounding

The glockenspiel, or orchestra bells, is a set of chromatically pitched steel bars arranged in a playing position similar to that of the piano keyboard. It's written in the treble clef.

The glockenspiel was originally played with a keyboard (Mozart's opera *The Magic Flute*). It's since been replaced with a manual technique using mallets in the player's hands. This method has greater dynamic range since different kinds of mallet heads can be used: yarn, rubber, wood or metal. The choice of mallet heads is usually the player's who chooses based on the dynamics of each passage. Single notes, intervals and three-note chords work if confined to an octave. The instrument has bright sonority with good carrying power. Accumulated, undampened vibrations from many notes produce a tonal blurring that's a characteristic asset. Its luminous resonance minimizes any dryly percussive sound. Relatively short solo melodic phrases have a distinctive charm in the soft-to-medium-loud dynamic range levels (*The Dance of the Apprentices* in Richard Wagner's *Die Meistersinger* and the *Scherzo* from Rachmaninov's *Second Symphony*. Its tone outlines melodic and rhythmic ideas well for short color dabs of single notes or intervals, and for splashy *glissandos* on very rapid *crescendos*.

EXAMPLE 28-17

The instrument doesn't respond to rapid double strokes.

The glockenspiel can effectively double the flutes, oboes, clarinet, harp, and strings.

The Vibraphone

Here's the range of the most common vibraphone available:

EXAMPLE 28-18

The vibraphone is an extra-large glockenspiel equipped with resonators, each containing revolving disks operated electrically. These resonators produce an exaggerated vibrato that causes continuous blurring and overlapping of successive tones. Composers may ask the vibist to turn off the motor to eliminate the exaggerated vibrato. Or, they may ask the vibist to adjust the motor speed to affect how fast or how slow the notes vibrate.

The almost exclusive use of soft mallet heads prevents any dynamics beyond the softer ones unless amplified. Top professional vibists can manage two mallets per hand and so do a maximum of four part harmony. This four-part harmony can be used in a pad or "snap-rolled" similar to a piano. It can also be arpeggiated.

Vibes have a foot pedal that acts like a piano damper pedal.

One of the more effective vibe parts in the symphonic literature is found in Holst's *The Planets*. Vibes are often used in studio work for highly coloristic work with flutes, piano, and harp. They can also be part of small jazz ensembles.

Vibes Discography

To hear the vibes and what they're capable of, you're referred to the music of Gary Burton and the Benny Goodman Quartet Album, *Together Again* featuring Lionel Hampton.

The Chimes or Tubular Bells

French, *cloches*; Italian, *campane*; German, *Glocken*

The chimes consist of a set of long tubular metal pipes usually hung on a specially constructed rack or frame. Their range covers an octave and a perfect fourth, with intervening chromatics:

EXAMPLE 28-19

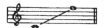

A gavel-like hammer is used for single strokes. Successive tones pile up jangling overtones similar to a carillon's. As these large bells speak slowly, avoid fast-moving notations. Single strokes, well spaced, give the best results. Bell tones, either real or imitated, have always fascinated composers. Note orchestral works of the nineteenth century: In the Carillon movement of Bizet's *L'Arlesienne Suite No. 1*, the composer has set up a 52-measure imitated-bell *ostinato*. A similar imitation occurs in the Angelus section of Massenet's *Scenes pittoresques*. Berlioz, in the final section of his *Symphonie Fantastique*, wrote for two chimes and six pianos. Kodaly combined chimes with other percussive instruments in his witty *Hary Janos Suite* (example 28-26). Find a comparison of real and imitative clanging church-bell sounds in the Coronation Scene in Moussorgsky's opera, *Boris Godunov* and the *Russian Easter Overture* by Rimsky-Korsakov. The realistic effect of chimes colors the final movements of *Iberia* by Debussy and by Albeniz in the *Arbos* transcriptions.

The Tam-Tam and the Gong

The tam-tam comes from the Far East and is rarely scored correctly. This large bronze disk measures some 28" in diameter and has a turned-down rim to minimize its high-vibration frequency. A smaller type, known as a gong, is often substituted for the larger tam-tam. Both have a strong low-pitched resonance and tonal power that limit their usefulness. Single strokes with a large beater are rarely used softer than mf>.

19th-century composers associated the tam-tam with gloom and despair (Tchaikovsky's Symphony No. 6). Later composers, however, scored it in various ways: as a super-cymbal (George Gershwin's *Concerto in F*; for its coloristic potential (Example P-7); and for its overwhelming tonal strength, as found in the final movements of *Pictures at an Exhibition* (Moussorgsky-Ravel) and *The Pines of Rome* (Respighi).

The Antique Cymbals

French, *crotales*; Italian, *crotali*; German, *antiken zimpeln*

Antique cymbals are tiny discs made in pairs, with definite pitch. They're held in the palms of the hands by small straps that let them ring after their rims are struck together. These bell-like cymbals are impractical, because their pitch variance has never been standardized. Since it's difficult to get these cymbals, orchestral bells are substituted. Debussy wrote briefly for them in the final measures of *Prelude to the Afternoon of a Faun*. Parts for antique cymbals with differing pitches were used by Berlioz in *Romeo et Juliette*, by Ravel in *Daphnis et Chloe* and by Stravinsky in *The Rite of Spring*.

Wooden Percussion

Xylophone

Marimba

Wood Block

Temple Blocks

Castanets

The Xylophone

French, *xylophone*; Italian, *xilofono*; German, *Xylophon*

The xylophone differs from the glockenspiel; its bars are made of wood instead of metal. There are two types: a folding set without resonators with a small-to-moderate range, and a more elaborate set mounted on a special frame with resonators with a chromatic compass of more than three octaves. The three-octave-type is the exception, not the rule. The treble clef is used for the varying ranges as seen below:

EXAMPLE **28-20**

The xylophone sounds *an octave higher* than written. Playing technique is about the same as for the glockenspiel, with different mallets available for dynamic variance. Its tone is dry, brittle and percussive. Slow melodies require a constant tremolo and aren't successful. Its best parts include short solos of rhythmic-melodic interest, outlining rapid figurations, accenting melodic and harmonic elements, and arpeggiated chords. Short, quick *glissandos*, ending on an accented note, add color. Intervals and three-note chords are feasible. Some contextual passages for xylophone are:

Saint-Saens *Danse macabre*

Prokofiev, *Scythian Suite*

Howard Hanson, *Merry Mount Suite*

Douglas Moore, *Pageant of P. T. Barnum*

Kabalevsky, *Colas Breugnon Suite*

Lambert,*The Rio Grande*

Gardner Read, *First Overture*

Joseph Wagner *Symphony No. 1*

The Marimba

The marimba is an elaborate xylophone, with a subdued, mellow tone usually played with soft-head mallets. Up to four mallets can be used as described in the vibes section. Instruments in this country have a four-octave compass equipped with resonators. It sounds an octave lower than the xylophone.

EXAMPLE 28-21

The Wood Block

The wood block is a hollowed-out, rectangular piece of wood with slots on each side near the top playing surface. Snare-drum sticks or hard xylophone mallets used with single stroke attacks point out accents and rhythmic patterns; dry, brittle, isolated tappings are meant for neutral percussive effects. Chinese in origin, the wood block has become an almost exclusively American adaptation. Parts for it are included in:

Aaron Copland: *Billy the Kid* and *Rodeo*

George Gershwin *Concerto in F*

Prokofiev, Symphony *No. 5*

Ravel, *Concerto for the Left Hand*

Joseph Wagner *Hudson River Legend*

Walton *Suite from Facade*

Temple Blocks

Temple blocks, also Chinese in origin, are round, brightly lacquered wooden blocks, usually five in number and roughly tuned to approximate the notes of a pentatonic scale. Various sticks and mallets make sounds resembling those associated with gourds of different sizes. Notation is with *x's* at various pitch levels without clefs.

The Castanets

Castanets are shell-shaped pieces of hard wood made in pairs. They're connected by string loose enough to permit manipulation by the fingers when held in the palm of the hand. However, since this style of playing requires a lot of skill, castanets are more often fastened to a wooden paddle so they can be played like a rattle or clapper.

Castanets have always suggested Spanish or Latin-American dance music, clicking out rhythms neatly and adding local color. European composers have used them occasionally without this connotation.

Other Percussion Instruments

For Latin instruments, aside from the castanets, there are maracas, claves, the guiro, bongos, timbales and congas.

Maracas are gourds filled with seeds or pebbles. They're generally used for steady ostinato patterns or to create a whirring sound when twirled.

Claves are two hard wood sticks that are struck together. Used mostly for rhythmic fill-ins or as part of a rhythmic ostinato.

The Guiro is a gourd with carved ridges on the outside. A stick is rubbed across the ridges to create a pleasant scraping sound. Used mostly for rhythmic fill-ins or as part of a rhythmic ostinato.

Bongos are small drums held between the knees while the percussionist is seated. They're played by slapping with the fingers at various positions of the head.

Timbales are a special type of suspended tom-tom hung from a stand. There are two timbales to a stand, 13" and 14" respectively. They can be played with the hands, special timbale sticks, or with mallets. They can be struck in the center, near the rim, or with a rim shot. This instrument is frequently used by film composers, separate from Latin rhythms, in action/ adventure scenes. Its sound cuts through sharply and crisply.

Congas are a tall vertical drum, usually 30" tall. Often used in pairs for a hi-lo sound. They're played with a special technique using the fingers and heel of the hand. Mallets can also be used.

The Mark Tree suspended has vertical metal bars (like organ pipes). Played by the fingers, you get a shimmering sound because of the multiple strikes.

The Bell Tree is an inverted cone with graduated bells that creates a long gliss.

Percussion and Synthesizers

Many of the sounds listed in this chapter (snare drum, pop bass drum, timpani, gongs, ride cymbals, hi-hat cymbals and Latin instruments) are found on most top-of-the-line sample-based synthesizers. In the absence of a percussionist able to perform these instruments, more than adequate sounds are available electronically.

The Drum Set

Symphonically, most often used in pops arrangements, but is a mainstay of studio recording for film scoring and pop music. Below is a typical set:

EXAMPLE **28-22**

The modern drummer will have at least three tom-toms: two top-toms, and a floor tom-tom. There will be two to three cymbals: ride and two crash cymbals. Also, there's a hi-hat, a bass drum, and usually a 5" metal or wood snare drum using plastic heads. Here's how to notate the drum set parts (cymbals have already been explained):

EXAMPLE **28-23**

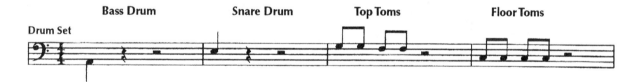

Note

Generally, for stage band work, most drummers prefer *not* to have a heavily notated part, preferring, for example, to have the rhythm of the trumpet line notated on the B line below middle C.

If you want a specific rhythm, simply tell the drummer, and with a top player, you'll get better than what you could possibly notate. If, however, you have a unique rhythm, by all means notate it, but give it to the drummer at least a day ahead of the session so you can see if this is what you really have in mind.

When the drummer has brief solo of one to four beats, write hash marks and the word Fill across the top.

Percussion: The Group

Not until the 20th century did composers stop scoring percussion ensembles to accentuate music's elemental rhythmic figures and pulsations. Until then there was only slight interplay of independent rhythmic patterns within the section. It was customary to make the lighter instruments (triangle, tambourine and snare drum) play together on rhythms taken from the melodic line. The heavier ones (cymbals and bass drum) emphasized the rhythmic pulse of harmonic progressions and/or strong beats of the measures. Likewise, no one experimented with percussive timbres and their coloristic potentials in the softer dynamics.

Recently, composers have expanded the scope of the section. They recognized the differences among the pitch levels, timbres and tonal strengths of each instrument. Their unanimous interest in the rhythmic vitality of music created a more diversified arrangement of percussion parts with an interplay of mixed rhythmic patterns within the section. Yet the goals of color and tension haven't been sacrificed. Finally, note the advanced accomplishments with percussion instruments at softer dynamic levels. Percussive timbres have become more subtle and provocative, adding a new dimension of *timbre sonorities*.

Note also that few scorings of the full percussion ensemble in orchestral *tuttis* include percussive instruments with definite pitch other than the timpani. Instead, they combine instruments with various indefinite pitch levels and place them according to the most prominent characteristics of the music. The following excerpts are devoted to the percussion ensemble to illustrate the development of independent parts for the section within a relatively short period of time. (The Britten excerpt, example 28-27, is for the percussion as a solo unit.)

EXAMPLE 28-24

EXAMPLE 28-25

EXAMPLE 28-26

EXAMPLE 28-27

Britten
The Young Person's Guide to the Orchestra

Books Used in the Preparation of This Volume

ADLER, SAMUEL. *The Study of Orchestration*. New York: W.W. Norton, 1982.

FORSYTH, CECIL. *Orchestration*. London: MacMillan 1914

GROVE, RICHARD. *Arranging Concepts*. Los Angeles: Alfred Publications

KARLIN, F/WRIGHT, R. *On the Track: A Guide to Contemporary Film Scoring*. New York: Schirmer, 1990.

KLING, H. *The Art of Instrumentation*. New York: Carl Fischer, 1905

KOECHLIN, C.L.E. *Traite de l'orchestration*. 4 Vol. Paris:Max Eschig, 1954-59.

MANCINI, HENRY. *Sounds and Scores*. Los Angeles: Northridge Publishing, 1962.

PISTON, WALTER. *Orchestration*. New York: W.W. Norton, 1955.

PROUT, EBENEZER. *Instrumentation*. Boston: Ditson.

READ, GARDNER. *Thesaurus of Orchestral Devices*. New York: Pitman, 1953.

RIMSKY-KORSAKOV, NIKOLAY. *Principles of Orchestration,* transl. by Edward Agate. New York: Kalmus Publications.

WAGNER, JOSEPH. *Orchestration: A Practical Handbook.* Los Angeles: Alexander Publishing, 1989.

WIDOR, CHARLES MARIE. *The Technique of the Modern Orchestra.* London: J. Williams, 1906.

Scores

Except for Borodin *Symphony #1* and Rimsky-Korsakov, *Capriccio Espagnole* (Kalmus Publications), all other public domain scores sourced and available from Dover Publications.

PROFESSIONAL ORCHESTRATION™. VOLUME 1
PROFESSIONAL MENTOR™ & AUDIO PACKAGES

The Professional Mentor™

More than a workbook. The *Professional Mentor™* is the heart of *Professional Orchestration™ Volume 1* because it turns *Professional Orchestration™* into a complete home study course that you can do on your schedule at your own pace. Here's how it works. With the *Professional Mentor™*, rather than taking a self-test to see if you know the material, you write one piece for each of the 13 solo instruments covered (the equal of roughly a semester's worth of work at college) before you do your "final" project – a full symphonic orchestration. With this approach, you create 13 publishable works that become the basis for your own publishing company, and, you can go to the next step, and create your own CD by doing a MIDI mock-up of your piece.

For electronic scoring, you get 13 solo compositions with MP3 and MIDI files created by composer Jay Bacal for the new Vienna Instruments sample library. Just load the MP3 and MIDI file into your sequencer. You'll see how Jay created the composition by studying velocity, expression, and mod wheel data. By the time you've gone through each instrument, including solo strings, you'll know how to approach doing a MIDI mock-up.

Professional Orchestration™. Volume 1 Audio Package #1

Learn on the run with our *Professional Orchestration™ Volume 1 Audio Package #1* covering a majority of the book's examples.

You asked for portable learning! Now it's here. Thanks to eClassical.com, you can download DRM-free MP3s covering a majority of the book's examples, so you're free to learn "on the run". That's because all the MP3s that we've licensed from eClassical.com are unrestricted. You can play them on your computer (Mac or PC), iPod or other MP3 player, your cell phone, or even convert them to an audio CD to listen to on your home stereo or on your car's CD player. With this portability, you're free to choose when you want to learn and where!

You get the complete movement the book example is found in. This means you hear the technique being studied within the context of the whole movement so you can judge its dramatic impact within the score. Because *Professional Orchestration™* comes with full page/full score examples, you can boost your MIDI mock-up skills by importing the MP3 into your sequencer, locate the position, then key-in the excerpts to recreate them using your favorite sample libraries.

New! Professional Orchestration™. Concert Package

To develop your familiarity with each solo instrument, the *Professional Orchestration™ Volume 1 Concert Package* gives you an average 20-minute concert with each solo instrument. Total number of MP3s - 78!

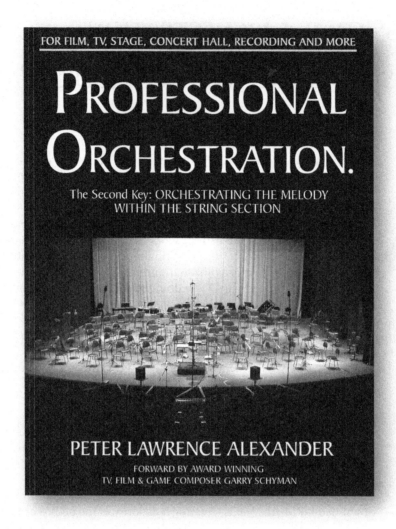

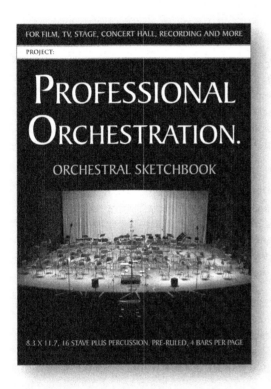
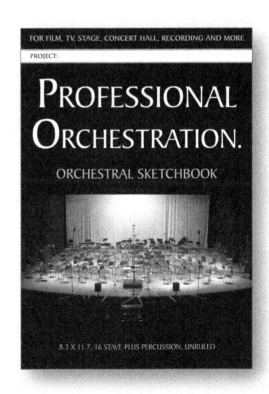

HOW RAVEL ORCHESTRATED: MOTHER GOOSE SUITE

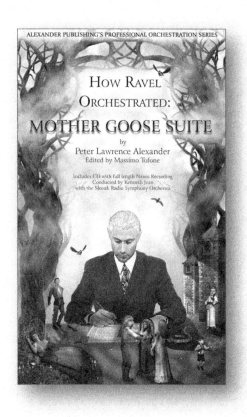

ISBN: 978-0-939067-12-1

Alexander Publishing's *How Ravel Orchestrated: Mother Goose Suite* is a breakthrough in orchestration instruction. For the first time ever, an American publishing company has completely re-engraved the classic work with the condensed piano part at page bottom in an oversized 8x14 format packaged with a complete downloadable performance of Mother Goose Suite from eClassical.com by Sir Neville Mariner and the Academy of St. Martin in the Fields. Thus, one book gives you a total portable package letting you learn on-the-go, anytime, anywhere.

For fast referencing, each bar is numbered at the bottom of the page (original rehearsal marks are also included). By including the piano part at page bottom, students of counterpoint will see specific devices that Ravel used, where, and how he orchestrated them. Jazz musicians and composers will also see how Ravel composed and orchestrated using altered DOM7 chords, mixolydian chord scales, and triads with the added 9th.

How Ravel Orchestrated: Mother Goose Suite is a good read. Preceding each movement is the complete short story that movement was based on. Now you can look at Mother Goose Suite to better understand the dramatic composition and scoring techniques that went into each work. By comparing back to the original story, you gain a better understanding of Ravel's approach. Following each movement is a brief orchestration analysis based on the *Eight Keys To Learning Professional Orchestration* as taught in the *Professional Orchestration™* Series.

REVIEW:

All I can say is fantastic! My students, and I were completely enthralled by the analysis you provided, as well as the score with the included piano part. Two of the students are jazz majors and were very excited about how Ravel was approaching harmonization from a chord/scale jazz harmony perspective. They really started to make a connection with Ravel's approach and what they have been learning in arranging class for big band; especially the jazz harmonization and line writing aspect of the score.

The piano part at the bottom of the score is a great teaching tool for orchestration students. All of my students stated that they would like to see more scores presented in this format. They all felt that they were gaining a better understanding on how Ravel approached orchestrating this movement because of the piano part that was included in the score. The next time I teach my orchestration class, this will be required reading for all of my students, it is that good. I love the new approach.

Dr. Rik Pfenninger
Plymouth State University

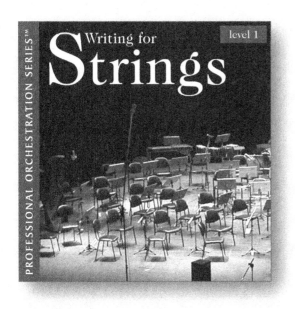
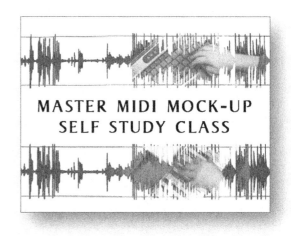